Not Just a
Pretty Face

Not Just a Pretty Face

Football, Fun and Despair

Luke Chadwick

MATHEW MANN

pitch

First published by Pitch Publishing, 2025

(pitch)

Pitch Publishing
9 Donnington Park,
85 Birdham Road,
Chichester, West Sussex,
PO20 7AJ
www.pitchpublishing.co.uk
info@pitchpublishing.co.uk

A CIP catalogue record is available for this book
from the British Library.

ISBN 978 1 83680 135 1

MIX
Paper | Supporting
responsible forestry
FSC
www.fsc.org   FSC™ C016779

Printed and bound on FSC® certified paper in line with
our continuing commitment to ethical business practices,
sustainability and the environment.

Typesetting and origination by Pitch Publishing
Printed and bound in India by Replika Press Pvt. Ltd.

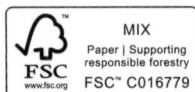

Contents

Foreword by Dion Dublin

I JOINED Manchester United shortly after the Class of '92 (Beckham, Giggs, Scholes, et al.) had won the FA Youth Cup. United always seemed to have a wealth of talented youngsters coming through, and I often watched the kids play at The Cliff after training. That's where I first became aware of a schoolboy by the name of Luke Chadwick.

Chadders was an unassuming lad determined to succeed. Great touch, incredibly fast, he quietly went about his business. He was a tall, skinny boy and, when I first saw him, I thought, *No chance.* Then, with the ball at his feet, he did something special, and my thoughts changed to, *Flipping heck. I wasn't expecting him to do that.* He let his football do the talking and that's what earned him respect.

During his time at Old Trafford, Chadders received tons of abuse about the way he looked. Fans up and down the country gave him stick. It was jealousy. Pure and simple.

Here's a young lad working hard, playing for United. What can we have a go at him about? He looks different, so let's pick on him because of his appearance.

I've never spoken to Luke about how it affected him, but I imagine it would have hurt. It must have been a hugely challenging time, but he dealt with it in an adult way. He got his head down, trained hard, worked hard. He ignored the haters.

I think it's a great idea that Chadders is telling his story because people don't know him. What will come out of this book is that Luke worked his nuts off to get to the top and play for the biggest club in the world. He's a good lad and a really funny guy.

We played against each other a few times over the years, but it wasn't until 2006 when he joined me at Norwich City that we became team-mates. We instantly formed a relationship that was based on mutual respect. Chadders held me in high regard because of my age and the clubs that I'd played for. He was a big Cambridge United fan and loved talking to me about the good old days. They were some of the best times that I had in football, so to have the chance to reminisce with a fan and a fellow pro was brilliant.

Luke loves chatting about anything because he'll have a story about it. He's got a story about everything! He was quick-witted and absolutely hilarious. He'd hold the room without even knowing that he was doing it. He'd start telling a story and then walk over to the fridge to grab a drink. Every pair of eyes in the dressing room would follow his movements as he sat down again. He'd still be telling the story when he got in the shower and, because everyone was hanging on his every word, we'd follow him into the shower so we could hear the punchline.

We haven't kept in touch as often as we'd like, but I was delighted when he asked me to write this foreword. He's a mate and I'll always have time for him.

Good luck, Chadders!

Chapter 1

Falling in Love

I WAS six years old when I fell in love for the first time. Not with a girl; at such a tender age I was yet to develop an interest in the fairer sex. No, my love affair was with the game of football, and it has lasted a lifetime.

I grew up in Meldreth, a sleepy village in south Cambridgeshire. The most exciting event of the year, the one that all the villagers looked forward to, was the annual fete, which took place each summer at the Holy Trinity Church, just around the corner from the council house that I lived in with my mum, dad and older brother, Carl.

We were fortunate enough to have quite a large garden with lots of space to run around and play in. My earliest memory is of playing football in that garden with Dad and Carl. Most of my childhood memories involve football.

I vividly remember the 1987 FA Cup Final; Coventry City beat Tottenham Hotspur to win their first FA Cup. Cup final day was a big thing back then, with the build-up to the match shown all day live on the BBC. My eyes were glued to the television most of the day, but at one point I went outside to the garden and watched Dad and Carl heading the ball to each other. I tried to join in, but I couldn't do it, so Mum came out, picked the ball up and tapped it between my head and hers, pretending that I was heading the ball.

My parents separated later that year. A few years after, Dad remarried and his new wife, Joy, became a part of the family until she sadly passed away after a long battle with cancer.

Even though my parents divorced, Carl and I still saw a lot of Dad. On one of our days out, Dad took me to watch my first-ever live football game, and my life was changed forever.

Cambridge United was our nearest professional club and my maiden voyage to the Abbey Stadium absolutely blew my mind. I don't remember the opponents from that day, but I'll never forget the emotions that I experienced being so close to the action; the smell of the turf, the sound of the crowd, the feel of the atmosphere – that was the moment when I fell in love with football. From that moment on, everything in my life revolved around football.

Not long after that match, Dad bought me my first Cambridge kit. It was all yellow with a black V-neck collar, black stripes down the sides, and 'LYNFOX' (the club sponsors) emblazoned in red across the middle. I wore that shirt at every opportunity and wouldn't take it off if I could help it.

Not long after I visited the Abbey Stadium, my grandma took me on another exciting trip – to Cambridge city centre to buy my first pair of football boots. It was such a momentous occasion and, after much deliberation, I chose a pair of Mitre Pulsa boots, the latest release with different types of studs. They were black (*all* football boots were black in those days) with the white sideways V logo on the side and Mitre written in white on the tongue.

The following week I turned up, shiny boots in hand, at Meldreth Primary School for the Saturday Morning Club. This was my first experience of organised football and, by the end of the session, my obsession with the beautiful game had begun.

* * *

I was an incredibly shy child. I don't remember this, but my mum has told me that I never wanted to go to nursery. As soon as we arrived, I begged her to take me home. I was a real mummy's boy and didn't want to go anywhere without her.

For the first two years of primary school, I cried my eyes out every morning when I was dropped off. Mum would always tell me to go in, but when my grandma took me, I knew that if I kicked up enough of a fuss, she'd take me back to her house and I'd miss school. They were the best days. I missed so many days of school that it got to the stage where my teacher created a reward chart, and I was given a star to stick on it every time I attended.

It wasn't that I disliked school as such, I just felt very uncomfortable when I wasn't with my parents, grandparents or Carl. I eventually came out of my shell and became quite popular at school – probably because I was good at sports – but it was a real challenge during those early days.

It didn't help that I had a speech impediment, which meant I struggled to get my words out and often said the wrong thing. I became very self-conscious, and my shyness intensified. Eventually, I saw a speech therapist who was a huge help and helped me to improve the way I spoke. I quite liked those visits because the sessions were held during the day, so I got to leave school early. Any excuse!

I longed for the summer holidays when we'd go up to Kirkham, Lancashire, to visit my dad's parents, my nana (Mavis) and grandpa (Harry). They owned a butcher's shop, and we stayed with them in the flat above. My middle name is Harry after my grandpa.

Like most kids that age, I didn't have any career aspirations. My grandad on my mother's side (Derek) and uncles all worked in the train industry, and I quite liked the idea of following in their footsteps. I was interested in trains as a young child. My maternal grandparents' house was attached to Meldreth railway station. I remember being incredibly excited when my grandad arranged for me to ride in the front of a train one day. I spent a lot of time with my grandparents and Aunty Diane, who lived with them. My grandad sometimes took me to school in his three-wheeled van, which was an adventure.

Dad was a delivery driver, driving vans and lorries all over the UK, and Mum worked at a place called Intascreen, an industrial printer. Back then the company was located in Meldreth, which was great as she could walk to work, but they've since moved four miles up the road to Royston – and she still works there now! She must have been with them for over 40 years.

So, although I didn't have any idea of what I wanted to do when I grew up, as soon as I started playing football, I knew that I wanted to play it as often as I could. It was so much fun.

I endured the various subjects my teachers were trying to teach me because being at school meant that I got to play football at breaktime and lunchtime – the green grass of the playing field when it was dry and the gravel on the playground if it rained. After school I'd hone my skills in the back garden, nothing technical, just having fun pretending to score the winning goal in a cup final.

During the school holidays, Carl and I would ride our bikes to the park to meet up with Robbie and Peter Askham, friends of ours who lived in the same village, and play football and cricket all day. When we felt hungry, we'd cycle to my grandparents' house, where my grandma (Lorna) would make us sandwiches and a drink. After we'd refuelled, it was back to the park to play various football games, like headers and volleys.

Carl was a talented footballer who did really well at grassroots level. He signed for Eternit Colts, a local junior team, and I stood on the side of the pitch and watched him play, desperate to be there out on the pitch myself, playing in a proper game. My time came when I was eight and I followed in Carl's footsteps by signing for Eternit Colts' feeder team, the Melbourn Tigers, coached by Colin Barnard and Martin Winter.

In August 1989, I put on the yellow-and-green Tigers strip for the first time and made my footballing debut in a friendly match against St Thomas Colts. We drew the game 1-1 and I scored our goal. I received the ball from midfield, took it around the goalkeeper and slotted the ball into the back of the net. This was the first goal I ever scored in an actual net. It was the first of many.

Grassroots football was very different then to how it is now. Perhaps the biggest difference is that we played on 11-a-side pitches with full-sized goals, which was absolutely crazy considering the size of us.

We were really successful during my first season. I was freakishly fast, much quicker than anyone else at my school, so I was put up front and I scored a ridiculous number of goals. My team-mates soon devised a system that fully utilised my pace; they'd smash the ball over the opposition's defence for me to chase after. Sometimes our keeper would launch the ball, which would often bounce over the defenders' heads for me to run on to, take it up to the tiny goalkeeper standing between the huge goalposts, and I'd knock the ball past him into the net.

There was one game when we beat Hitchin Rangers 29-0, with yours truly bagging 13! It was a complete mismatch and probably wasn't great for anyone's development, but that didn't stop us from scoring goal after goal.

After that match, everyone at school knew my name, which was a bit strange. I didn't court the spotlight and I was still really uncomfortable in most social situations. Once I'd got to know people, I was absolutely fine; it was just hard at the start because I was so timid. The football pitch was the one place where I felt truly free; somewhere I could express myself. The game gave me an opportunity to display my personality and I had to learn to accept the attention that inevitably came my way.

My goalscoring exploits garnered interest from the local newspaper, the *Royston Crow*. It gave me a real buzz to see my name in the headlines, and after my 13-goal haul against Hitchin when I won the Pro Hot Shot award, which was a bag of football-related goodies, given out weekly to local kids who'd achieved something special in junior football. Mum took me to the *Royston Crow* offices to receive my award. There was a photographer there to capture the moment when I was presented with my bag, and I felt so awkward. I loved reading about myself in the newspaper, but I certainly didn't enjoy having to pose for a photograph that I knew would be in the paper.

By the end of the season, I'd scored an incredible 104 goals! Unsurprisingly, I received the top-scorer award at our end-of-season presentation evening.

The only disappointment during my inaugural football season was the cup final against Radburn Rangers, which was held at Garden Walk, the home of our local semi-pro side Royston Town. At the time it was the best ground I'd ever played at; there was a stand along the touchline and even floodlights. But rather than savouring the excitement of the occasion, like all my team-mates, nerves got the better of me. There was an enormous amount of pressure on my young shoulders; I was the one who scored the goals, I was the match-winner. Everyone expected me to do well.

Radford were a very good team, and I wasn't having as much joy as I usually did during the match. I struggled to make an impact and I came off injured with the scores level. I can't recall if I was genuinely injured or if I'd just told the coaches that I was, to get out of the game, but what I do remember is that the game felt too important. I crumbled in what to me felt like a high-pressure situation. We lost the game in a penalty shoot-out. I was devastated.

Despite that setback, football had consumed me and there was no doubt in my mind that I was going to become a professional footballer. My dream was to play for Cambridge United, the club that I'd fallen head over heels in love with ever since my first visit to the Abbey Stadium. My passion for Cambridge coincided with the best period in the club's history.

Cambridge United didn't become a Football League club until 1970, eventually reaching the dizzying heights of the old Second Division (now Championship), before plummeting back down to the Fourth, where it languished until 1990. That was when former player John Beck was appointed as manager.

During his first season at the helm, Beck led Cambridge to the quarter-final of the FA Cup and won promotion to the Third Division. Twelve months later, the Us reached the quarter-final of the cup again and also claimed the Third Division title. The following year, Beck was on the brink of achieving a third successive promotion, but a play-off semi-final defeat to Leicester City ended Cambridge's dream of reaching the inaugural Premier League. It was a magical time to be a supporter.

I knew each member of the team off by heart and can still reel off the names of all the players because I watched them intensely each week. Everyone who donned the gold shirt was a hero to me. Dion Dublin and John Taylor, the two main strikers, stood out because I played in the same position, but others like Chris Leadbitter, Lee Philpott, Colin Bailie and Phil Chapple were also held in high regard. Gary Clayton, a midfielder, was the player I used to look up to. I don't know why because he didn't always start the games, but he had a knack for coming off the bench and grabbing a goal. I've actually got a photo of Gary on the wall behind the desk that I work at.

Phil Chapple presented me with an award at one of my junior club presentation evenings and that was amazing for me as a young supporter. I couldn't believe that I was shaking hands with someone who actually played for Cambridge. I was star-struck.

Cambridge got a bit of stick from the purists because of the particular brand of football that John Beck set them up to play. It was very direct, but at the same time very entertaining.

The aim was to ping the ball out wide for the wingers to get it into the box. The ground staff would let the grass grow long in the corners to stop the ball from running out of play when the defenders launched it down the flanks. This style of play created so many chances for Dublin and Taylor and I always found the games exhilarating.

The most exciting match that I ever attended was in January 1989 when Chris Turner was the manager and John Beck was still a player. I'd written a letter to the club asking if I could be a ball boy at one of their home games. I couldn't believe it when I received a reply inviting me to be a ball boy for the match against Tranmere Rovers. I was only eight years old at the time and felt so nervous standing on the side of the pitch. My spot was directly in front of the away fans, and they were shouting and swearing all game – I'd never heard language like it before and I stood there like a statue, feeling terrified!

In the second half, I was moved to a different area, in front of the home fans, who were a bit better behaved. One of the kids in the stand dropped their yellow balloon and it blew onto the sideline. The child's dad asked me to pass it back to him, but I didn't know if I was allowed to even look at, let alone speak to, anyone in the stand, so I completely ignored them, and the balloon flew off into the sky!

It was such a great day for me, that feeling of being so close to the pitch and to my heroes. It was surreal when the ball came to me, and I had to pick it up and throw it to one of the players. The whole day felt like a dream come true.

That was the only time I was lucky enough to be a ball boy, so for the rest of the matches I had to be content to watch the game from my seat in the Main Stand or, when that was sold out, I stood in the Habbin Stand with Dad and Carl. When I got older, I'd go with my school friends or the lads I played football with and stand in the Newmarket Road End, behind the goal. That was my favourite.

Dad was from Bury and was actually a Bury fan, but he took a keen interest in his local club. Carl was a Cambridge fan, but I was a fanatic. I loved everything about the club and was desperate to go and watch them every week. I used to check the fixture list on Teletext and then pester my parents to take me.

Teletext was my go-to source for all the latest football information in those pre-internet days. It's where I developed my extensive knowledge of football. Every day after school I'd head into the lounge, pick up the remote control, and key in the magic number 302. Within seconds I was presented with an Aladdin's cave of football news. I devoured everything I read and eventually learned the names of almost every player who played in the top four divisions of English football.

Mum did the pools each week and received the latest card on a Monday for the matches taking place the following Saturday. I studied each and every game and then went and played them out in the back garden, doing the commentary in my head (sometimes out loud if I was on my own) and pretending to be players from both teams. There wasn't a great deal of football on TV in those days, so although I knew the name and position of each player, I had no idea what most looked like – or even how good they were!

I recognised the top-flight players, of course, because their images appeared in the *Shoot* and *Match* magazines that I used to read whenever I could get my hands on a copy. I also collected Panini stickers, mainly during the international tournaments, but my biggest passion was VHS tapes. Whenever anyone asked me what I'd like for my birthday or when I compiled my annual list for Santa, I always requested a football video tape. If I had any money, I'd go to Woolworths (sadly, like Teletext, no longer here) and peruse the tapes sitting on the shelves before finally selecting the latest addition to my growing collection. *101 Great Goals, Goals Galore, Best of the Eighties.* I watched them all, over and over again.

By the time I'd turned nine, football had taken over my life – and I couldn't have been happier.

After my successful debut season, I left the Melbourn Tigers and joined Eternit Colts. Eternit was a local company that produced fibre cement, and they sponsored the team. I settled in well at my new club and continued to score goals at will, which made me feel more comfortable. Whether it was the coaches or my peers, I always felt better when people told me that I was good. It wasn't long before my form attracted the attention of the county team, and I played a few games for the Cambridge League's representatives.

Then I received the best news ever – Cambridge United wanted me to attend a trial at their School of Excellence. I was absolutely buzzing, especially as my team-mate Michael Wagstaff, Waggy as he was known, was also invited.

For three weeks, on a Monday night, we travelled to Bottisham College for an indoor session. It was about half an hour away from home, and one of our coaches used to drive us there and back. Unfortunately, the training was absolute chaos. There were so many kids in the sports hall – health and safety wouldn't allow it now – and it was impossible for anyone to give the best account of themselves.

At the end of the three-week trial, I was told that I wouldn't be invited back. Waggy didn't make it either. To say I was heartbroken is an understatement. That was the first time I'd ever experienced rejection in football.

I went straight from my final session with training to Cubs. I was still wearing my kit and shin pads when I arrived, and the Akela asked me how the session had gone. Tears welled up in my eyes as I explained to her what had happened. I'm not making excuses, but the way the sessions were run meant I hadn't been given the opportunity to show the coaches what I could do. Not that I'm still bitter!

I was upset, obviously, but I was also resilient, and it didn't really prey on my mind once I'd got over the initial disappointment. It helped that I was still scoring goals for fun when I played for Eternit Colts and Cambridgeshire Schools, and that gave me a huge amount of inner confidence. A massive reason that I enjoyed a lengthy career in football was the success that I enjoyed during my formative years. I honestly believe that things would have been very different for me if I'd grown up somewhere else, somewhere with a hotbed of footballing talent. I grew up playing against little village teams in Hertfordshire and Cambridgeshire and my pace and ability at that age ensured I stood out.

One day, I received a letter, completely out of the blue, asking if I'd like to play for a team called East Anglia Boys. They were a big club, ran by Martin Lacey, that went on tours overseas and I'd still be allowed to continue playing with my mates for Eternit Colts.

My first tour with East Anglia was over in the Netherlands, and I found it very tough. Mum and Carl came with me and the team on the coach and I was the only one there who had a family member with them. I wasn't able to mix with the other children particularly well because of my shyness and, as a result, I didn't do very well during the tournament. I was a substitute most of the time, which was something that I wasn't used to. East Anglia Boys was a very strong side and we beat most teams by a margin of seven or eight goals and inevitably reached the final.

During the final of the tournament, our goalkeeper suffered an injury, and I was brought on to replace him between the sticks. We already had a solid lead, and the opposition didn't have enough of the ball to trouble me. We won the match convincingly. At the full-time whistle, I burst into tears. It was the first time I'd ever cried after a game. I don't know if it was because we'd won the tournament or because I'd struggled to bond and felt completely out of my comfort zone for the entire five-day trip. All I know is that I felt overcome with emotion and that memory has stuck with me.

I eventually settled in, made friends, rediscovered my form and I went on further tours with East Anglia Boys, to Belgium, Denmark and even out to America.

The second time that I cried on the pitch was at the end of one season when Eternit Colts were playing in a title decider. We should have won that match but didn't and I felt so guilty because I'd missed a penalty (not the last one I'd miss either!). I was distraught and, as I trudged off the pitch, Mum came over to me and said, 'You play football because you love it, Luke. Don't ever let it make you cry.'

I'm eternally grateful to her for giving me that advice and I called on her words throughout my career whenever things weren't going well for me. Every time I encountered a challenge, I took myself back to those early days of playing football.

Football is one of the things that makes you happy. That's why you do it became my mantra.

I tried to keep that childhood innocence when the game was all about fun and enjoyment. Obviously, it changes slightly when it becomes a job, but I constantly reminded myself of how lucky I was to be doing something that I loved.

I didn't have a lot of natural technical ability, I developed technique later on, but what did come naturally was my speed, and that allowed me to score goals. I spent hours and hours on my own playing football in our back garden or at the park with my friends. We had a cow field next to our garden, with a fence in between to stop the cows from coming too close. Concrete pillars separated the fence panels, and I used them to play one-twos. When I finished my career, I realised that one-twos were one of my biggest strengths.

It's a totally different structure for kids now, with fantastic coaches who hold the relevant badges to help children improve their technique. I don't think I'd have enjoyed that, though. I was lucky to be given total freedom to play football and that's what kept my enjoyment going. In my opinion, there's no greater teacher than actually playing in a game. When you spend that much time doing something, you're bound to get better.

I was starting to think that I was going to become a professional footballer. In fact, I *knew* that I was going to become a professional footballer. I wasn't being arrogant; I just couldn't envisage a future that didn't involve me making a living playing the beautiful game. My life was centred around football. Anything else was just an inconvenience.

To achieve my dream, I knew that I had to move to bigger and better teams. I couldn't just continue to play with my mates, or I wouldn't get noticed.

When I was 11, I joined a club based in Newport Pagnell, near Milton Keynes. Roy Ferguson was the manager, and he was building a top team with the best local talent. It wouldn't be the last time I was managed by a Mr Ferguson!

The quality of players – both team-mates and opponents – was a big step up from the Colts, but that didn't faze me at all. I was one of the top performers for East Anglia Boys, and they were a team full of lads who were playing schoolboy football for pro clubs.

From there I had trials at Ipswich Town and then Norwich City. I went on a trip to Wales with Norwich, but the lack of public transport meant that I couldn't sign for either of them.

I didn't do very well at school because I just wasn't interested. I probably performed worse when I started to have trials with professional clubs because in my mind I didn't need to worry about school or concentrate. What was the point?

In 1993, at the age of 12, I was presented with a fantastic opportunity – I became a School of Excellence player for Premier League giants Arsenal. Although it was around 50 miles from my house in Meldreth to London, it was fairly easy for me to get there because I could catch the train from my grandparents' house to Finsbury Park. From there it was a short walk to the famous marble halls of Highbury.

I did feel a bit more pressure when I stepped up to play for the Gunners, but the pressure was more about the social aspect than the football side of things. The second that I stepped onto the football pitch I felt at home and all my shyness evaporated. As soon as I started scoring goals, I gained the respect of my peers and that helped me to build relationships and make friends. Obviously, the games were more challenging than those at a grassroots level, but I never felt that I was out of my depth. The biggest change for me was that I had to get used to not scoring ten goals a game!

Two players that I played with at Arsenal stood out: Stuart Taylor and Ashley Cole. Stuart was a fantastic goalkeeper who excelled at that age and went on to have a fantastic career with Arsenal, Aston Villa and Leicester City, among others. Ashley was an unbelievable player who played as a left-winger then, before becoming one of the best left-backs in the world, winning every trophy going and playing over a hundred times for England.

The only downside was that I wasn't allowed to play for Eternit Colts or East Anglia Boys anymore, although I was still able to represent Cambridgeshire Schools on a Saturday, before playing for Arsenal on the Sunday. I was churning out games without thinking too much about it. I loved playing in matches, but I didn't particularly enjoy the training that came with signing for Arsenal.

Training took place in the indoor hall at Highbury on a Wednesday evening but, more often than not, I'd make up a tummy ache and ask Mum to let them know that I wouldn't be going. That's no reflection on my coaches, they were fantastic; I just didn't like the structure that surrounded the sessions. I was a playground player; I wanted the ball to myself so I could dribble and score, and I found training to be a real chore.

It was a huge boost to my ego when I told my school friends that I was playing for Arsenal. Everything was going to plan, and I was loving life. I didn't think things could get better. But then the biggest club in the world came calling – Manchester United.

Chapter 2

From Boy to Man (United)

SO, I was playing for Cambridge Schools on the Saturday and Arsenal on the Sunday. School football was massive at that time; that was where you gained recognition, more so than playing for a pro club.

Every Monday I eagerly awaited the delivery of the *Cambridge Evening News*, the newspaper that covered our games, as I enjoyed reading about my goalscoring exploits for my county. One season I broke the record for goals scored in a single season. The previous record was 18; I got over 40!

When I was 14, I played a match against Essex Schools, and before the game my manager told me that there was a scout from Manchester United in attendance. And what was more exciting was that he was there to watch *me*. That was a huge thrill. United had just won the inaugural Premier League – their first league title in 26 years – and was a club very much on the rise. My heart was pounding with excitement, although there were also a few more nerves than normal.

Essex was renowned for having a very strong team – Bobby Moore, Jimmy Greaves, Glenn Hoddle, Tony Adams and David Beckham have all represented Essex in the past, and a future

England captain, John Terry, lined up against me that day. I think Joe Cole also played in that game.

I was desperate for a good performance that would convince the scout that I was Red Devil standard. Unfortunately, we were beaten 6-1, and although I scored our goal, I didn't do a great deal else. I hadn't stopped running, trying to make an impression, and I was exhausted as I trudged off the pitch at the end of the match, feeling a little dejected. I wished I'd been part of the Essex side because I know I'd have scored a few more goals.

As I was getting changed, my manager told me that the scout had been impressed and that someone from United would be in contact. *Wow*, I thought. I certainly wasn't expecting that after suffering such a heavy defeat.

Later that week, I returned home from school to find a white envelope addressed to me. My heart pounded as I opened it and extracted a typed letter on the official Manchester United paper. I was invited to a week-long trial during the next school holidays. That letter was magnetised to our fridge for months!

For the first time, I couldn't wait to get to school the next day so that I could tell everyone that I was having trials with United. Yes, Arsenal is a huge club, but this is Manchester United we're talking about.

Although I was a Cambridge fan, I had always held an affinity to United. A massive reason for that was the number of youngsters who were breaking into the first team. The Class of '92, who were beginning to break into the first team, weren't much older than me, and it was exciting to watch these talented players develop into world-class stars. I'll never forget Alan

Hansen's infamous quote on *Match of the Day*: 'You'll never win anything with kids.' Look at what they achieved.

The two United players I looked up to were Ryan Giggs and Eric Cantona. Giggs came into United's side at a really young age and was an exciting player with bags of skill. Cantona was a huge hero of mine. He was a fantastic player with an arrogant streak that made him so good. I didn't know it at the time, but many years later I'd have the privilege of playing alongside Eric during Ryan Giggs's testimonial match.

As the date of my trial approached, I began to feel a sense of trepidation, mainly about meeting new people, but also for the first time I had some doubts over whether I was good enough. United is the biggest club on the planet and I imagined that the other 14- and 15-year-olds who were already there would have been out of this world. So, I was excited and fearful in equal measure.

When the big day came, Mum dropped me off at the train station, where I began the arduous journey to Manchester. There were no direct trains, so I travelled from Meldreth station to Cambridge, Cambridge to Ely, and finally Ely to Manchester Piccadilly – it took almost five hours in total.

When I arrived in Manchester I was met at the station and taken to the Castlefield Hotel, on Liverpool Road, just on the outskirts of the city centre. There was a group of other trialists staying at the hotel, including David Healy and Michael Stewart – two lads I became good friends with – and I immediately felt at ease. The way we were treated, how we were spoken to, everyone seemed so happy that we were there.

I spent a week training with a group of talented youngsters in my age group and it was amazing. No disrespect to Arsenal, but the set-up at United, the whole environment and atmosphere, was different to anything I'd experienced before. I felt part of something special from day one.

At the end of the week, we played a match against Nottingham Forest at Littleton Road, home to United's academy. I felt immense pride when I pulled on the red United shirt for the first time, and although I knew it was only a friendly game for the under-15s, I was still very aware that I was representing this great club.

Before kick-off, I sat on the bench in the dressing room, gathering my thoughts, and then I saw a familiar face enter the room – Sir Alex Ferguson. The legendary manager introduced himself to us (as if he needed to because we all obviously knew who he was!), told us how pleased he was to meet us and wished us luck for the game. It was such a surreal moment; I'd only ever seen him on the television standing on the side of the pitch. He had a reputation as a fearsome character, but he was so warm towards us. It was extraordinary that Sir Alex took time out of his extremely busy schedule to come and watch us play.

Under the watchful eye of the greatest manager of all time, I put on an impressive display, scoring two goals with a performance that left everyone in no doubt of what I was capable of.

After the match, I got changed and was given a lift back to Piccadilly station where I embarked on the reverse rail journey that I'd taken a week earlier. Five hours later Mum greeted me at Meldreth station with the news that Sir Alex had phoned her that afternoon, asking for her permission to sign me. I thought she was pulling my leg at first – I mean, who could imagine that the manager of the Premier League champions would phone the mum of a 14-year-old kid? – but she managed to convince me. I later learned that he did that with every single player he wanted to sign, regardless of whether they were a schoolboy or an international superstar. He wanted the best players at his club, and he knew how powerful a call from him would be. It worked too. As soon as I knew that Sir Alex Ferguson had made the effort to phone, there was no way I was ever going to say no.

Manchester United's offer put me in an awkward position, though, because Arsenal also wanted to sign me. I'd already decided that I wanted to join the Red Devils, so I asked my mum to call Terry Murphy, head of youth development at Highbury, to tell him that I was signing for United. Terry, who was a brilliant man, always supportive of me, didn't want to take no for an answer and asked if he could come to our house with Bruce Rioch, the Gunners' first-team manager, to try to persuade me to stay. I'd already made up my mind, but there was no way we were going to tell Terry that the Arsenal manager wasn't welcome at our house.

A few days later I was sitting on my sofa in the front room – probably catching up with the latest football news on Teletext – when a big Mercedes-Benz pulled up outside. Terry and Bruce got out and walked up the path towards our front door, while I sat there absolutely petrified.

Over a cup of tea, Terry offered me a two-year schoolboy contract, followed by a two-year YTS (Youth Training Scheme), and then a guaranteed one-year professional contract. It's very rare to be offered a pro contract at that age – only the international schoolboys were usually offered one – so that shows how highly Arsenal valued me.

United had only offered me two-year schoolboy forms with no guarantee of a YTS contract, let alone a pro deal, but Manchester was the place that felt right, that was where I wanted to go. I obviously didn't say that on the day, though. I thanked Terry and Bruce for their time and told them I'd think about it.

Mum later phoned Terry and told him that I wouldn't be signing for Arsenal. I know they weren't very happy about United taking me from under their noses and they made their feelings very clear to the powers that be at Old Trafford.

And that was it, I signed schoolboy forms with Manchester United. Every weekend and all my school holidays were spent in Manchester, training and playing under the watchful eyes of Paul McGuinness and Warren Joyce.

The lads who lived closer to Manchester took part in mid-week training sessions but, because of the distance, I couldn't attend, so the club arranged for me to train with the Stevenage Borough under-16s. It was bizarre.

During my first session, it was clear that there was a gulf in quality between me and the Stevenage players, and they were looking at me wondering why I was there. In the end, the coach asked me to referee the game because I was quite a bit better than everyone else. I didn't like training at the best of times, but I certainly didn't want to spend my Wednesday evenings refereeing a practice game, so I didn't go back. I didn't tell Manchester United, and I don't think Stevenage told them either.

I was loving life. The only problem I had was that I still had two years of school to get through before I could, hopefully, move to Manchester on a full-time basis on a YTS.

I was never particularly studious and didn't work as hard at school as I could have done, but after signing for United I downed tools completely academically. I'd swan around corridors wearing my Manchester United jumper thinking I was the Big I Am, and probably being seen as that by the younger kids at school. I used it to my advantage.

I had to finish my lessons earlier on a Friday so I could get to Manchester at a decent time, so my timetable was changed to accommodate me. My teachers decided that I'd only take GCSEs in maths and English so that I could focus on passing my core subjects. My parents were always supportive of me, and they didn't mind that football took priority. If I was happy, they were happy. And I was ecstatically happy that I didn't have to take most of my classes!

I had quite an easy life compared to my schoolmates. They'd be sat in geography class, and I'd be in a different room pretending to read a maths book, but not really doing very much. I ended up leaving school without any GCSEs, which is a real shame, and something I regret now.

The only good thing about school was that I was able to continue representing the school football team and the county, playing alongside my mates.

I couldn't get enough football and I soon signed up for Foxton, one of the adult village teams. Their manager had asked me if I'd play for the men's side, and I stupidly agreed. I'd played for Cambridge Schools in the morning, and I was due to play for Foxton in the afternoon, but my PE teacher, Mr Yallop, got wind of it and gave me a right dressing-down. Mr Yallop was hugely supportive of my blossoming football talent throughout secondary school. He made it clear, in no uncertain terms, that there was no way I should be playing at that level where I ran the risk of picking up an injury.

The lure of a game of football was something I could rarely ignore. I later played alongside Carl for my local village team, Barrington, a few times, which I loved. One match was a cup tie against Great Chisel. We won 6-5 and I scored a hat-trick. Unfortunately, someone found out that I wasn't a registered player and Great Chisel made a complaint to the local FA, which resulted in us getting kicked out of the tournament. I still get reminded about that!

I enjoyed playing against adults on those few occasions. Yes, I got kicked around a bit, but that never bothered me. When I'd been at primary school, playing on the playground, I'd be dribbling past everyone and I'd get absolutely smashed to the ground, cutting my knees open. I always gave as good as I got. As my career progressed, I actually quite liked it when I was kicked because it meant that I was doing something right. I accepted that tackles are as much a part of the game as a good piece of skill. Eventually, I was strongly advised – and rightly so – that I was an idiot for risking my future and I stopped playing for the village teams.

Away from football, I spent a lot of time with my mates, doing the usual stuff that teenage boys get up to: having the odd dance with a girl at the school disco and drinking from a bottle of White Lightning cider at the park – although I sometimes poured mine away because I hated the taste!

As much as I enjoyed socialising with my mates, the highlight of my week was undoubtedly my trips to Manchester. The standard there was so high and, at first, I didn't think that I was as good as the other lads, particularly those who played in my position. There were four strikers in my age group including me, and they'd all played for England Schoolboys. I hadn't, so in my young mind that meant they were better than me. It wasn't that I felt I didn't deserve to be there; I just knew that I wasn't at the top of the tree with regards to the other people in my age group.

Despite four strikers competing for two spots, I managed to get a lot of game time because Paul Wheatcroft and Ian Fitzpatrick were at Lilleshall (the National School of Excellence) most of the time, so I often started up front with George Clegg, a left-footed, talented forward, who became a close friend.

It's certainly easier to play football when you have better players on your side. We had Michael Stewart, who later won four caps for Scotland, and Wayne Evans, a talented Welshman, in midfield. Both were very good passers of the ball and I quickly realised that if I got into good positions, they'd find me and, inevitably, I'd score.

Paul McGuinness and Warren Joyce coached the under-16s. Paul was a fantastic coach, who oversaw all the youth teams, and Warren, who was still playing for Hull City at the time, had a great personality and was always supportive of me.

Every day was so much fun, even though there was a certain element of seriousness. It was drummed into us that we were representing Manchester United, and we were expected to win every game, whether it was a meaningless friendly or a cup final.

During the school holidays, the club would sort us out with tickets to watch the first team play at Old Trafford and that was incredible. I'd previously enjoyed going to the Abbey Stadium to watch Cambridge, but Old Trafford was a completely different kettle of fish. Sitting high up in the stands, looking around the stadium – the hallowed turf, the imposing stands, the sound of 70,000 fans – it was magical. I experienced such a thrill from being there, watching so many world-class players in the flesh. I watched those games as a fan. I certainly didn't sit there thinking that one day it would be me out there. It all seemed so far away.

Ray Medwell was the scout who spotted me, an incredible man who has sadly passed away. Ray did so much for me and on more than one occasion he'd drive down to Meldreth to pick me up and take me to Manchester when the trains weren't running. He took me to Old Trafford in October 1995 for the game against Liverpool when Eric Cantona made his long-awaited return following the ban he'd received for his infamous kung-fu kick on a fan. There was an unbelievable atmosphere inside the stadium, and when Cantona scored the winning goal from the penalty spot, the noise levels went up a few more decibels. Before the game, Ray had taken me to the United Megastore and bought me a United tracksuit. He was such a generous, kind man and he was a huge factor in my becoming a professional footballer.

That's the thing with Manchester United: they knew that it wasn't a case of just assembling the best players and letting them get on with it. Everyone at the club went to so much trouble to ensure every single player felt welcome and special. It was a totally different set-up to every other club. The staff went above and beyond, nothing was ever too much trouble. That was huge for me, especially with my introverted personality. It wasn't just that I wanted to be part of the club, I *needed* to be there.

My schoolboy contract expired in the summer of 1997, and I set my sights on taking the next rung of the ladder –

earning a coveted YTS contract. Several of the boys, mainly the international players, had already been offered YTS contracts, but my future was one of the last to be decided on.

A month or so before the decision was made, we went on a tour to Austria and played a few games out there. For the first time in my career, I played a little further out wide than my usual role as a centre-forward. I thought I'd done really well; I set up a few goals and certainly didn't feel that I'd let myself down.

The youth development officer at United was Dave Bushell, another guy who had a huge impact on my career. Dave didn't come with us to Austria, and he phoned me to ask how I thought it had gone. I replied that I'd played well, but he told me that he was concerned that I'd only scored one goal. He then explained that they were still in discussions about my future and that they'd make their decision in due course. I was a little surprised that he hadn't told me that I'd be fine, but I remained pretty confident. *There's no way they'd have made me travel up to Manchester every weekend for two years and not take me on*, I thought.

In May 1997, those of us who hadn't yet been offered a contract were summoned to Old Trafford to find out what our futures had in store. Sir Alex Ferguson was there, as were Paul, Warren, Dave and Ray. We were split into two groups: one group was told they were being released; the other was offered YTS contracts. Looking back, it was a pretty awful way to do it and it would never in a million years happen like that now.

Fortunately, I was one of the players the club wanted to keep, which was amazing. Sir Alex congratulated us all and outlined his expectations, although I was too excited to remember what he actually said!

During the long journey back to Meldreth, my face displayed a permanent grin, knowing that I was going to be leaving school – not that I did a lot there anyway – and playing football every single day. That was the absolute dream. After a short summer holiday, it was time to leave home and move up to Manchester to begin the next part of my journey.

Chapter 3

Fun and Games

IT DIDN'T dawn on me that I'd be moving away from home, until my dad drove me up to Manchester in the summer of 1997 to begin my new life. I remember it fondly as it was the day after the school leavers' prom. That was the moment it all began to feel real.

There were various houses stationed around Salford, near the academy training, that United used as digs. I was placed into a house on Littleton Road and shared a room with Jason Hickson, another first-year YTS and a great lad who I'd got to know well during my time as a schoolboy. Our landlord was John Lancaster, an incredible bloke, who looked after us and prepared our evening meals.

Despite the support from John and Jason, I found the first few weeks really challenging. I felt homesick, almost from day one and, during those early days, I phoned home every night in tears, telling Mum that I wanted to come home. At one stage I begged my dad to come and pick me up. I even asked him to phone Cambridge United and see if they'd take me on so I could continue my football career while living at home.

Dad spoke to Dave Bushell and explained how I felt. Dave was shocked because I hadn't said anything to him, but I was too scared. That was when I realised what a fantastic club Manchester United is. The coaches, staff, my team-mates, everyone did their utmost to make me feel welcome. Nothing was ever too much trouble, and everyone bent over backwards to help me to settle. I was allowed to go home almost every weekend, which cured my homesickness, and the coaches constantly checked in with me to see how I was feeling.

From that moment on, everything changed: I embraced the city and cherished the fact that I was playing football every single day. I soon became accustomed to life as a young footballer, and my time on a YTS ended up being two of the best years of my life.

After breakfast, Jason and I would walk to The Cliff, United's training ground, to get changed. The youth-team players would then get on a bus to Littleton Road where we'd train for a couple of hours. I don't think any of us had grasped how hard it was going to be physically. I went from not training at all to suddenly training every day. I found it very demanding on my young body.

When I started training with the youth team on a daily basis, I quickly realised that there wasn't a big gulf between where I was compared to the others. These youth internationals who I'd imagined to be superhuman were just kids, like me, trying to make their way in the game.

The technical side was something that I knew I needed to improve. I was always effective because of my pace, but sometimes I'd let myself down technically with my crossing or shooting, so I had a lot of work to do.

After training, it was back to The Cliff for lunch, followed by our chores. In those days, YTS jobs were very much part of the daily grind. I wasn't used to doing chores – I hadn't done much around the home as a teenager – so having to do these tasks was a bit of a shock to the system.

Each of us was responsible for cleaning the first-teamers' boots. I was allocated to Gary Pallister and David May and it's safe to say that I was pretty useless! I'd frequently forget to clean them and on one occasion an angry Pallister pulled me aside and reminded me that his boots needed to be cleaned every day. After I'd received that pep talk, I made sure I did them every day. Well, most days!

I was also responsible for cleaning the first-team dressing room. I was paired up with the youth-team captain Steven Rose. There was a lot of sweeping and mopping so we had to work out between us who was doing what. To be honest, Steven ended up doing most of it because I was useless at sweeping too. It wasn't necessarily a case of me not wanting to do my chores, it was the fact that I was absolutely shattered after training and couldn't really do the job to the high standards that were expected of us.

At the end of each day, Steven told Eric Harrison, Neil Bailey or Dave Williams, the men who were in charge of the youth team, that all our jobs had been completed and they'd then go around and check that everything had been done correctly. Only when they were satisfied would we be allowed to go back to our digs. By the time we returned to the digs in the evening, we were exhausted, so after dinner (prepared by John) Jason and I would go back to our room to rest, sleep and prepare to do it all again the following day.

Despite the hard work, we socialised together as a team. There was a room above the training ground that was kitted out with a pool table, table tennis table and dartboard, and we were given free cinema tickets, so we were never bored. A lot of lads were playing a computer game called *Final Fantasy 7*, a strange game where you had to travel from world to world. I got quite heavily into it and found myself playing into the early hours of the morning. I have quite an addictive personality and wouldn't let myself go to bed until I'd finished a certain level. After a while, I noticed that my lack of sleep was affecting my performance in training, so I stopped playing it.

One of the biggest perks was that United had a contract with a taxi company so we could get a taxi to wherever we wanted. That stopped a few years later and we were probably a reason for that because we were getting taxis here, there and everywhere!

It was a brilliant part of my life. I was with my mates doing what I loved every single day. It was a special time, although there was one part of being a first-year YTS that I was absolutely dreading – the initiation ceremony. Initiations are commonplace within football clubs. These days they typically involve a new signing singing a song or performing a dance in front of their new team-mates. They're designed to be embarrassing, but it's a way of breaking the ice and helping the team to bond.

Back in my day initiations were brutal. At United, it was called Fun and Games, but for me it was anything but. Just the thought of it put the fear of God into me. The good news was that it took place within the first two weeks. The bad news was that the build-up to it seemed to take forever.

I knew all about Fun and Games because the second-year YTS lads, who'd been through it a year earlier, took great delight in winding us up. 'Fun and Games next week, lads,' they'd say after training. I was shitting myself at the prospect of having to show myself up in front of the first team, reserves and my team-mates. It was one of the reasons I'd wanted to leave in those early days.

There were various things that we had to do, crazy things and a lot of the stuff shouldn't really be spoken about. One of the reserves (I can't remember who) donned a wig and I had to pretend he was a girl and chat him up. You can imagine how uncomfortable I found that with my introverted personality. What made it a million times worse was that the room was full of some of the best players in the world, players I'd looked up to, such as Peter Schmeichel, Ryan Giggs, Roy Keane and David Beckham, and I was being made to look like an idiot in front of them.

When that was out of the way, the treatment table was put across the centre of the dressing room to act as a net, and I had to have an imaginary tennis match against one of my team-mates.

'Pick up your imaginary tennis racket, Luke,' one international player instructed.

'Don't forget to grunt like the female players do at Wimbledon,' said another.

I was about as far out of my comfort zone as I could be. That day was one of the most awkward days of my life, but I experienced a great feeling of relief when it was over. I wondered why we were made to do it but, when it was all over, I felt – rightly or wrongly – that I was now part of the fabric of Manchester United. The whole thing, although intimidating, was done in jest, in the spirit of fun.

While we're on the subject of uncomfortable moments from my early years at United, I should probably tell you another embarrassing story. When you get a group of 16- and 17-year-old boys together, they're inevitably going to talk about two things: football and girls. Thanks to the hours I'd spent reading Teletext, I could talk about football all day long, but it was a different matter when it came to girls. One day, the lads were talking about their girlfriends. It seemed that all my team-mates had one.

'What about you, Luke?' I was asked. 'Do you have a girlfriend?'

I felt the eyes of all the lads boring down on me as they waited in anticipation for my response. The honest answer was that I didn't have a girlfriend, but I couldn't say that. I was desperate to fit in and didn't want them to think that I was different. I panicked.

'Yeah,' I replied. 'She's called Claire.'

I thought that would be the end of the matter but, back at digs, Jason would regularly speak to his girlfriend on the phone, and he wondered why I didn't want to speak to mine. I was deep in the lie and too afraid to come clean, so I had no choice but to continue with the charade. The next thing I know, I'm having pretend conversations with my imaginary girlfriend on the phone every couple of days. In the end, the pressure became too much for me, so I had a fake argument with her and ended the relationship on the phone in front of Jason. That was a huge weight off my shoulders, and I enjoyed the single life again!

The Cliff, in Broughton, Salford, had been used as a training facility by Manchester United since the late 1950s. When I joined the club in 1997, The Cliff was where the players spent most of their day. There were three dressing rooms: the first team, reserves and youth team. But apart from the changing rooms, there was no segregation, so you'd see the first-teamers all the time. It was so surreal to be walking down a corridor and see Gary Neville walk past. Or standing in line for food at the canteen behind Denis Irwin. I was in awe, and it took a while for me to get used to being so close to all my icons. I felt intimidated around these superstars and wouldn't speak to anyone unless they spoke to me first. I felt much more comfortable among my peers.

The Cliff was where we played our youth-team matches. During my first-year YTS, there was an A team and a B team. There wasn't an age limit on either team, but usually the B team was formed of first-years with a few second-years, and the A team consisted of second-years and a smattering of young pros. In my second year that changed to under-17 and under-19 teams.

There was so much quality within our squad. Wes Brown was the standout player in the youth team. He was a year older than me, a local lad, who'd signed a professional contract at the age of 17. Wes was always head and shoulders above the rest of us. He was an incredible central defender who was highly rated at the club, and rightly so. He was already playing a lot of reserve-team football and made his first-team debut later that season. When he dropped down to play with the A or B team, it filled the rest of us with confidence, knowing that he was on our side.

There wasn't a 'Wes Brown' in our year, but there was a John O'Shea. John joined slightly later than the rest of us because the school system in Ireland works differently and he had to finish his exams first. I could see immediately that John was a special defender. I'd got to the point where I could take the ball past my peers most of the time, but John was much harder to get by. He went on to have a fantastic career at United and Sunderland, and also won over a hundred caps for Ireland.

Richie Wellens, another second-year YTS, was a talented midfielder who I loved playing with because of his ability to pick me out when I'd made the runs. Richie is another who made a living from the game, notably with Blackpool, Leicester City and Doncaster Rovers, and is now a successful manager.

One of the best players in our team was Wayne Evans, a Welshman, who was a really gifted footballer. Unfortunately, it didn't work out for Wayne at Old Trafford, but he did carve out a good career in non-league football.

There were four strikers, including me, in my year – Michael Clegg, Ian Fitzpatrick and Paul Wheatcroft – plus Alex Notman and David Healy in the year above, so I had a lot of competition for a role up front.

Before one game for the B team – away at Burnley – I was told that I'd be playing on the right wing. I'd done well in training, impressing people with my work ethic, and the coaches had noticed that I was having a lot of joy when I was running with the ball, so the idea was to try me in a wide position. I'm not sure if the plan was for that to become my permanent position but I had a really good game, scoring a brace and setting another up.

From that point on, the coaches felt that my future was as a winger rather than a centre-forward and I didn't play as a striker again. I could play on either flank and, because I'd had that initial success against Burnley, I was happy to go along with the coaches' wishes. I certainly wasn't the kind of person who'd knock on the manager's door demanding to play up front. Over time I recognised that I was more effective out wide because my strengths were moving with the ball, my electrifying pace and how hard I worked.

One thing that made the coaches think favourably of me from my first day was that I always gave 100 per cent. There are so many variables during a game of football, so many things that you can't control. But the one thing that I could control was how hard I worked, so I made sure that I ran until I could run no more. The minimum expectation at any level was putting a shift in. So hard work was never an issue for me – unless it was cleaning the dressing rooms, of course!

As the season progressed, I was playing regularly and getting lots of assists and goals. I adapted to my new role like a duck to water but I knew that, if I was to make a career in the game, I needed to learn what to do when we were out of possession. During those early games, I'd stand on the sideline, waiting for us to retain the ball, and then try to run past everyone when I received it. That was fine in the A or B team, but I needed to adapt if I wanted to play at a higher level.

In our B league, there was a team called Marine, obviously not a pro club but their youth team used to play in our division for some reason. We played against them in a terrible game where we were awful. We were so bad that their goalkeeper scored! He kicked the ball out of his hands, and it bounced over our keeper into the net. I was playing on the left wing and Eric Harrison kept telling me to tuck in. I now know that he wanted me to tuck in tight on the opposition's midfielder, but at the time I had no idea what he was going on about. I was too shy to ask him what he meant, so I just carried on hogging the touchline. His instructions gradually turned into moans as I ignored him. That's something that sticks in my mind because I wasn't doing what was expected of me. It was a steep learning curve and I dedicated myself to understanding how to play without the ball.

Winning is an important part of the culture at Manchester United, and the FA Youth Cup is a big thing. Since its creation in 1952, United have won the FA Youth Cup a record 11 times, with the 1992 cup-winning side producing the core of the historic treble-winning squad. Phil Neville, Ronnie Wallwork and Michael Clegg had won the FA Youth Cup in 1995 and they'd progressed to the first team, so we all knew how important a good cup run could be for our development.

We entered the Youth Cup at the second-round stage, but before that we had a game against Wigan at Springfield Park in the Lancashire Cup. I didn't expect to be selected because the cup squads were usually formed of second-year players, with only a handful of first-years. But to my surprise, I started the match on the right wing. I played exceptionally well, setting up a couple and scoring one myself in an emphatic 6-0 victory.

I didn't know it at the time, but that game changed the coaches' perception of me from 'just one of the players' to 'one of the best'. It was also the match when I began to win the respect of my peers. I remember Wes Brown telling me how well I'd done, and his feedback made me feel ten feet tall.

Following my performance against Wigan, I was delighted to retain my place in the starting line-up for the FA Youth Cup second-round tie away at Blackburn on 2 December 1997. That was a really tough draw as they had a strong team featuring the likes of future England international David Dunn, and

Martin Taylor, who went on to make over 400 appearances during his career.

We drew a poor game 1-1 and I didn't have any impact whatsoever. Afterwards, Sir Alex, who often attended Youth Cup games, came into the dressing room and was fuming, telling us that our performance was unacceptable. He called out a couple of players but didn't say anything to me personally, which I was quite happy about, even though I knew I'd played badly.

That was the first Alex Ferguson hairdryer that I'd witnessed, although it wasn't a full-blown one because he knew he was dealing with young kids. I'll never forget sitting in that dressing room at Ewood Park, staring at the floor. I deserved a telling-off but luckily I managed to avoid one. Obviously, it was scary when the great man was shouting at you, but worse than that was the feeling that you'd disappointed him. All you ever wanted to do was your best for him and, in turn, the football club.

The good news was that we hadn't lost the match, and the replay was to be held at Old Trafford a few days later. I'd not yet played at the Theatre of Dreams, so I was feeling excited when I arrived at the stadium for the replay. My excitement turned to devastation when I found out that I'd been dropped, not just from the starting line-up, but from the entire squad. That was a huge wake-up call; I'd gone from doing really well and gaining favourable reports to not even making the bench for the most important game of the season. I was left with a feeling of emptiness in the pit of my stomach. I accepted that I probably wouldn't be named in the first XI, but I'd expected to be included as a substitute because I was always capable of impacting a game. It made me question whether I was actually good enough to be at a club like Manchester United.

I learned how cut-throat football can be. The FA Youth Cup is built up into a huge thing at United, with the tradition, and maybe that was why I'd crumbled against Blackburn. I'd been so overawed by the occasion when in essence it was just 22 kids playing a game of football, albeit in a large stadium.

As I gained experience, I began to look at games as just that – a game. The pitches are the same size, the rules are the same. The more I played the more I understood that the most important game of the season is the one you're playing at that moment in time. There's nothing before, nothing after, just the one you're playing in.

Sadly, we lost the replay 3-2, after extra time, and that was us done. It was so disappointing, going out at the first hurdle, and it was little consolation that Blackburn finished as runners-up in the cup that year, losing to Everton in the final.

Chapter 4

Bambi on Ice

TOWARDS THE end of my first year on a YTS, I was having an issue with my groin that was causing soreness after games. I went for some tests and found out that I had a hernia and needed an operation. I missed the last few weeks of the season. After the op, I spent the summer back in Meldreth. I couldn't do a lot in terms of exercise because I was recovering from my hernia, so I spent the time resting and recuperating.

The highlight of the summer (apart from the annual church fete, of course!) was the 1998 World Cup held in France. Like most of the nation, my eyes were glued to the television, watching England progress to the round of 16 where we lost to Argentina on penalties. I watched most of the games in the Barrington Social Club with my mates and I remember making out that I was a lot closer to the four United lads in the England squad than I actually was. I was trying to impress my friends by pretending that Paul Scholes, Gary Neville, David Beckham and Teddy Sheringham were my mates when in reality they didn't have a clue who I was!

When I returned to Manchester for pre-season training, I felt 100 per cent fit and raring to go. I was looking forward to getting back into the swing of being a young footballer. Over the previous 12 months, I'd felt that I'd become one of the better players in the youth team, although I was aware that I still had a lot of improving to do.

The first year had been challenging because I was part of the youngest of the full-time groups at the club and I didn't know what to expect. I found the second year much more comfortable because I was one of the older players in the youth team, felt settled in my digs with John and Jason, and I could just focus on my football. Plus, I didn't have to worry about Fun and Games this time!

I didn't set myself any targets; I just focused on one day at a time. I aimed to give my all during training sessions and games and see where that took me.

A couple of months into the 1998/99 season, I made my reserve-team debut in a Pontins League fixture away to Leicester. There were over 20,000 fans packed into Filbert Street – by far the biggest crowd I'd played in front of at the time – and the hairs on the back of my neck stood up when I came on as a second-half substitute. We won 6-2 with Jon Greening bagging a hat-trick. From then on, I spent the majority of the season playing for the second string, although I made a few under-19 appearances too.

Back in those days, reserve-team games were proper football, a mixture of up-and-coming youngsters and seasoned pros who were out of favour or recovering from injury. It wasn't unusual to be coming up against an international, which was great for my development. It was a buzz to play against someone who'd played a lot of first-team games, and I relished the chance to pit my wits against these experienced stars. Mark

Delaney and Lee Sharp were two opponents who stood out. I loved the challenge.

Apart from the few appearances I'd made as an ineligible player for Barrington, this was my first real taste of men's football. I was full of confidence because I'd been doing so well against lads my age, and I started having a lot of joy with the reserves. I was encouraged to play to my strengths, and I just felt so free. I was fearless in those days, and I'd try to run with the ball every time I got it. That was the start of MUTV, where all our games were broadcast to subscribers, and I had a lot of people raving about my performances. I flourished under the spotlight.

We played most of our reserve games at Bury's ground, Gigg Lane, but for the bigger matches we'd play at Old Trafford. They felt like proper games, ultra-competitive. My debut at the Theatre of Dreams came against Leeds United Reserves. There was a big crowd there and I played really well, even managing to score a goal with a diving header of all things. I know it wasn't a first-team game in front of 70,000 people, but just to have played at Old Trafford in any match was a dream come true.

I knew that I was improving each week, and after a handful of appearances for the reserves I was summoned to the manager's office for the first time. Lee Roche, a defender who'd also made the jump up to the reserves, had also been asked to see Sir Alex, so we went together. We sat down and listened intently as the great man told us how pleased he was with our progress and then he stunned us by saying that he was offering us both a professional contract. To say that I was ecstatic is an understatement. He didn't talk about figures, he just told us that we'd receive details of the terms of the contract through the post. There was no negotiation, it was just expected that we'd sign. Why wouldn't we?

A few days later I received my new contract and was over the moon. I was being offered a three-year deal starting at £500 a week, increasing to £600 the following year, and then £700. Rochey, who was from nearby Bolton, wasn't too happy because he was offered £100 a week less than me. The reasoning was that it cost me more to travel home, and I certainly wasn't going to argue!

As if that wasn't enough, the contract also included a £10,000 signing-on fee, broken down over three years. The day I signed the deal, £3,500 appeared in my bank account. I'd never seen that much money before – I felt like a millionaire. If there's one thing a young professional footballer needs, it's a decent wardrobe, so I went out and spent a large chunk of my signing-on fee on some extremely dodgy new clothes!

Although I was now a pro, I was still only 18 so there was no obligation for me to find my own place to live. The club preferred the young players to stay in digs – where they had someone looking out for them – and that was fine with me. I was still very much a kid and liked living with John and Jason.

I managed to train with the first-team players on a few occasions, but they were limited to the international breaks when those who hadn't been called up by their countries dropped down and trained with us. Even though I was now a professional footballer at Manchester United, I knew I was a million miles away from being a *proper* professional.

It's a big step up from the youth team to the first team, and it usually takes a while to make that transition. One of the few who was fast-tracked was Wes Brown, who'd made his first-team debut the previous year and became part of the squad for most of the 1998/99 season. There can be a lot of jealousy in football when your peers go on to achieve things that you don't, but I was always happy to see my mates making that step up.

The big thing about being a young player at Manchester United was that there was always a pathway to the first team. That was one of the reasons why the best young players in the country signed for United; everyone knew that there would be an opportunity. The Class of '92 lads were a prime example. I knew that if I kept on developing and performing like I had been, I'd get a chance. Don't get me wrong, I never for one minute thought that I'd replace Ryan Giggs or David Beckham in the starting line-up. They were two of the best wide men in the world. The goal for me was to try to get into the squad and maybe come on for five minutes here and there. Just to get onto the pitch and enter the same arena as all those superstars would be an achievement. But that was all far away in the distance.

The 1998/99 FA Youth Cup pitted us against Everton, the holders, in the third round. They were one of the best youth teams around and had future Premier League players Tony Hibbert, Leon Osman and Francis Jeffers in their line-up, so it was a tough draw. We weren't as strong as we'd been the season before because, well, we didn't have Wes Brown anymore. We'd also lost another key player in future Northern Ireland international striker David Healy, who was now too old to play for the youth team.

We were drawn at home, and although United usually played their FA Youth Cup games at Old Trafford, we played Everton at Gigg Lane because the first team was playing Middlesbrough at home on the same day. Sir Alex wasn't in attendance either because he was preparing for the Premier League match, and that was a huge disappointment, especially as I put in a great performance, scoring two goals. To be fair, Everton battered us on the day, but I equalised with just a few minutes left on the clock to give us a 2-2 draw.

After the game, I was asked to do an interview for BBC Radio 5 Live. I was still quite introverted, but I was absolutely buzzing after my brace, and being interviewed on the radio made me feel like a real footballer. It was probably a terrible interview, though!

A few weeks later we went to Goodison Park for the replay, and we got beat 4-0. We were totally outplayed. Unfortunately, Sir Alex *was* watching that game. He was sitting next to Dave Bushell, who was telling the manager how well I'd been doing. Sir Alex turned to him and said, 'Well, today he looks more like Bambi on ice than a footballer.' When Dave passed on that feedback, it brought me right back down to earth.

I finished the season strongly, scoring a really good goal against Oldham in the Manchester Senior Cup Final at Boundary Park. We won 3-0 and I got to lift my first piece of silverware, which was nice.

And that was it for the youth and reserve teams; our season had finished. But the first team still had lots to play for. Three days after we played Oldham, I was at Old Trafford to see United lift the Premier League trophy, and a week later I travelled down to Wembley with the rest of the reserves and youth-team players to watch Manchester United win the FA Cup.

And then it was time for the big one, the Champions League Final. The club flew every member of staff out to Barcelona for the final, which was amazing. We travelled to Spain on the morning of the game and were taken to a fish restaurant on the harbour where we had a couple of beers. Then we moved on for a few more beers and ended up somewhere we probably shouldn't have been.

As kick-off approached, we went to find the coach that was going to take us to the stadium, but no one could remember where we were supposed to meet it! Instead, we got on the metro, worse for wear, not having a scooby doo where we were going! We probably shouldn't have drunk as much as we did but we were celebrating the end of our season and I think we got caught up in the excitement of what was an historic occasion.

We eventually found the Camp Nou and took our seats behind the goal where Ole Gunnar Solskjær and Teddy Sheringham scored the late goals that won United the Champions League and an unprecedented treble.

After the game, we got on the coach and headed back to the airport. I wasn't a particularly big drinker, but I'd been drinking for most of the day and was completely gone by that stage. The club had chartered several planes, and we were herded onto one and flown back to Manchester. It was a long day, but a memorable one. And one that I'll certainly never forget.

Chapter 5

My Hero and the Villans

I RETURNED to Meldreth in the summer of 1999 thinking that I'd made it. I'd enjoyed my best-ever season and was receiving lots of praise from my coaches. I even read an article where Sir Alex Ferguson was quoted as saying that he had high hopes of me breaking into the first team the following year. That was brilliant to hear but probably gave me a bit of a big head.

I'd been dating my future wife, Hayley, for a few months, but we had a bit of a separation during the summer, so I went out to Ibiza with my mates. We drank all the time, ate a load of rubbish and I did very little running or fitness work. As a result, I returned to Manchester for pre-season in the worst possible shape to start my first full season as a pro. If I'm honest, I thought it was going to be easy. My YTS days were behind me, which meant that I didn't have to do any chores, my wages had increased to £600 a week (plus I received another £3,500 as part of my signing-on fee), and I had the security of two more years remaining on my contract.

The reality was completely different. If anything, it was going to be harder now because I'd be playing against tougher opponents each week. I learned a lot about how not to behave as a professional footballer. I soon realised that the only thing that had changed was that I was a year older. I was still a long, long way from becoming a first-team player. I needed to continue to work hard and do the same things that had got me to this stage, or my journey would end very quickly.

There's a fine margin between success and failure in football, and there's a huge difference for those who make it compared to those who don't. A few of the lads, like Wes Brown, John O'Shea and David Healy, were on their way to becoming internationals, but others, including my former roommate Jason, weren't offered professional contracts and drifted out of the game.

I moved into the reserve dressing room and, although we trained in a separate group from the first team, pre-season gave me an opportunity to play alongside some of the treble-winning stars. On 30 July 1999, I was part of the squad selected to play against Bristol Rovers in a testimonial match for former Manchester United left-back Lee Martin. Martin had famously scored the winning goal in the 1990 FA Cup Final replay to claim United's first trophy under Sir Alex. The manager wanted to do something to help him out.

I played the full 90 minutes on the left wing. We had David May at the back, David Beckham on the right, Paul Scholes in midfield and Ole Gunnar Solskjær up front. The rest of the side consisted of my mates from the reserves, such as Dave Healy, Lee Roche and John O'Shea. I enjoyed playing alongside the big hitters, but it helped massively that I was doing it with lads that I knew. Jim Ryan, the reserve-team coach, took the team, but Sir Alex was watching, and I felt I gave a decent account of myself.

That game aside, I didn't enjoy a particularly good start to the 1999/2000 season. My development had stalled, and I wasn't progressing as much as the club expected of me. Complacency had set in. I'd played a lot of reserve-team games and I think I needed something different to take my game to the next level.

All the young players knew that there was always a potential opportunity for us to play in the League Cup (sponsored by Worthington at the time). For years Sir Alex Ferguson had used the competition to rest the senior players and blood some youngsters. The idea was to give the fringe players a taste of first-team action to see who could cut it at that level, who would rise to the occasion.

Manchester United were due to play Aston Villa in the third round of the League Cup on Wednesday, 13 October 1999, and during the build-up to the match there was a lot of excitement among us reserve-team players, as we wondered whether any of us would be involved. Most of the regular first-teamers had played in Alex Ferguson's testimonial against a Rest of the World XI on the Monday night and, with a Premier League fixture against Watford on the horizon, we expected the manager to rest some of the big stars for the visit to Villa Park.

On the eve of the game, I left my digs in the morning and took the short walk across to The Cliff as usual. While I was getting changed, I was told that I, along with a few other lads from the reserves, would be part of the squad for the League Cup tie. I was absolutely buzzing.

After a brief warm-up with the first team, we were split into two groups; those who'd played in Monday's friendly were in one, and I was in the other with my mates from the reserve team – including Michael Clegg, John O'Shea, Lee Roche,

Dave Healy, Richie Wellens – and a sprinkling of senior pros, preparing for the League Cup tie. It would have been great to play a competitive match alongside all the big stars – Beckham, Scholes and Ryan Giggs – but having so many of my mates alongside me in my first senior squad made the situation a little more comfortable. Saying that, and this might sound selfish, the only thing I was interested in was whether or not I'd play. At the end of the session, I found out that I'd be starting the match. I couldn't wait. After training I walked back to my digs with a huge smile on my face. *This is it*, I thought. *This is the moment I've been waiting my whole life for.*

I slept sporadically that night, as you can imagine. A combination of nerves and excitement kept me awake deep into the early hours. It's pretty hard to switch your mind off when you know that in less than 24 hours you're going to play for Manchester United!

The following morning, I travelled with the squad down the M6 to Birmingham. We arrived at the Marriott Hotel, near Villa Park, and enjoyed lunch before going to our rooms to rest and relax ahead of the match. I'd been allocated a room on my own and didn't know what to do with myself as it was all new to me. When I played with the reserves and youth team, we'd travel straight to the stadium, play the game and then come home. This felt like the right way to prepare, though. It made me feel like a real footballer.

It was a long afternoon. I was just hours away from playing the biggest game of my life, so sleep was out of the question, and I found it hard to relax. I wiled away the hours chatting to friends and family on the phone. After what seemed an eternity, it was time to board the coach and travel the short distance from the Marriott to Villa Park. My nerves and excitement turned up a notch when I caught my first glimpse of the famous old stadium that I'd seen on TV so many times.

The smile I'd been wearing all day vanished as soon as we got off the coach and I heard the Aston Villa fans who'd gathered in the car park. There were boos, jeers and lots of hostility aimed towards all of us, but especially Mark Bosnich, our goalkeeper, who'd recently left Villa for United. It was startling for me as a young player to feel such hatred from opposing fans, but it was something I eventually got used to. I had to – that was the reaction we got whenever I travelled with United.

My smile returned when I stepped onto the pitch for the warm-up. The ground began to fill with spectators, and I looked around in awe, pinching myself as a reminder that I was about to play a proper game of football in such an iconic venue.

The whole day had been full of firsts, and in the visitors' dressing room before kick-off I experienced another – a Sir Alex Ferguson team talk. These days young players often travel with the squad on a matchday so they can see first-hand what it's all about, but this was my first adventure with the first team, and it was all new to me. I loved every minute, especially when I saw my name and number on the back of my United shirt. 'Chadwick 39'.

Just moments after Sir Alex finished delivering his pre-match instructions, we congregated in the tunnel and lined up alongside our opponents. United's side that evening consisted of three world-class players – Jordi Cruyff, Ole Gunnar Solskjær and Mark Bosnich – plus a bunch of skinny kids. In contrast, Villa's team – who'd finished sixth in the Premier League a few months earlier – was full of household names, including Ugo Ehiogu, Gareth Barry, Alan Thompson, George Boateng, Julian Joachim and their England international striker Dion Dublin. Dion had been a hero to me when I was growing up and he was a massive reason that I developed a love for football and dreamed of being a professional footballer. My childhood memories of watching Dion play at the Abbey Stadium suddenly came rushing back as it dawned on me that I was about to play against him. It was such a surreal moment.

I was playing on the left side of midfield and was up against Welsh international right-back Mark Delaney, a very good one-v-one defender. I honestly thought that I was going to have a field day. I thought it was just a case of doing my usual trick of knocking the ball past the defender and running around him to get on the other end, but it proved to be a lot more challenging than that. I quickly learned that this level was a lot harder than anything I was used to. The innocence of youth!

I don't have huge recollections of the match itself, but one overriding memory is towards the end of the game when Dublin and our defender Ronnie Wallwork were involved in a bit of a tussle, just handbags really. I ran over and got in between them, although I have no idea what I thought I was going to do, especially when I realised how big and strong Dion was! Luckily the ref came over and calmed things down.

When the final whistle blew, I felt exhausted. Absolutely shattered. All the adrenaline and energy had been drained from my body during those gruelling 90 minutes and it took me a few days to recover. Despite the fatigue, my overwhelming feeling was one of immense pride. I knew my parents and Hayley (we were back together by then) were somewhere in the ground and it's great to know that they were there to experience that moment with me, although at the time I was purely focused on what it meant to me.

Despite losing 3-0 to a stronger, more experienced side, I thought we did alright. I wasn't brilliant by any stretch of the imagination, but I was relatively pleased with my performance. The experience was invaluable, and I learned so much from the occasion. To be honest, I don't think many people would have expected us to win that game but defeat still hurt. And the manager, during his post-match team talk, let us know in no uncertain terms that, although we were young, inexperienced players, it was unacceptable for a Manchester United team to go to Aston Villa and lose by three goals.

I glanced around the dressing room at the lads I'd played with over the years, and they were all just staring at the floor. Inside, I'm sure that they, like me, were absolutely buzzing from having made their debuts, but no one was brave enough to look up and risk making eye contact with Sir Alex after a defeat. That was the last thing you ever wanted to do.

After the euphoria of making my debut, I went straight back to the reserves, which was what I expected. Maybe if we'd gone through to the next round, I'd have had another outing, but I knew that my first-team exploits had ended at Villa Park. For the 1999/2000 season at least.

The competition for a place in the first-team squad was so fierce and I wasn't ready to be involved with them on a regular basis. I planned to continue working as hard as possible every single day and just see where that took me. If I performed well, I might be able to force my way into the squad for a Premier League match, but it seemed an impossible task at the time. I wasn't progressing enough playing with the reserves. I needed a change of environment, somewhere I could play regular first-team football and continue my development.

That opportunity soon came in the form of the Belgian Second Division side Antwerp.

Chapter 6

A Royal Adventure

IN DECEMBER 1999, Mick Phelan, Manchester United's reserve-team manager, told me that I'd be going on loan to the Belgian Second Division team Royal Antwerp, United's feeder club. I flew over to meet the manager, Regi Van Acker. He told me that he'd watched me play for the reserves and was so impressed with my performances that he'd asked Sir Alex Ferguson if he could take me on loan. It made me feel special, knowing that I was wanted.

I was delighted to join Antwerp and thought the move would give me exactly what I needed. Even though I'd made my United debut, in all honesty I was further away from regular involvement with the first team than I'd been the season before. Antwerp were giving me a chance to play competitive football week in, week out, something that could only help my development.

Everything about the move – completely new surroundings for a short period, living in a different country, regular involvement – appealed to me, and I couldn't wait to get started.

After enjoying the festive period in Manchester, I moved to Belgium in January 2000 to begin a new adventure. My girlfriend, Hayley, came over with me and we moved into a hotel, located in the Diamond Quarter, close to the city centre. Hayley, who was from Barrington, Cambridgeshire, returned to England after a week or so to resume her college studies. I found it hard not being able to see her as often as before. There were plenty of phone calls, though – no text messages in those days – and we both had pagers, so we were able to keep in touch regularly.

At first, living in a hotel was a novelty, but I soon went stir-crazy. After a couple of months, I rented a flat in the city centre with my brother Carl, who'd moved over to Belgium to keep me company.

I was lucky that two of my close friends from the youth team – George Clegg and Kirk Hilton – were also on loan at Antwerp, and they helped me to settle in. United and Antwerp had created a link in 1997 that allowed Manchester United to send promising young players to the Belgians to gain some first-team experience. Danny Higginbotham was the first to make the move and a total of 29 others – including John O'Shea, Tom Heaton, Danny Simpson and Jonny Evans – were sent to Antwerp, until the relationship ended in 2009.

Antwerp is a very diverse city, in the north of Belgium, with a large Jewish community. It was very different compared to living in Meldreth or Manchester, but I embraced the new culture and grew as a person from the experience.

I was welcomed by my new team-mates and got on well with everyone, although I was my usual reserved self. The youth-team dressing rooms I grew up in featured predominantly British and Irish players, whereas Antwerp's squad consisted of players from all over Europe and Africa, so I found it strange at first, sitting in the changing room, listening to multiple languages. But most Europeans are a lot more educated than us Brits when it comes to learning languages and the majority of my team-mates spoke English, which was a huge help.

Royal Antwerp, the oldest football club in Belgium, was languishing in the Second Division when I joined, and the aim was to win promotion. The lads were doing well, and my first challenge was to get into the first team. That's not easy when a side is winning games and sitting near the top of the table.

At that time, pretty much every team in England played 4-4-2; games were played at a frenetic pace and you were on the move all the time. Belgian football was slower, but much more technical. Antwerp, like most of our opponents, employed a possession-based style of play, where teams would keep the ball in circulation as long as possible. That allowed me to stand out because I was a direct player, someone who travelled with the ball more or less every time I received it. I was totally different from the type of players being produced in Belgium.

The other major difference was that the games all meant something. When I was playing for United's reserves, you'd often play against some big names, which was great, but it was still reserve football and there was nothing on the line. The three points up for grabs in league games made a world of difference to the supporters and would impact the amount of money my team-mates could earn. The result at the end of the 90 minutes was so important and I got caught up with that. A lot of players can be quite selfish when they're on loan, focusing solely on their performance, but I felt an instant connection to the club and wanted to help Antwerp have a successful season.

I made my debut on 8 January 2000, coming off the bench in a 2-0 defeat away to Royal AA Louvieroise. A week later I made my home debut against KFC Dessel Sport – it's one of the most memorable matches of my career.

Our stadium, Bosuilstadion, was quite dated but always produced an electric atmosphere. There were smoke bombs in the stands, passionate fans generating a Continental feeling – and that was just during the warm-up! Aged 19, I was fearless. When I received the ball for the first time, I ran with it and the crowd was off their feet with excitement. The fans' reaction gave me so much confidence and before long I'd scored my first professional goal. It was one of the most exhilarating experiences of my life and, to top it off, the crowd started singing my name. I couldn't believe it. It wasn't that long ago that I'd been sitting in the stands, chanting the name of my Cambridge heroes and now I was on the receiving end. We won the game 5-0. What a day!

At that moment, if I'd been offered the chance to stay in Belgium for the rest of my career, I'd have happily taken it. I was addicted to first-team football. Playing in front of fans each week, winning games – there was just no better feeling. I was excelling in my performances and loving every minute.

I scored my first, and only, senior hat-trick on 23 March 2000, in a 5-1 home demolition of KV Kortrijk, and we went on to win the league title by a staggering 19 points. On the day we were crowned champions, the supporters ran onto the pitch and lifted me onto their shoulders. I had my shirt ripped off and nearly lost my boots and shorts too as fans clamoured for a souvenir. A photo appeared in the newspaper of me being carried off the pitch by the jubilant supporters. I didn't have my shirt on and looked like a right skinny little thing.

It was such a fantastic day, but I found it quite hard to celebrate and really enjoy the moment. I felt a little awkward, wondering how much I'd actually done to help the team. I looked around and saw my team-mates lost in the moment, absolutely buzzing, but I didn't feel the same way. I almost felt deflated; the season was over, and our target had been achieved. It was the same feeling I experienced throughout my career; I always found it difficult to celebrate team achievements, which is a real shame. I get more joy out of my career now when I look back than I did at the time.

At the end of the season, Manchester United brought a reserve team over to Antwerp to play against us in a friendly. We won 1-0 and I assisted the goal. It was brilliant to see all the lads, but strange playing against United. Mike Phelan spoke to me afterwards and gave me some nice feedback about my development.

That summer I was called up by England for the UEFA Under-21 European Championships, which were being held in Slovakia. As part of the preparations for the tournament, we stayed in Oulton Hall, Leeds, at the same time that the senior squad was there. Steve McClaren, assistant manager of both Manchester United and England, told me that everyone at the club was pleased with how I'd performed in Belgium.

'When you come back to United, you'll be part of the first-team squad,' he said. I was shocked. I didn't even think he'd know who I was, for a start! I'd expected to just slide back in with the reserves, and the thought of spending pre-season with the big hitters invoked a bit of fear.

After the tournament, I was staying with my mum when Steve McClaren rang. He told me that they'd decided to send me back to Antwerp for another season to gain more experience. I was delighted with the news. I'd loved my first season and felt comfortable over there.

Hayley had finished college that summer, so she moved out to Belgium with me to share the experience. We rented a little flat in the city centre, just a 25-minute walk from Antwerp's stadium. It was the first time we'd lived together so everything was new. Nutrition wasn't a big thing back then and I was hardly domesticated, so we ate a lot from Pizza Hut or food from other local takeaways. Neither of us could cook, but it didn't matter because we didn't have an oven. We had a hob, a frying pan and a saucepan, so unless you could boil it or fry it, we didn't eat it.

We did get our first taste of the big time when Mariah Carey was performing in Antwerp. Tickets were impossible to get, but an agent who was desperate to represent me sorted me out with a pair. A courier on a motorbike delivered them to me at the training ground, which was so cool, although the lads gave me quite a bit of stick!

I settled in quickly off the pitch. On it, I soon discovered that the standard of opposition was a lot better in the Belgian Pro League (top flight) compared to the Second Division. We'd lost a few of the players who'd got us promoted and I don't think our squad was as strong as it had been the previous season, but we were all determined to avoid relegation.

It didn't really worry me that we'd gone from a team winning most games to one that might struggle. I relished the prospect of pitting my wits against the best players in the country. It gave me an opportunity to show everyone what I could do. I understood that you'll win, lose and draw games, but in football you can only take care of your performance, so I focused only on doing my job. Hopefully, that was as part of a winning team, but as long as I could say that I'd done my best after each game, I'd be happy. I was always fairly grounded and never took defeats too badly, nor did I get too carried away after a win.

Four games into the season, we'd lost three, won one. Our next opponents were Anderlecht, the champions. Our stadium was packed to the rafters, with a hostile environment because the two sets of fans hated each other. Anderlecht were in the same Champions League group as Manchester United, so we knew they wouldn't be pushovers. We gave them a good game, but unfortunately lost 3-0. After the match, I walked back to my flat through a park and I saw groups of supporters fighting each other. I zipped my jacket up to the top to hide my chin, desperately hoping that no one would recognise me!

Despite the club's struggle in the league, my performances were earning rave reviews. One of the national newspapers wanted to interview me as I was regarded as one of the best young players in the league. I hadn't received any media training and was a little uncomfortable but managed to stumble my way through using a host of cliches – every other word I said was 'obviously' and I threw in at least one 'at the end of the day'. That's how footballers are supposed to talk, right? When the paper went on sale, I rushed out to buy a copy. I was so proud that there was an article about me in a national newspaper, and I wanted to take a copy home and show it to my parents. I couldn't understand Flemish, but I skimmed the article, nevertheless, and froze when I saw a paragraph containing words and phrases that I could understand.

'Dentures a la Bugs Bunny.' 'Acne.'

My heart sank and shame swept over me. I couldn't understand why the media were poking fun at my appearance. This was supposed to be an article about me as a footballer, not a piss-take of how I looked. I'm pretty sure that the rest of the piece was complimentary, but the damage had already been done. I felt embarrassed and wanted to go out and buy every single copy and destroy them, so no one else could read the article.

It had been mentioned to me previously that I looked different, with spots on my face and teeth that stuck out but, in my mind, I was a completely normal teenager who just wanted to play football. At school, you have banter and mickey-taking with your mates, and I always gave as good as I got. This was different. I naively thought that when I left school and became an adult, the childish behaviour would stop. I had no problem at all with people writing negative things about my performance on the pitch, but my appearance? That was personal. It had crossed a line. But what could I do? There was no way in the world that I was going to contact the journalist or complain to the newspaper, so I just brushed it under the carpet and tried to ignore it.

It didn't affect my game. I continued to play well, although I became paranoid and anxious whenever I was mentioned in the papers. I'd always, as many players do, check the match rating I'd been given by journalists. Sometimes you got so lost in the game that it was difficult to assess whether you'd had a good game or not, so the ratings were either confirmation that I'd played well or a kick up the backside that I needed to improve. But now, instead of focusing on the ratings, I scanned the articles to see if those words materialised again. As far as I know, my appearance wasn't mentioned in Belgium again and I naively thought that that would be the end of it. Little did I know that jokes about my appearance would plague the early part of my career and have such a detrimental impact on my mental health.

I scored my first top-flight goal away to Lierse. You can't replicate the feeling of scoring a goal and sometimes your emotions take over. As soon as the ball hit the back of the net, I ran to the away fans like a lunatic to celebrate. My reaction to scoring was always impulsive; I was never cool enough to have a planned celebration.

Manchester United's youth development officer, Dave Bushell, and my old landlord, John Lancaster, came over one weekend to watch a game and we had a good catch-up afterwards. I have a lot of respect for Dave and appreciate the honest feedback he always gave me. Other than that, I had very little contact with United during my loan spell. I felt pretty much forgotten about, which was perfect for me. I was happy out there and enjoying my football.

Some time in October 2000, Regi called me into his office. I thought he was going to tell me that I was joining the club permanently. I'm not sure why I thought that, but I did feel a little excited at the prospect. Instead, he told me that Manchester United wanted me to return immediately. He was disappointed because he'd be losing one of his better players. I was disappointed because I was enjoying my football and loved the city.

So, Hayley and I packed our bags, said our goodbyes and headed back to Manchester. I assumed that I'd be spending the rest of the season in the reserves. I couldn't have been more wrong.

Chapter 7

Who's Luke Chadwick?

WHEN I returned to Manchester, I booked into a bed and breakfast in Sale, near United's training ground, Carrington (they'd moved from The Cliff while I'd been in Belgium), while Hayley and I began house-hunting for a more permanent residence.

As expected, I was back with the reserves and, although it was good to see my mates again, I missed the competitiveness that came with first-team football.

At the end of October 2000, I was called up to the squad for a League Cup tie away at Watford. Just like the Aston Villa match the previous season, our side consisted mainly of younger players with a handful of bigger names. But it wasn't my debut this time, so I didn't experience any nerves. I'd gained invaluable experience with Antwerp, and I was full of confidence.

I lined up on the right wing, and came up against Paul Robinson, a good left-back who I knew well from the England Under-21s. I enjoyed a lot of success against Robinson that night and had a hand in two of our goals in a deserved 3-0 win. In the dressing room afterwards, the manager said, 'Well played, Luke.' Those three simple words meant so much coming from

Sir Alex Ferguson. He was complimentary about me in the newspapers too.

I was still training with the reserves but soon found myself named in the squad for a Premier League game against Coventry City at Highfield Road. Seeing my name on the team sheet and warming up with the lads was unreal. That was when I started to feel part of it all. I didn't get on the pitch – I hadn't expected to – but it felt like a real turning point.

A week later, on 11 November 2000, I made my Premier League debut, as a substitute, in a home match against Middlesbrough. I'd spent most of the game warming up on the touchline, desperate to step onto the pitch. I'd played there for the reserves, of course, but this was the first time I'd ever witnessed a packed Old Trafford from pitch level.

We were winning 2-1 when Sir Alex beckoned me over and told me to get ready. I looked at the scoreboard and saw that 90 minutes had been played. I knew I wouldn't have much time, but I didn't care.

As I slapped hands with Dwight Yorke and took my position on the left wing, the stadium announcer's voice boomed around the ground. 'Replacing number 19, Dwight Yorke, is number 36, Luke Chadwick.' The supporters clapped and cheered and I'm sure most turned to the person sitting next to them and asked, 'Who's Luke Chadwick?'

I was in a heightened state of excitement, with adrenaline flowing through my body. I ran around like a headless chicken because I didn't want my first Premier League appearance to end without me touching the ball. Fortunately, I went on a couple of little runs, although they didn't lead to anything. I was on cloud nine at the end of the game.

Walking down the tunnel, Roy Keane patted me on the back and said, 'Well done.' I thought he was taking the piss because I'd only been on the pitch for two minutes, but he was being genuine. Although a very minor one, I'd played a part in our victory. At Manchester United, we won together and lost together. That game was massive for me, an incredible honour.

A fortnight later I travelled with the squad to Derby. Sitting in the Pride Park dressing room before the match, Sir Alex read out the line-up and he said my name. There had been no indication that I'd be starting, and I thought I'd misheard him until the lads came over to offer their congratulations.

I played on the right wing, coming up against Seth Johnson, another one of my England colleagues, who was playing left-back. He kicked me in the air early on, but then I had some real joy against him and made a positive impact on the game. I forced their keeper to make a save with a left-footed shot from outside the box that normally wouldn't have reached the goal, and I was pleased with my performance when I was substituted with 15 minutes to go.

The following week, I moved into the first-team dressing room and was involved in more or less every squad for the rest of the season. I didn't expect to play in every game. I knew I was a bit-part player and I accepted that. I was happy to deputise for David Beckham or Ryan Giggs when they were injured or needed a rest. Being a back-up to two of the best wingers in the world at the time was a huge honour.

It was a big thing, becoming part of the first-team squad, but I found it quite difficult to adjust. I still played the same way that I had as a kid: with freedom and a smile on my face. On a football pitch, regardless of my opponent, I always tried to express myself. I had confidence in my ability as a footballer and felt capable of producing performances worthy of United.

In training I was a bit more anxious and uptight, and it took a while to integrate with those big stars that I was still in awe of because of who they were and what they'd achieved. I suffered from imposter syndrome when I was with the lads off the pitch. On the pitch you get lost in the game so that was okay; it was before and after that was the issue. I found it so challenging trying to walk into a dressing room full of superstars.

The pre-season friendlies and my two League Cup outings had been fine because there had been safety in numbers – a couple of the big hitters, but most of the team were my mates. The difficulty now was that it was all these world-class players and then me; the numbers were stacked against me. When I'd been a reserve-team player, on the rare occasions that I'd been told I'd be training with the first team, rather than feeling excited my heart sank a little because I was fearful of being in that environment.

I should point out that the lads were all incredibly supportive and it was an inclusive dressing room. I certainly wasn't made to feel unwelcome. The odd player checked to make sure I was okay, but it was my responsibility to learn how to step up into this intense environment of excellence. I had to adapt.

Everyone could see how nervous I was the first time I trained with the senior players. During the warm-up, I heard one of the lads behind me making fart noises because he knew I was shitting myself. That made it easier for me because it broke the ice, and I had a good session. We ended with an 11-a-side game and I was on the left against Gary Neville and David Beckham. Talk about a baptism of fire! I was forced to step out of my comfort zone and I did really well. When I started training with the lads day in, day out it became second nature, and I grew accustomed to it.

Roy Keane was the club captain, a role that he took very seriously. Off the pitch, Roy was always supportive of me and all the young players. As a young, shy teenager, I'd seen him on the TV shouting and screaming and I thought he was an intimidating character until I got to know him better. There was an ongoing joke among the younger players that you didn't want to be on Roy's team during training because if you gave the ball away, he'd give you the mother of all bollockings. When I played with Roy, I was terrified of making a mistake, and probably still would be if I played alongside him today!

If I didn't have a good training session, he'd tell me in no uncertain terms that I had to improve, that I had to do better. But it wasn't personal, he'd say the same thing to anyone, and I wholeheartedly respected him for that. Roy held his team-mates to the same incredibly high standards that he maintained. I'd never dream of saying anything back to him, but a few of the more established pros did. That was their prerogative and they'd earned the right to do so. I was still a kid, trying to forge a career in the game and I took on board all feedback, and saw it as an opportunity to improve and try to reach the impossibly high levels of my team-mates.

Training sessions at Manchester United were always so intense. The possession games and the 11-a-sides were seen as just as important as the match on a Saturday. That was very different from what I was used to, but that's where our high standards were developed. That's where our winning mentality came from. Sometimes training games were like a war zone because everyone was so desperate to win.

I spent a lot of time training with David Beckham, doing crossing drills and the like. He was an incredible player to watch and learn from. It would amaze me to see him hit perfect crosses pretty much every time, whereas I might do one good one in every three. But when I did, he'd say, 'Great cross, Chad,' and that gave me a huge buzz, coming from the best crosser in the world. Although I stepped in to play in the same position as David, we were very different players. His technique was out of this world, and he was capable of doing unreal things with the ball, but he wasn't as quick as me, which meant I offered the team something different if he was injured or on the occasions when he moved into the centre of midfield.

I felt I was more like Ryan Giggs, although we were still quite different in our styles. Ryan ran with the ball a lot, which is something I enjoyed doing. He was someone I looked up to enormously, so quick and nimble with the ball. Watching him every day and seeing the things he could do blew my mind. Ryan spent a lot of time with me, passing on advice and feedback.

Those little snippets from world-class players were huge for my development, especially when they said positive things. Everyone enjoys receiving praise, but when you're getting it from Beckham and Giggs it means even more.

Paul Scholes was the best player I've ever played with and I'm sure 99.9 per cent of his former team-mates would say the same thing. He was an absolute genius. Very quiet, but he had the full respect of his peers. He'd drive the fitness coaches mad because as soon as he stepped onto the training pitch, he'd start smashing balls around and the coaches would be screaming at him to stop and do a warm-up first. Scholesy just loved football. Despite playing in such a highly talented squad during his long stay at Old Trafford, he always seemed to stand out. Scholesy was known as the 'manager's son' because he was Sir Alex's favourite.

I had a good relationship with Scholes's midfield partner Nicky Butt. Nicky was a real joker and a huge personality in the dressing room. He took me under his wing and went out of his way to help me settle in.

Another member of the famous Class of '92 was Gary Neville. Gary was a real voice in the dressing room. He'd arrange the nights out and Christmas parties; whatever was going on, he'd be in charge of. People used to say he was a bit busy, but I thought he was incredible, a real mainstay of the club, and someone that everyone looked up to.

Denis Irwin was Mr Consistent. I don't think he ever had a bad game, although I do remember one training session when I had the best session of my life. I kept getting past him, which was a rarity as he was a top, top defender.

Jaap Stam was another defender who I had some joy against in training. We were doing one-on-one drills and I managed to knock the ball through his legs and get around the other side. I was delighted with that and thought everyone else would have been just as impressed. No one said anything to me or even made eye contact, which was strange because I'd just nutmegged one of the best defenders in the world. A few minutes later I ran towards him with the ball, and he kicked me 15 feet up into the air. When I got back to my feet, I realised that I probably shouldn't have megged him! That moment aside, Jaap was a really nice guy, who spoke to me a lot. He was very quiet but had a big presence, and he was one of the most important players in the team.

Teddy Sheringham was someone I loved playing with. He'd watched me play for the youth team at The Cliff and used to look out for me. Teddy had great football intelligence and is someone I have a huge amount of respect for.

Ole Gunnar Solskjær was an absolute diamond of a man. What sticks out the most about him is his work ethic, both on the training ground and in the gym too. When he first joined United, it was obvious that he was an incredibly gifted goalscorer, but his critics suggested that he didn't really have the physicality for the Premier League. Ole worked so hard in the gym to gain strength, and the goals he scored make him a living legend at Manchester United.

The main man at Manchester United was Sir Alex Ferguson. He has a public persona of a scary man who's angry all the time, but that couldn't be further from the truth. Yes, he'd shout at you if you did something wrong, but his words were always carefully considered, and he was always in control. He was a born winner and wanted the best for United and his players.

I tried to keep out of Sir Alex's way most of the time. I reasoned that if I wasn't getting told off, then I must have been doing alright. I always felt fully supported by the manager. He'd known me since my first game as a trialist when I was a 14-year-old, so he knew that I was a shy, quiet boy. But he saw me as a brave player and that was something he loved. I didn't do everything right, that's for sure, but I gave everything that I could in and out of possession, working as hard as I could, and he respected my work ethic.

Sir Alex was a genuine, lovely man. Back in March 1999, I'd received a call-up to the England Under-20 squad for the World Youth Cup, which was being held in Nigeria. During the build-up to the tournament a threat was made against the England and United States teams, but because of the level of security provided to us, the powers that be decided that we'd still be going.

At the same time, my mum had a health scare, and I made the decision not to go to the World Youth Cup. The coaches were supportive and allowed me to go home for a few days. Fortunately, my mum was okay.

When I returned to Manchester, I saw Sir Alex in the canteen, and he came over to ask how my mum was. I didn't think he'd know anything about the situation. Obviously, football was the be-all and end-all, but Sir Alex always went the extra mile to ensure that everyone was okay as a human being. I'll never forget that moment.

I'll also never forget the time I was summoned to his office when I was a YTS player. An agent had contacted me as they were keen to represent me. It was flattering and I thought it was a massive thing, but when you're a young player there isn't really a lot that they can do for you. Still, I mentioned it to Eric Harrison, and he told Sir Alex.

When I walked into the manager's office, he said, 'I hear you've been approached by an agent, Luke.'

'Yes,' I replied, feeling my heart rate begin to rise.

'Well, you won't be signing with them,' he said. And that was the end of the matter.

Not to be deterred, the agent saw me as a promising player, and they kept in touch in the hope that I'd sign with them in the future. When I started playing first-team football, they got me a boot deal with Diadora. That was a big thing. They paid me £5,000 a year for two years, which topped up my wages, and best of all I got an incredible amount of merchandise. The agent who wasn't my agent drove me up to the Diadora factory in Widnes a couple of times and we'd fill up his car with so much gear it was crazy – we could barely see out of the back window! If you visited Barrington, Cambridgeshire in the early 2000s, you'd have seen half the population walking around wearing Diadora tracksuits and trainers!

At the start of December 2000, I started another Premier League game, this time against Charlton Athletic at The Valley. We went in at half-time with a 2-1 lead and I thought I'd done okay. The only bad thing was taking a left-footed shot from the edge of the box that hadn't gone anywhere near the goal. During his half-time team talk, the manager said to me, 'When have you ever fucking scored with your left foot?' I didn't know how to reply, so I just sat there with a stupid grin on my face. I think he was about to go off on one of his rockets, but my smile disarmed him. 'Next time you're in that position, find someone to pass to,' he said softly.

We drew the match 3-3, and while waiting at Heathrow for our flight back to Manchester, Sir Alex told me that he wanted to discuss a new contract with me. I wasn't expecting that after almost receiving a hairdryer just a few hours earlier!

A few days later, I went to Sir Alex's office at Carrington with Ronnie Wallwork, another young player who'd also just broken into the first team. The manager offered us each £2,000 a week and said that the contracts would be ready to sign in a few days.

I was more than ready to sign, but I spoke to a couple of the senior players, and they thought that I was underplaying my worth. I also discussed it with some of my England Under-21 team-mates and found out that many were on a lot more than that.

When Sir Alex called me back into his office to ask if I was ready to sign my new contract, I plucked up the courage to share my opinion. I told him that some of the Under-21 lads were on £6,000 a week and I felt I was on a par with them.

'I'll give you £6,000 a week then,' said Sir Alex.

I didn't know what to do and felt completely out of my depth, so I asked for some time to think about it. I spoke to Roy in his role as club captain, and he passed me on to his lawyer. We didn't meet, just had a couple of telephone conversations, but he took over negotiations and I ended up with a fantastic contract that was worth £12,000 a week.

It was an astonishing amount of money for a 20-year-old. More than I'd ever dreamed of. It allowed Hayley and me to buy a duplex apartment in Sale. It was a beautiful place and we kitted it out nicely, with a corner bar and a huge television.

I hadn't passed my driving test at that time, so I relied on Hayley if I needed to go anywhere. She was driving a Peugeot 106 but had always wanted a Volkswagen Beetle, so we bought one of those too. We had a screen put in that came down from the roof so I could play the PlayStation in the passenger seat, which was great for the long drives to Cambridge and back.

Life was good.

Chapter 8

We Are the Champions

THE CHRISTMAS party was an event everyone at Manchester United looked forward to. Not only was it an opportunity for us to let our hair down away from the pressure of our quest for trophies, but it was also a chance for us to bond as a team. Whenever we had team social events, most people had a few beers and got quite merry. I probably drank a bit more than the others because I still felt uncomfortable around the lads, especially in a social environment, and the alcohol gave me a little Dutch courage.

We went out early doors, and by mid-afternoon we'd moved on to a nightclub called The Living Room. Some strippers were performing, and they asked for a volunteer to join them on the stage. Volunteering was the last thing on my mind, but someone shouted my name, and the next thing I knew I was being led to the stage by a scantily clad dancer. I sat in a chair, surrounded by the girls, who slowly began removing their clothes while my famous team-mates cheered them on. One of the dancers put an ice cube in my mouth, which slipped down my gullet, and I began to choke. I leaned forward and someone whacked my back until the ice cube was dislodged from my throat and I could breathe again. Can you imagine the headlines if a Manchester United footballer had choked to death on an ice cube that a stripper had put in his mouth? I called it a night after that bit of excitement!

Festivities aside, I played in the biggest game of my career a week before Christmas. It was a complete disaster. Manchester United v Liverpool has always been a huge game. There's a lot of rivalry between the two most successful teams in England and there's a lot at stake.

I was named as a substitute and watched the game from the Old Trafford bench. We were really poor, and it was no surprise when Liverpool took the lead through a Danny Murphy free kick just before half-time. With ten minutes to go, the manager decided to change to a more attacking formation and brought me on for Denis Irwin. The tactical change meant that we were a little exposed at the back, though, and when a long ball was played over the top, I found myself as the last defender, chasing Vladimír Šmicer. He was grabbing hold of me, we became entangled, and he went down.

As soon as the referee blew the whistle, I knew what was coming. I looked up and saw a red card and my game came to a premature end. I was distraught as I jogged off the pitch thinking I'd let everyone down in such a big game. Strangely, I received a massive round of applause from the Old Trafford crowd as I headed down the tunnel.

I sat in silence in the empty dressing room, with my head in my hands, dreading the moment the rest of the lads came in and gave me the inevitable bollocking. Eventually, I heard the banging of studs against the floor and then the dressing room door opened. A couple of players came over and told me that I was unlucky and that there was nothing I could have done.

Then Sir Alex walked in. He was not happy with the result or our performance and tore into a few of the lads. He kindly told me not to worry and that it wasn't the end of the world, so I managed to get away scot-free.

On the way back to the apartment, we had to go to Sainsbury's in Wythenshawe to get something for dinner and I walked in with my cap pulled down over my face, hoping that I wouldn't be recognised. I spent the rest of the weekend hibernating at home. It's not right to go out when you've just lost to Liverpool.

But there was a silver lining to the first – and, as it would turn out, only – red card of my career. I'd be suspended for the Boxing Day game against West Ham United, so I asked Jim Ryan if I could spend Christmas in Cambridge. He looked at me blankly and said that I was in the starting line-up against the Hammers. 'It'll be a good test for you as you'll be coming up against Stuart Pearce,' he said.

I was sure that I wouldn't be able to play because of my red card so I plucked up the courage to speak to the manager. He hadn't realised that I'd be suspended but, when I told him, he allowed me to go home for Christmas, which was nice.

I was back in the squad for the trip to Newcastle on 30 December 2000. I was in awe of St James' Park; it was incredible to see the size of the stadium from the pitch. We drew the game 1-1 but the only thing I can remember from the match is that it was freezing. I've never been that cold on a football pitch, before or since. I'm sure Newcastle is a lovely city, but I certainly wouldn't recommend going there in December!

I scored my first-ever senior goal for Manchester United on 13 January 2001 in a Premier League match away at Bradford City.

After a really poor first-half performance, the score remained 0-0 at the interval. Roy had a go at Giggsy, and they got into a bit of an argument in the dressing room. I was a substitute and Sir Alex told me to make sure I was ready to go on.

I replaced Phil Neville in the 65th minute, and we took the lead seven minutes later when former United keeper Gary Walsh had an absolute stinker. He went to clear the ball, but completely missed it and Teddy Sheringham pounced, slotting the ball into the empty net. A rejuvenated Giggs scored our second. He was unplayable in the second half, and I wondered whether the argument with Roy had wound him up. Whatever the reason, he was unbelievable.

With three minutes remaining, Beckham played a lovely through pass for me. I controlled the ball with my right foot and knocked it in with my left to make it 3-0. I had no idea what to do, so I raised my arm and ran to the United fans before being embraced by my team-mates.

After the game, we were waiting around for the team coach. Bradford's stadium is quite old, and there was an old holding cell that was used to house any supporters who'd been causing trouble. We were standing next to the cell and a drunk United supporter inside was congratulating me on my first goal.

My only disappointment from that day is that ITV had the broadcast rights to the Premier League that season, so I didn't get to watch my goal on *Match of the Day*.

We were supposed to be flying out to Spain for some warm-weather training, but Sir Alex told me to stay at home. I think it was going to be a bit of a jolly-up and I was quite relieved. I spent the next few days training with the reserves, feet firmly back on the ground.

I've already mentioned the huge rivalry we had with Liverpool, but in terms of challenging for the title, Arsenal were our biggest threat. They were ferocious matches against the Gunners, with the two captains, Roy Keane and Patrick Vieira, usually at the heart of the battle.

You could feel the difference in atmosphere during the build-up to the big games. There was a certain edge to the matches against Arsenal, Liverpool and Leeds because they were the only three teams who could potentially take the title away from Old Trafford.

Arsenal had beaten us 1-0 earlier in the season, with a wonder goal from Thierry Henry, and most pundits were expecting another close game when we played them on 25 February 2001. I was named as a substitute, and it was sheer joy watching United that day. We were 5-1 up by half-time, which was incredible, and by the time I made my bow with 15 minutes remaining, we were cruising. That was probably the biggest game I ever played in, because of the stature of the opposition and the calibre of players I was coming up against. It was a pinch-me moment being on the same pitch as Henry, who's such an icon. Teddy rounded off the scoring to give us a 6-1 victory. It was a great feeling to be part of the squad that won so emphatically. That result gave us a 16-point cushion at the top of the table.

A week later I scored my second United goal, opening the scoring in a 1-1 draw away to Leeds United. I came on at half-time, replacing the injured Nicky Butt. Elland Road was always a difficult place to go as a United player. We seemed to receive a hostile welcome wherever we went, but Leeds had a nastier edge to it. I remember getting some heavy abuse when I was warming up on the touchline in the first half. Nothing personal, just the general 'who are ya?' and 'you wanker'. My opponent was Danny Mills, a good defender who I respected, but I felt I'd have an opportunity to run at him or dribble past him and create something.

My overriding memory of that game is my goal. Scholesy played the ball through to Solskjær who, by his standards, took quite a weak shot that I expected the Leeds goalkeeper, Nigel Martyn, to gather. I was always taught to follow the ball in just in case. This time my gamble paid off. Martyn spilled the ball, my eyes lit up and I tapped it in and ran away like a lunatic. I was hoping that there would be no more goals so I could say that I'd scored the winner, but Leeds, who were probably the better team on the day, equalised later on through Mark Viduka and we ended up hanging on for a point. Leeds reached the Champions League semi-final that season, so it was a good result overall.

Our dream of FA Cup glory was ended when West Ham United knocked us out in the fourth round with one of the most bizarre goals that I've ever seen. I was a substitute on that cold January afternoon. Deep into the second half, Frédéric Kanouté played a ball through our defence that Paolo Di Canio ran on to. Fabien Barthez stood still and raised his arm, hoping for, or expecting, the linesman to raise his flag. I was standing next to the linesman and could see that he had no intention of flagging for offside. I don't know if Fabien was playing mind games or if he genuinely believed that Di Canio was offside, but the Italian wasn't fooled and calmly slotted the ball into the net. The goal stood and we lost 1-0.

It was a very strange situation, but Barthez was like that. He was always trying new things. Very eccentric and aloof, not in a bad way, he was just his own man. I think Roy Keane had a go at him afterwards, but I don't remember the manager saying anything to him.

Walking out of the tunnel at Old Trafford to start a game had been an ambition of mine ever since Ray Medwell took me to the Theatre of Dreams when I was still a schoolboy. My dream came true in a Premier League match against Everton. That was a huge moment, although I was surprised that I'd been named in the starting line-up. I was experiencing excitement and nerves and was lost in thought during the manager's team talk. As we lined up in the tunnel, I realised that I hadn't checked where I should stand on set plays. I shit myself. How could I have been so stupid?

When the match kicked off, I was praying that Everton wouldn't win a corner or a free kick as I had no idea where I should position myself. My heart sank when the Toffees were awarded a corner in the first few minutes. I wandered over to the edge of the penalty box, feeling like a lost sheep, before Jaap Stam shouted at me and told me where I should be. Everton didn't score from the corner, but I learned a valuable lesson, and I made sure to always listen to pre-match instructions.

I didn't have a great impact on the game, even though we won 1-0. I wasn't brilliant on the ball, but I worked so hard out of possession that Sir Alex gave me a lot of praise for my work ethic. I'd come a long way since the days when I didn't understand what tuck in meant!

One of the worst moments of my career happened not long after the Everton game. I'd become obsessed with the Channel 4 show *Big Brother*. I'd missed the first series because I'd been living in Antwerp, so I made the most of series two. Hayley was working shifts at Manchester Airport by this stage, and when she was working through the night, I'd take my duvet into the living room and watch the live feed on E4, to see if I could get an early scoop of what was going on.

One night I must have fallen asleep at some unearthly hour, and I was awoken by Hayley. I looked up at her, still half asleep, and asked her why she was home so early, hoping she wasn't ill. It turned out that she wasn't back early, it was 10am. Training started in half an hour! My heart sank as I realised that I wasn't going to be able to get to Carrington in time. Panic washed over my body as I imagined the bollocking I'd receive from the manager. I couldn't very well tell him that I'd slept in because I'd been watching *Big Brother*! I had to think of something.

I called my mum and asked her to phone Carrington and tell them that Hayley had fallen over, and I had to take her to the hospital. It was an awful lie, but I didn't know what else to do.

The next morning, I went into training (I'd set an alarm this time) and I couldn't believe it. The first person I saw was Sir Alex, walking down a corridor towards me. I didn't have time to change direction and my heart was pounding as I waited for the inevitable confrontation.

'Luke, I heard that Hayley had an accident. How is she?' he asked with genuine concern.

'She slipped over and landed on her wrist,' I replied, convinced he'd see right through my lie. 'It's not broken, just sprained.'

'That's good,' the manager said before continuing his walk down the corridor to his office.

Hayley used to ferry me around and she enjoyed getting dressed up and watching the matches in the players' lounge at Old Trafford. For the next few games, I made her wear a Tubigrip bandage on her wrist. If anyone asked her if she was alright, she had to tell them that she had a badly sprained wrist. It was certainly an awkward moment, and I learned another valuable lesson. I never overslept again, that's for sure.

United's Champions League journey was progressing well. The format in those days was different from how it is now. Instead of a group stage and then the knockout rounds, there were two group stages and then the quarter-final.

I made my Champions League debut in the penultimate game of the second group stage, away at Greek side Panathinaikos. I came on as a substitute and don't think I did particularly well. The pitch was dry, and it was so hot. I fell over the ball a couple of times, but I did manage to get half an assist for Paul Scholes's last-minute equaliser. I took a wayward shot that ended up at his feet and he tucked it away. I'm not sure if it really counts as an assist, but I'm claiming it anyway!

I started our next Champions League game, at home to Sturm Graz. It was a very special night; the atmosphere under the lights for a European game felt different, it was electric. Before the match, the stadium announcer read the team line-up but just said the first name of the player, and then the 65,000 in attendance chanted the surname. I was at the end, and I was thinking how embarrassing it would be if the announcer said 'Luke' and the crowd fell deathly silent. Fortunately, they roared the 'Chadwick', and I got a huge thrill from hearing my name reverberate around Old Trafford.

I played on the right-hand side for the first hour and then moved over to the left. I had a few dribbles and the crowd got excited. I had a hand in two of our three goals and was pleased with my performance. The pundits were talking favourably about me on the TV after the game, which was fantastic.

Our Champions League adventure came to an end in the quarter-final against German giants Bayern Munich. We lost the first leg at home 1-0 and a week later travelled to Munich for the return leg. Mick Hucknall was with us at the hotel when we had our pre-match meal, which was surreal because my mum was a huge fan. We used to have his cassette playing in the house all the time when I was growing up.

I was named as a substitute and was sitting in the dugout at the Olympic Stadium watching the starting XI line-up for the customary pre-match photo when I noticed that there weren't 11 United players on the pitch; there were 12. There was one person I didn't recognise at all. It was bizarre, but he was a grown man wearing the full white United away kit and he even had football boots on, so I assumed he was supposed to be there. Maybe he'd won a competition, and his prize was to line up with the lads.

I later found out that the imposter was Karl Power, a prankster who'd somehow managed to sneak onto the pitch with the lads. He did the same thing at Headingley later that year, walking out with the England cricket team, pretending to be a batsman. I don't know how he managed it!

The Germans scored two first-half goals and led 3-1 on aggregate at the break. Giggs pulled one back for us early in the second half and then I came on as a replacement for Wes Brown when we were desperately chasing a goal. I wasn't a great goalscorer, but I could run around and pull defenders out of position, which would create space for others.

I had a really good chance to score, and I probably should have shot but crossed it instead. Unfortunately, we lost the game, which was a huge disappointment, but I was on a massive high because I'd been trusted by the manager in such a high-stakes match. Bayern went on to win the Champions League that season.

When I was walking off the pitch, Munich's striker Roque Santa Cruz – who later played in the Premier League with Blackburn Rovers – asked me if I'd swap shirts. It wasn't anything I usually did, but I was buzzing that he'd asked me and was more than happy to oblige.

Back to the Premier League, I found myself in the starting line-up for the Manchester derby on 21 April 2001. City weren't rivals in the same way that Arsenal, Leeds and Liverpool were because they were struggling in the league and were never a threat to us in our hunt for trophies, but it was still a big game. Sir Alex made sure we all knew how important the match was for the supporters; they wanted the bragging rights when they returned to work on Monday morning.

I think we were suffering with a hangover from our Champions League defeat because we put in a lacklustre performance and didn't really get going. We drew the game 1-1, but no one remembers the score. People remember it for Roy Keane's tackle on Alf-Inge Haaland that resulted in our captain receiving a straight red card. It was a terrible challenge, and the ref was always going to send him off, but it was made worse when Roy admitted in his autobiography that the foul was intentional. The FA dished out a huge fine and gave Roy an additional five-game ban.

Sir Alex was disappointed with our performance and gave out a few bollockings in the dressing room but didn't say anything to Roy because our captain was nowhere to be seen. That was a huge concern to me because Hayley, who drove me to most games, was working and Roy had given me a lift to Old Trafford and was supposed to be dropping me back home. I didn't know how I was going to get back – I certainly didn't fancy getting on the tram after a tense Manchester derby – so I sat in the dressing room waiting patiently.

I must have been in there for a couple of hours, sitting there on my own while the cleaners swept the floor and scrubbed the showers, when eventually Roy put his head through the door and said, 'Come on.' I have no idea where he'd been, but I followed him out to the car park, and we sat in an awkward silence while he drove me back to Sale. When we arrived at my apartment, he said, 'If you're going out tonight, just be careful.' I thanked him for the lift, and he drove off. I'd have loved to ask him what was going through his mind, but I was way too shy (and a little scared) for that.

Despite that disappointing result, we won the Premier League at a canter, finishing ten points clear of second-placed Arsenal. It was United's third title in a row, becoming the first team to do so in almost 20 years. We were presented with the trophy in front of a packed Old Trafford, and for some reason I was second or third in line to receive it. When I lifted it above my head the lid fell off and nearly took off my nose!

I was incredibly proud to have been part of such a talented squad, but I didn't feel that I was a massive part of it, and I felt a little awkward when we were crowned champions. The lads were jubilantly celebrating a fantastic achievement, but I struggled to join in with the celebrations. In those days you had to make ten appearances to qualify for a medal (it has reduced to five now) and I'd played 16 times in the league, scoring two goals, so I had contributed, but I'm not sure how much I'd *really* contributed. I'm pretty sure we'd have won the league had I stayed in Antwerp for the whole season.

The club held a party for us at the five-star Lowry Hotel in Manchester, which I attended with Hayley and a couple of our friends from Cambridge, Ian 'Gibbo' Gibson and Doug Perry. The press took photos of us walking in, which was bizarre. Victoria Beckham and Katie Price were also there, and I felt a little out of my depth among the high-profile partners of my team-mates. Fame and celebrity never interested me, and I always found it a little embarrassing when I was recognised while on a night out (not often!). I certainly wasn't someone who'd walk to the front of a queue and try the old 'do you know who I am?' routine. I don't think it would have got me very far, to be honest!

I felt totally drained at the end of that season. Although I hadn't played loads of games, the intensity of being in such a high-profile environment had taken it out of me. I'd started the season with Antwerp expecting to be embroiled in a relegation battle and finished it as a Premier League champion. It was such a whirlwind year, and I was thankful for the rest.

I was also mentally exhausted. I'd developed an air of arrogance and that was the only period in my life where I didn't live up to my expectations as a human being. I'm not making excuses, but I wasn't emotionally intelligent enough to show vulnerability and admit that I was struggling mentally. I was becoming even more introverted; my anxiety levels were through the roof. And all because of a TV show called *They Think It's All Over.*

Chapter 9

They Think It's All Over –
I Wish It Was

THEY THINK *It's All Over* was a television show that ran from 1995–2006. Presented by comedian Nick Hancock, two teams, each led by a former England captain, David Gower (cricket) and Gary Lineker (football), competed against each other in a light-hearted sporting quiz. Like millions of others, I'd watched the show and laughed along with the jokes. That was until *I* became the joke.

The night before our home match against Derby County on 5 May 2001, I was relaxing at the flat when I received a text message from a friend: 'Nice appearance on They Think It's All Over tonight!'

Although I had a deep sense of foreboding, I turned on the TV and watched the repeat. About ten minutes into the episode, a photograph of me appeared on the screen and Hancock said, 'This photo of Luke Chadwick was ruined when Luke Chadwick turned up.'

My heart sank and I felt instant dread, followed by huge embarrassment, knowing that the popular show was being beamed into millions of homes around the UK. I'd felt uneasy when my appearance had been mocked in the Belgian newspapers, but this was much worse because it was on a much bigger scale.

I was mortified, but perversely I couldn't stop watching. A few minutes later, another photograph of me appeared on the screen and Hancock said, 'Iron Maiden's biggest hit is "The Number of the Beast", and if you want to know the number of the beast, Luke Chadwick wears the number 36.'

That was enough. I switched off the TV and sat in silence, staring at the blank screen in front of me, while negative thoughts danced around in my head. *Everyone is laughing at me. Is this what I've got to put up with for the rest of my career?*

I hoped that it was a one-off, but sadly that was just the start. The build-up to each episode was excruciating as my anxiety levels ramped up and I prayed that I wouldn't be mentioned. I became strangely obsessed with the show. Even though it made me feel terrible, I couldn't stop tuning in because I wanted to watch an episode that didn't mention me. Then I'd be okay.

But every week my photo was accompanied by another derogatory comment about the way that I looked. As soon as the latest joke about my appearance had been told, I switched the TV off and asked myself when it would end. Wondering if it *would* ever end.

The turmoil that I went through was because of my total lack of emotional intelligence. My whole focus up to that point had been football and I'd never taken the time to develop myself as a human being, which meant that I didn't have a clue how to deal with this situation. In my mind, I'd be weak if I showed any vulnerability or told anyone that the insults were hurting me, so I swept my feelings under the carpet. If anyone ever asked me about the show, I'd tell them that I wasn't bothered. But that wasn't true; it bothered me a great deal.

Hayley was always there for me and that meant so much. Having someone who I loved and knowing that she loved me was a huge source of strength, even though I didn't talk to her about it. I hate to think about how it would have been had I been alone. I'm sure I'd have ended up in a much darker place.

Apart from going to training and matches, I didn't want to leave the sanctuary of my flat. I became a bit of a recluse. Hayley would want to go shopping at the Trafford Centre or into the city centre for dinner, but I preferred to get a takeaway and stay in. The young lads at United would invite me on a night out but I'd turn them down. The flat provided solace. I felt safe there, knowing that no one could say anything to me like they could on the streets. I was convinced that if I went out to public places, people would shout abuse at me or they'd be laughing and pointing at me because of my appearance. *There's that funny-looking guy from the TV. Let's laugh at him.*

I'm sure that wouldn't have happened if I had ventured out, but the internal feelings were so powerful at that time. The jokes on *They Think It's All Over* lasted seconds, and most viewers would have forgotten about it by the time the closing credits appeared, but I saw it as a much bigger thing than everyone else – of course I did; it was me they were taking the piss out of. I honestly believed that people only knew me because of the way that I looked, not because I was a footballer.

The fact that the comments weren't about football was the big issue. As a footballer, you can live with people saying that you're a bad player. You can do something with that feedback, learn from it, and improve your game. But this was just about the way that I looked – something I had no control over – and it wasn't right that I was targeted. I felt it was unfair and unjust. I just wanted it to go away.

I never felt any anger or hatred towards anyone on the programme. If they knew how bad it was making me feel, they'd have stopped, I'm confident of that. But how could I tell a big corporation like the BBC to stop making jokes about me? I felt powerless to defend myself. I longed for the day when they'd had enough of me and moved on to another victim. I know that isn't right but that's how I felt.

But then it started spreading and the newspapers and magazines began to mention my appearance in their match reports. Even *The Guardian* joined in: 'Manchester United's Christmas party turned ugly on Wednesday night, though it had nothing at all to do with the presence of Luke Chadwick.'

I wasn't seen as a footballer anymore; I'd become a figure of fun. It was the fact that this was on a mass scale that caused me so much stress and anxiety.

We now know that mental health can affect anyone, but back in the early 2000s there was a stigma attached to it. Especially for a highly paid Premier League footballer. I didn't recognise the symptoms I was experiencing at the time, but looking back it's clear that I was dealing with mental health challenges. My approach was to push things to the back of my mind and ignore them, which is completely the wrong thing to do when you have problems. It was a different world then with regards to mental health. Back then it was a case of 'man up and get through it', and that was my attitude. I just couldn't allow myself to open up and tell anyone how bad it was actually making me feel.

I'm pretty sure that if I'd had the confidence to seek someone out and talk about it, I'd have received the support I needed because Manchester United is an incredible football club. A couple of my team-mates told me not to listen to all that rubbish, which helped. David Beckham was in the press a lot because of his appearance – different haircuts, wearing a sarong, etc. – but we were at two completely different ends of the spectrum, so I never reached out to him for advice.

The football pitch and training ground were the only places I could forget about everything. During a game, I was in the moment and able to switch off from all external distractions. Even the insults and jeers from opposing supporters didn't bother me because they were aimed at every single United player.

It's not nice but we've come to accept it. Football is a strange world and it's crazy what being in close proximity to a football stadium does to people. All that emotion seems to bring out the worst in people. But, as I say, I could cope with it on the pitch. Where it did affect me was walking out of the away grounds back onto the team bus. I'd get loads of abuse because of my appearance – some really awful stuff that I'm sure the culprits would be embarrassed about if they could hear now what they'd said to me – and that did bother me because I felt so alone. I couldn't say anything back, so I'd look at the floor and walk dejectedly onto the coach, telling myself that this was the price I had to pay for the privilege of playing for the biggest club in the world.

I don't think the verbal abuse that I received had any impact on my performances. It's certainly not an excuse for me not having a glittering career at Old Trafford, but that period of my life was clouded to a certain extent because of the challenges I was facing.

I lost myself a little bit at that time and I got above my station. I felt the whole world was laughing at me and my defence mechanism was to become arrogant. I developed a bit of an ego. When I went back home to Cambridge, if anyone said anything negative to me, my automatic response was to tell them about the amount of money I was being paid. There are huge challenges with going from not having anything to earning thousands of pounds a week. I started to think I was more important than others because I had more money.

It changed me as a person for a short period, but what I realised was that money doesn't make you happy. The unhappiest period of my life was the time when I was earning the most money. That wasn't the real me, but I'd reconciled it in my head that, although I was getting bullied, I was rich. Fortunately, it didn't take me long to rediscover some humility and get back to being me.

During this challenging time, I didn't ever change the way that I felt about myself. I never looked in the mirror and felt disgusted by what I saw. I didn't beat myself up too much. The shame and embarrassment that I felt was because I knew that others were laughing at me. I'd be prominent in lists of the ugliest footballers, which was incredibly hard at the time, but it taught me a great deal. It forced me to understand myself. I recognised that it doesn't matter what you look like, it matters what you're like as a human being. For me, now that my career is over, I prefer for people to judge me on who I am as a person and how I behave towards others, not for my skills or achievements in football and certainly not for my looks.

The reason I was seen as 'looking different to others' was because I suffered from a protruding jaw that was prone to locking, teeth that stuck out and a bad case of acne. I always knew that I'd have to wear braces and have an operation at some point, but I kept putting it off. If I'd had the procedure done when I was younger, it would have been more straightforward, but my biggest fear as a child was going to the dentist. I still don't like going. I always kicked up such a fuss that Mum wouldn't take me.

In 2001, I decided to go ahead with the operation that would straighten my teeth and make me look more 'normal', even though I didn't think I looked abnormal. At first, I had to wear braces to straighten my teeth and then, in 2003, I went through a procedure that involved surgeons breaking my jaw and resetting it. I didn't have it done to look different, it wasn't vanity. It was for health reasons, to stop my jaw locking.

My acne eventually disappeared, but not before I'd spent an absolute fortune on expensive skin products designed to get rid of the spots. None of them worked. The only other thing I'd tried was concealing the spots. When I was about 16, I went to a nightclub in Cambridge with some friends. While getting ready, I used some of my mum's foundation to try to cover up the spots, but when I was standing in the queue a girl looked at me and shouted, 'This boy's got make-up on!' That was so embarrassing, so I didn't wear make-up again.

Eventually, the jokes ran out and the mocking stopped. Another person became the target. Although it took a long time, I managed my feelings internally and came out of the situation a much stronger person.

During the Covid lockdown, everyone was in a mad place in terms of what the world had become, so I decided to come away from the terrible jokes I often told on social media and do something more positive. I wanted to put an inspiring message out there, one that might spark a feeling and help someone who was going through a challenging time. I reminded people that they should speak up – not bottle it up like I did – as that's the first step to overcoming mental health challenges. I used my experience of *They Think It's All Over* as an example and naively thought that everyone would take it as a positive message.

I was surprised by the reaction to my post; the media outlets across the UK all reported it, and I was bombarded with interview requests. The narrative became distorted, and the story turned into an attack on the show and the people involved with it. Gary Lineker and Nick Hancock, in particular, were vilified and targeted on social media and that's not what I wanted to happen. I didn't want to put any individuals under any pressure because of what I'd said. Hancock and Lineker both apologised to me, which was nice, but not necessary. I accepted their apologies wholeheartedly, although I also felt guilty that they were receiving stick because of what I'd said.

But if my post helped just one person, then it was all worth it.

Chapter 10

Big-Time Chadwick

THE SUMMER of 2001 was a busy one for Manchester United. Firstly, Sir Alex rocked us with the news that he'd be stepping down as manager at the end of the 2001/02 season. According to the newspapers, there were some tensions between the manager and the board, although, as a young player, I kept well away from football club politics.

Everyone within the club was shocked. Most of us were saddened. So many of us had known Sir Alex since we were children, and some saw him as a father figure. The manager had played a massive part in our lives and development, not just as footballers, but as people too. He was more than *just* a manager. He was Manchester United.

It was a strange situation because usually when a manager goes there's an announcement and then they're gone. But with Sir Alex announcing his decision almost a year in advance, we had to endure the endless speculation around his successor. That caused some uncertainty and uneasiness within the squad as the players were wondering if they'd still be at the club the following year.

I didn't feel particularly fearful for my future because I wasn't yet a bona fide member of the first team and didn't know if I'd still be at the club in the long term anyway. I couldn't imagine what it would be like at Manchester United without Sir Alex, though, because he meant so much to everyone.

The next big piece of news was the news that Steve McClaren, Sir Alex's assistant manager, left us to become as manager of Middlesbrough. Steve, who'd joined United during the treble-winning season, was a fantastic coach who'd helped me to improve as a player and he was a big miss. McClaren did a great job at Middlesbrough and in 2022, after several high-profile managerial jobs, he rejoined Manchester United as Erik ten Hag's assistant.

Mike Phelan, my old reserve-team manager, became Sir Alex's right-hand man until the summer of 2002 when he was replaced with the Portuguese Carlos Queiroz. The training sessions changed massively, but I didn't pay too much attention to the ins and outs of the coaching staff. I did what I was told, kept my head down, and tried to continue my development.

Two of McClaren's first signings at Middlesbrough were my team-mates Jon Greening and Mark Wilson, and the newspapers linked me with a move to Teesside. I was happy at Old Trafford and had no desire to leave, although it was quite exciting to think that other clubs were interested in me. I aimed to break into the first team on a more regular basis and with Greening, a wide player like me, leaving, I was hopeful I'd have more opportunities.

Despite winning our third title in a row, Sir Alex strengthened the squad with two big-name signings. Dutch striker Ruud van Nistelrooy, who'd have joined us a year earlier had he not suffered a knee injury, was the first arrival. Ruud had garnered a reputation in the Netherlands as an incredible goal machine. Although I'd watched videos of some of his goals, I'd never seen him play until the first day of pre-season training when he gave us a glimpse into the quality he possessed. He was an absolute animal in front of goal. Ruud's finishing was second to none, the way he'd strike the ball with both accuracy and power. I knew he'd make the runs and my job as a winger was to try to find him at every opportunity because I knew he'd do the rest. I knew instantly that he was going to be a great success for us. He had that X factor; he was built to play for a club with the size and stature of United.

Making way for Ruud was Teddy Sheringham, who rejoined Spurs on a free transfer. I was disappointed to see Teddy leave as I always enjoyed playing with him. He was different to the other strikers at the club in the way that he played; he wasn't always in the box looking to score goals, and he was just as effective in creating opportunities for others. Teddy liked the ball played into his feet and more often than not he'd make something happen.

Midfielder Juan Sebastián Verón became United's record signing when he arrived from Lazio a couple of weeks after Ruud. Seba came in to massive fanfare, and rightly so because he was world class. He was an exciting signing and an unbelievable player. At times during training he was unplayable, but it didn't really work out for him at Old Trafford. He was such a free spirit on the pitch, going everywhere to get the ball, but his style didn't really fit into the rigid 4-4-2 structure that we played most of the time. I don't think he ever really got used to the frenetic pace of the English game, where he didn't get the same amount of time on the ball that he'd enjoyed in Italy.

Another new face at Carrington was Roy Carroll, a Northern Ireland international goalkeeper. Roy was expected to succeed Fabien Barthez in the long term. He was a great addition to the squad – and to our card table too.

We spent a lot of time on planes and coaches travelling to and from matches, so we had to find things to do to while away the time. The manager, Roy Keane, Denis Irwin and Ole Gunnar Solskjær often played the popular card game Hearts, while others listened to music or read books. Wes Brown, John O'Shea, Michael Stewart, Roy and I had our own table where we religiously played a card game called Shithead. Each player starts with nine cards and the idea is to lose them all. The last player to hold cards is the loser.

We'd play Shithead from the minute we stepped onto the team coach until the moment we arrived at our destination. It was so much fun. No money exchanged hands, but we were all competitive so it did get quite raucous at times and, occasionally, Sir Alex or one of the senior pros would tell us to keep the noise down. It was great entertainment and helped to ease some of the pressure we felt as young professionals.

I started pre-season as a fully fledged member of the first-team squad and went on the pre-season tour of Asia. We visited Singapore, Thailand and Malaysia. The tour was a promotional exercise as much as it was a footballing one, but I was looking forward to the experience. The only tours I'd been on previously were youth ones and I didn't really know what to expect. When packing, I just took all my Manchester United stuff: tracksuits, T-shirts and a couple of pairs of trainers. When we arrived in

Singapore, Sir Alex told us that we could have a night out. I wouldn't be able to get in anywhere wearing a tracksuit, so I went to the boutique in the hotel and spent an absolute fortune on a pair of trousers, a top and some shoes.

We went to the Raffles Hotel and drank Singapore slings – when in Rome, and all that! I was told that I was expected to do a little speech as it was my first tour with the lads. After knocking back a few extra slings to help combat the nerves, I stood up and thanked everyone for how welcoming they'd been and told them that I was honoured to be on my first trip with United.

Later that night we moved on to a nightclub where there was a specially roped-off VIP area set aside for us. This was 2001 and Beckham mania was at its peak; everywhere we went we were surrounded by screaming fans.

I got a bit restless, though, so went for a little wander to explore the rest of the club. I wasn't worried because I didn't think anyone knew who I was. I ended up on my own, dancing on a podium in the main room of the club, being cheered on by the locals. I was having a great time, but then a security guard grabbed me off the podium. 'What are you doing?' he asked as he dragged me back to the rest of the lads. Not many people get kicked *into* a VIP area!

Back at the hotel a few hours later, everyone was saying goodnight and heading back to their rooms, but I didn't want the night to end. I got talking to some journalists in reception and, because I was a little worse for wear, I agreed to go out with them for a couple more drinks. Just as we were leaving the hotel, Dwight Yorke pulled me away and led me back to my room, telling the journalists that I wouldn't be going out with them. I'm so grateful to Dwight because that could have turned into a complete disaster.

What a night!

I enjoyed the tour. It was nice to visit some new countries and get a few more games under my belt. We beat Malaysia All-Stars 6-0 in front of 100,000 fans in our first game, with Ruud taking just six minutes to open his account for the club. I was pleased to get on the scoresheet too.

Next up was Team Singapore, who we brushed aside 8-1. The highlight of that game was seeing our goalkeeper Fabien Barthez come on as a second-half substitute – on the left wing! Barthez was eccentric (aren't all keepers?) and during training he'd never want to go in goal. During small-sided games, he'd spend more time on the pitch than between the sticks. He was a frustrated outfield player and during the Singapore game Sir Alex granted him his wish. He did alright, to be fair, although I don't think he was ever going to take Ryan Giggs's place!

The final game of the tour was a 2-1 win over the Thailand national team in Bangkok.

The tour was good preparation for when our season began against Liverpool in the traditional curtain-raiser, the Charity Shield. Wembley was being redeveloped at the time, so the match was held at the Millennium Stadium, Cardiff, an impressive arena. The roof was closed during the match, which generated an incredible atmosphere.

It has its critics, but the Charity Shield (now known as the Community Shield) isn't a glorified friendly; it's an important match that means something to the players. We always saw it as an opportunity to set out our stall for the season ahead, to get into that habit of winning matches from day one. And games between Liverpool and Manchester United are never friendlies.

I was a substitute. The warm-up area was behind one of the goals, which meant I had a magnificent view of the action. I didn't get the call to go on, but I didn't expect to play because we had some new players that I thought Sir Alex would want to bring on ahead of me.

Unfortunately, we lost 2-1 to our big rivals and the manager was furious, telling us that we needed to up our levels. We'd won the league at a canter the previous year, and I think complacency had set in towards the end as we finished the season with three consecutive defeats. The last thing we wanted was for those poor performances to creep into the 2001/02 season. But that's exactly what happened.

Newly promoted Fulham were the visitors to Old Trafford for the first game of the new Premier League campaign. I came on as a substitute and was lining up against Jon Harley, a left-back I'd played with for England Under-21s. He was a good defender, but I expected to have quite a bit of success against him. However, although I ran with the ball as usual, I wasn't able to get past him as often as I thought, and I didn't have a great game. Mind you, I should have had a penalty when I was brought down in the box. I thought it was a stonewall penalty, but the ref disagreed, and I was fuming. I know a lot of people feel the big decisions always go in United's favour, especially at Old Trafford, but I can honestly say that I've never seen any big-club bias – and I've been on both sides. We won the game 3-2, with a brace from Ruud on his home debut, but it wasn't a great performance. We scraped through, and Louis Saha was outstanding for Fulham.

After draws with Blackburn Rovers and Aston Villa we lost our best defender when Jaap Stam was sold to Lazio following the publication of his book, *Head to Head*, which was an inside story into the workings of Manchester United. I didn't read the book but, apparently, he was quite critical of some of my team-mates. I couldn't understand why he'd have done that. Jaap was a massive player, a vital cog in the machine that had churned out a trio of Premier League titles during his three years at the club, but Sir Alex had expectations and we all knew that if you stepped out of line, there was no way back, regardless of who you were. Jaap wasn't the first, and he wouldn't be the last.

Our dressing room was tight-knit and I'm sure that Jaap would have had some questions to answer had he remained, but I don't think he'd have been ostracised because ultimately all anyone really cared about was what happened on the pitch. As long as you did your job and helped the club win games and trophies, then it didn't really matter who liked who.

We had a huge squad, with lots of different nationalities, cultures and personalities, and, naturally, not everyone is going to be best mates. It's well documented that Andy Cole and Teddy Sheringham didn't get on off the pitch, but that never affected their performances or the way they played together. As soon as you cross that white line, all differences are put aside, and you focus on the common goal – winning the game.

Although we were disappointed to see a defender of Jaap's calibre leave, we accepted that the manager's decision was final. We just had to get on with it.

Jaap's replacement was Laurent Blanc, a world-class defender who'd captained France during their World Cup and European Championship triumphs. Laurent was no stranger to the high-pressure environments you have at big clubs, having represented Barcelona and Inter Milan, but he was the wrong side of 30 when he joined us, and he'd maybe lost that yard of pace that's so vital and can make all the difference at the highest level.

The move saw Laurent reunited with his France team-mate Fabien Barthez. Before international matches, Laurent had kissed Fabien's head and the pair repeated this ritual before United's European games, although it didn't bring us the same good fortune that it had the French national team.

Laurent and Fabien are legends of the game, but also thoroughly nice guys. Fabien didn't speak much English and my French was non-existent, but we had a good relationship, and he always took the time to speak to me – even if it was in broken English! During one team night out in Manchester, I'd had a bit too much to drink and went outside to get some fresh air. That's where I bumped into Fabien and Laurent, who were smoking. They asked me how I was and offered me a cigarette. Although I didn't smoke, I didn't want to appear rude, so I accepted one and ended up having a crafty fag with two World Cup winners in the small garden of a Manchester nightspot. It was so surreal!

I made my first start of the season on 8 September against Everton, and I made sure I knew where to stand for set pieces this time! That was the first time I'd played alongside Verón – who opened the scoring in the eighth minute – and I thought he was excellent. Although I set up a goal for Andy Cole in our 4-1 win, I wasn't as involved in the game as I'd have liked. I wanted to get on the ball more and, instead of hugging the touchline, I kept drifting inside to try to affect the game. The manager wasn't happy with me, and he kept shouting at me to stay wide.

I played one of my best games for United in a 3-1 victory over Sunderland at the Stadium of Light. I set up two goals (one an own goal, the other for Andy Cole) and won the man-of-the-match award. Sunderland always gave two awards: one to a home player and another to an away player, so I had to go to one of the hospitality lounges after the match to collect my prize, which was a bottle of champagne. I got thoroughly booed by the home fans of course!

Sitting on the coach ride back to Manchester, I felt proud of my performance and started to think that I was a better player than I actually was, but I didn't make these feelings known to anyone other than Hayley.

The victory at Sunderland was our third of the season and we were sitting third in the table, just one point behind Leeds United, who occupied the top spot. So far, so good. But then we embarked on a terrible run that saw us tumble down the table.

We played Bolton at home at the end of October 2001. That was a really tough match. Kevin Nolan, a fantastic young midfielder, opened the scoring before Verón equalised. The score remained 1-1 when I came on in the second half and we were chasing a winner.

In contrast to the Sunderland game, this was one of my worst performances in a United shirt. I was so ineffective; trying to get the ball and run with it but having no joy. That was a major flaw in my game. If I couldn't get past defenders by using my pace, I didn't have a lot else in my armoury that I could use. I didn't recognise that at the time and kept running down blind alleys without success. Continually trying to do the same thing, often to the frustration of my team-mates and the crowd. There were a couple of times during that game when I lost the ball or was tackled, and I heard groans from the supporters.

When Michael Ricketts scored Bolton's winning goal with six minutes to go, the groans around the stadium turned into boos. Losing at home to Bolton Wanderers is unacceptable for Manchester United and the crowd was right to let us know. After the success of the previous three years, I think that we'd become so used to winning games that it was almost a foregone conclusion that we'd win the league every season. It's quite easy for a young player to slot into a confident, winning team when everything is rosy in the garden. The Bolton defeat really opened my eyes to what a high-pressure environment there is at United. You have to win games and you have to win them in style.

There was uproar in 2019 when Liverpool were forced to play two games on consecutive days, but 18 years earlier Manchester United and Arsenal had done the same thing. The Champions League fixtures originally scheduled to be played on 12 September 2001 were postponed as a result of the horrific attacks in New York the previous day and that resulted in a small fixture congestion. On 4 November 2001, United played Liverpool, and Arsenal took on Charlton Athletic, and then we faced the Gunners at Highbury the following day.

So, the big hitters travelled to Anfield (where we lost 3-1) and the youngsters and squad members (of which I was one) went to London for the League Cup tie. For some reason, Paul Scholes (who'd been on the bench for the Liverpool game) was selected for the Arsenal match, but he told the manager that he wouldn't be playing, and he remained in Manchester. There were rumours on the train to London that he hadn't turned up, others speculated that he'd refused to play. Whatever the reason, it was completely out of character for Scholes, who was a wonderful footballer and a consummate professional. There was a real hoo-ha and, although the story was kept hush-hush, we wondered whether Scholesy had played his last game for the club – especially considering what had happened to Jaap a couple of months earlier. But fortunately for United, Sir Alex and Scholesy cleared the air and Paul spent his entire career at Old Trafford.

I'd watched many games at Highbury when I was attached to Arsenal. I'd trained in the indoor arena, so this was my first time actually playing on the pitch and it felt very special. Unfortunately, the performance – not just from me, but the whole team – wasn't good enough and we lost 4-0 with Sylvain Wiltord scoring a hat-trick. Sir Alex was furious afterwards. In two days, we'd lost to two of our fiercest rivals, and he didn't mince his words.

There was an international break after that match, and I'd been called up to the Under-21 squad. I didn't really want to go, and the manager was usually more than happy for us to pull out of international duty and stay in Manchester if we said we were carrying an injury. So, I told the physio that I'd picked up a knock and therefore couldn't go away with England. He went and spoke with the manager, and I overheard Sir Alex say, 'No, he's fine. He can go.'

That told me that I hadn't played very well. I realised then that I wasn't doing myself justice with my performances. I didn't admit it to myself but maybe I'd become big-headed and I'd dropped my standards because I just expected to turn up and play well. I always worked as hard as I could, but I wasn't applying myself. I wasn't capable of mixing my game up and I didn't learn from my mistakes and use them to keep on improving.

Although I was still getting plenty of game time, the Sunderland game aside, I wasn't having as big an impact as I'd had the previous year and that's when doubts started to creep in. During my breakthrough season, I was just grateful to be involved and I did as I was told. But now I wanted to show everyone what I could do – to shine more and become one of the more effective players. It wasn't anything to do with the competition I faced, it was something inside me. Instead of remaining patient, I felt that I had to make the most of my sporadic appearances. I knew that I wasn't going to start each week, but if I could get ten or 20 minutes and set up a goal or two, I'd have more opportunities. I should have been playing to my strengths and doing the things that had got me to United, but instead I was chasing everything, desperately trying to make something happen. I wanted goals and assists and tried too hard.

When I returned from international duty, the Scholes story was plastered all over the newspapers and apparently the leak had come from the agent of an England Under-21 player. As soon as I stepped foot inside the training ground, I was told to go straight to Sir Alex's office. I found the manager scary at the best of times, so to be summoned to his office was absolutely terrifying.

'Did you say anything to anyone about Paul Scholes while you were away?' he asked.

I was shitting myself. 'Er, no, Boss,' I replied. 'I don't really know what's going on. Even if I did, the last thing I'd do is speak publicly about the ins and outs of Manchester United in a negative way.'

The fear on my face and the shakiness of my voice, more than my words, let Sir Alex know that I was innocent. I never found out who the leak was.

I didn't play for United again until Saturday, 1 December when I made a brief cameo in a 3-0 home defeat to Chelsea. The game was already over when I took to the field, and we were having a really tough time of it. I fully expected the hairdryer in the dressing room, but the manager surprised us all by telling us to take the next day off and report for training on the Monday and we'd go from there.

What I should have done is have a low-key weekend at home, but the combination of my poor performances, United's drop in form and the abuse I was receiving each week on the television led to me making the wrong choices. I thought I was 'big time' and decided to get a chauffeur to drive me back to Cambridge where I had a night out with my friends. I took a bit of stick about my appearance from a few people inside a nightclub, and my response was, 'I'm a Manchester United player and I earn loads of money.'

During the drive back to Manchester on the Monday morning (yes, I paid for another chauffeur), I used the time to have a good think about my actions. I began to question what I was doing to help the deteriorating situation at Old Trafford. Thinking of myself as a big-time Premier League footballer wasn't going to help anyone. Although I did play for United, I'd achieved very little in my career in terms of appearances and trophies. I realised that I'd come away from the person I was. I'd lost humility and wasn't acting as the human being I'd like to be.

I was named in the starting line-up for our next match, a home game against West Ham, and I was determined to get back to my best. However, I put in another poor performance and was subbed off before the hour mark. To make matters worse, Jermain Defoe scored the only goal of the game as we fell to our sixth league defeat of the season and our third in a row. We plummeted to ninth in the league table.

The newspapers the following day reported on a club in crisis. The squad that I was part of had always been there or thereabouts. No one really had any experience of being at a club who sat mid-table and it was a strange situation to be in. We needed to re-evaluate where we were and gel as a group in order to get a run of games together.

I'd seen my match ratings continue to drop and I wondered if I was actually good enough to play at the highest level. Obviously, when you're only 21, you magnify any negativity, but I did start to think that maybe my time at Old Trafford was running out.

I was having some issues with my pelvis and hips, nothing serious, although the uncomfortable feeling was restricting my movement, so I missed a few games. During my absence, United won eight league games, which propelled us back to the top of the table.

On Wednesday, 18 December 2001, we went out for the Christmas party. Although I managed to avoid strippers and ice cubes this time, it was still a memorable occasion. We started with a mini pub crawl around Manchester city centre and then we went to the Living Room in Deansgate. After a couple of drinks, we were driven to the Rossetti Hotel in Piccadilly. I was in a minibus with Seba Verón and some of his mates from Argentina. This was only a few months out from the 2002 World Cup where England would be facing Argentina in the group stages. As we travelled through the busy streets, Seba's mates were banging on the windows and shouting, 'Argentina, Argentina,' to the passers-by.

The festivities continued at the Rossetti, but at some stage Ryan Giggs and Roy Carroll had a bit of a row and had to be separated before it kicked off. There was also a bit of trouble elsewhere, although nothing to do with me. I'd been nowhere near any of it.

The newspapers got hold of the story – as they always seem to – and printed it alongside a photo of me, Giggsy and Nicky Butt, taken earlier that evening. The manager was absolutely raging, and I made the mistake of walking past him in the corridor two days after the party. Although I was playing for the reserves that evening, I thought I'd be the least of his worries, but he'd obviously seen the photo of me printed next to the story and I was guilty by association. 'You're fined two weeks' wages,' he said without even breaking stride.

Flipping heck, I thought. *I wasn't expecting that.* The Christmas party cost me £24,000!

After training, we had our Christmas dinner, which was traditionally served by Sir Alex and his coaching staff. I was one of the last to be served and sat watching everyone else enjoy their starter while I patiently waited for mine. Then I saw my 'waiter' walking over holding a steaming bowl of soup. Sir Alex slammed it down in front of me and said, 'That's the most expensive meal you'll ever eat, son.'

Incidentally, I scored a brace for the reserves that night.

Chapter 11

The Three Lions

THE END of 2001 also marked the end of my international career.

I'd dreamed of representing my country since watching England in the 1986 World Cup. My knowledge of football was still in its infancy, but I was mesmerised by Diego Maradona. I, like many people across the country, cried when he went from hero to villain with that handball 'goal'.

By the time the 1990 World Cup came around, I had a much better understanding of the game. England had a great run and I honestly thought we were going to win the tournament until the heartbreaking penalty shoot-out defeat against West Germany. Italia '90 really brought football to life; the passion of the fans, Gazza's tears and Gary Lineker's goals. Lineker had a boot deal with Quasar at the time and I begged my mum to buy me a pair like his. Cameroon's Roger Milla was another hero of mine back then. My friends and I used to copy his dancing celebration on the playground.

England struggled a bit after that tournament, although I remember being excited by Aston Villa's Tony Daley during Euro '92. He was an incredibly fast winger who always seemed to pop up providing assists on my *100 Greatest Goals* videos.

During the summer months in between seasons, I'd wear my Three Lions shirt in the garden, pretending that I was representing my country. It was always a big ambition of mine to play for England Schoolboys, but it never happened for me. They used to play their matches at Wembley before the senior games. When I was 12, I went to trials at Lilleshall, England's headquarters in those days. I did okay but missed out on a place in the last 30. That was a huge disappointment and I had to put my international dreams on hold for six years.

In August 1998, I was invited back to Lilleshall for a trial with the England Under-18 squad. I travelled down with my team-mate Lee Roche, who'd also been invited, and that made it easier for me. Former Sheffield Wednesday and Leeds United manager Howard Wilkinson was in charge, and he had the ex-England captain David Platt by his side. Howard was the manager who rated me higher than anyone else throughout my career and he took to me straight away. He loved the way I ran with the ball, and I knew from that first day that I'd be named in his squad.

On 2 September 1998, I made my England Under-18s debut against the Republic of Ireland at Tolka Park, Dublin. Ireland, with Robbie Keane, Stephen McPhail and Richie Partridge in their side, had recently been crowned European Champions.

I remember singing the National Anthem before the game, but I felt a bit self-conscious and probably mumbled it. I certainly didn't belt it out like Stuart Pearce and Tony Adams did! It was such a proud moment to pull on the Three Lions shirt, and it was extra-special to know that my dad was in the stands watching me.

Those who'd expected a close game were in for a surprise as we ran out 5-0 winners. I had a great game on the right wing, setting up three of our goals. We had the newspapers delivered to our hotel the next morning and I couldn't believe it when I saw my name plastered all over the back pages. To be named man of the match on my international debut was unbelievable.

A month later I was part of the team that beat a strong Italy side 4-2 on their own soil. It was a real joy playing with the likes of Stuart Taylor, Gareth Barry, Wayne Bridge, Steven Gerrard, Scott Parker and my United team-mates Rochey and Richie Wellens. I was surrounded by immense talent, but I had no doubts in my ability.

In March 1999, I was called up for a three-game tour in Spain. We stayed in little chalets in Cadiz, a holiday resort on the south coast. I didn't know much about nutrition back then, so I had chicken and chips from the buffet table most nights. It felt strange, more like being on holiday than on a football tour. I found it a real drag, to be honest. Although I loved playing for England, I hated going away with all the other kids. I wasn't very sociable in those days and found it challenging being away from home for long periods of time.

We drew 1-1 with the host nation in the opening game, with Joe Cole making his debut. Joe was an unbelievable talent. We followed that win up with an 8-0 victory over Andorra. I scored our fourth, which was an incredible feeling. I always wanted to score a goal in an England shirt and that goal alone made the trip worthwhile. We finished the tour with a 2-1 victory over Israel and that was the end of time with the Under-18s.

The Under-21s manager Peter Taylor took over at Leicester City in the summer of 1999 and his replacement was Howard Wilkinson. I found out through Teletext that I'd been named in his first squad. I couldn't believe it when I saw my name among the other members of the squad, many of whom were playing week in, week out in the Premier League: Jamie Carragher, Frank Lampard, Emile Heskey. This was in September 1999. I was just 18 and had not yet made my United debut.

The game was being played at the Madejski Stadium and we were told to report to a hotel in Reading. I felt so nervous. I felt that I belonged with the Under-18s because they were all the same age as me and very few had played for the first team, so they were in the same position as me. The Under-21s felt like a huge step up. I was convinced that I'd turn up at the hotel and be sent home, told it was some kind of mistake.

I didn't know what to wear so I got dressed up in a shirt and tie and arrived about an hour and a half before everyone else. When the other lads arrived, they were wearing their England tracksuits and I felt completely out of my comfort zone. I was sharing a room with John Curtis, another United player, although not one I knew well as he was in and around the first team.

The day before the match we had a practice game against Reading's reserves, and I was named in the first XI, playing right wing-back. It was mad. I don't think any of the other lads could believe that this kid who'd never made a first-team appearance was likely to start the following evening. I got a bit of banter from them about how Wilkinson must be my dad! When I think back to those days, I can still hear him shouting to the lads in his broad Yorkshire accent, 'Get t' ball t' Chaddy.'

Sure enough, I played the full 90 minutes in a 5-0 win over Luxembourg. It was incredible. A few weeks later I received my England cap through the post, which was nice.

I won my second cap on 8 October 1999 against Denmark. I actually scored in that game and was buzzing, until the referee ruled it out for offside. It was a convincing 4-1 victory. I worked so hard in that game and left everything on the pitch. Our coach was Liverpool legend Sammy Lee, an incredible person. He was leading the cool-down after the game and my legs had completely gone. I could barely move when he took us for a little jog, but I didn't have the courage to tell him that I couldn't do it, so I pushed through the pain barrier.

By the time I made my third appearance I was playing for Royal Antwerp. I felt like a big hitter being flown in from Belgium to represent my country. I played the full 90 minutes as we beat Argentina 1-0 at Craven Cottage.

The following day, I was flying from London City Airport to Antwerp. The man sitting next to me was reading the sports pages in *The Times* and there was a huge picture of me playing for England. I felt a bit awkward because I hated the attention, and I spent the rest of the flight hoping he didn't recognise me. He didn't.

I took a taxi from Antwerp airport back to the flat I was sharing with Carl. I didn't have a key on me, so I rang the doorbell. No answer. I pressed it again, but still no answer. The joy of representing my country evaporated as I started stressing about whether I'd be sleeping rough that evening. Eventually, one of my neighbours let me in. It was quite late, and he didn't look very happy with me for waking him up. When I got to my flat, I noticed that the door was open. Not unlocked, actually open. My brother was passed out snoring on the floor. He'd obviously had a good night!

In March 2000, we played Yugoslavia in a play-off match where the winner would qualify for the European Championships. I was called up to the squad but had a stomach bug and didn't want to travel and join up with the squad. Instead of being honest and telling the FA, I decided to ignore them. The FA rang me several times. Howard rang me several times. I just blanked them. Again, I wasn't being rude, I just didn't like saying no to people. To be honest, I'm surprised I received another call-up after that.

The lads won 3-0 and I was selected in the squad for the Under-21 European Championships that took place in Slovakia in the summer of 2000. I didn't want to be there, though. I hated every single moment of that trip. None of my club team-mates were there and I didn't really know anyone. I wasn't comfortable in the environment. I didn't train particularly well, and I didn't start a single game. I spent the whole trip waiting to come home. It was a disastrous tournament for the whole team as we went out in the group stages. Italy, with Andrea Pirlo, Gennaro Gattuso and Francesco Coco, beat us 2-0 in the opening group game. We beat Turkey 6-0 in the next match, but then lost 2-0 to Slovakia.

I didn't start for England again until 14 November 2000 when we played Italy in Monza. Within ten minutes of the kick-off the fog had become so thick that we couldn't see from one side of the pitch to the other. At one stage I had the ball and couldn't see more than ten yards in front of me. We were taken off the pitch and waited in the dressing room for almost an hour to see if it cleared. It didn't and the match was abandoned. Strangely, I got a real buzz when I heard that we couldn't continue the game. For some unknown reason, I got excited when a game was called off.

We always seemed to struggle against the better, more technical nations such as Italy because we were such an attacking team that played on the front foot and didn't defend very well. And there was no one more technical than Spain. We played the Spanish at St Andrew's, Birmingham, on 27 February 2001. They battered us 4-0. A young lad by the name of Xavi pulled the strings in the middle of the park. I wonder what happened to him! Shola Ameobi made his debut for us that day. He was the one shining light, putting in a great performance, while the rest of us were terrible.

I kept my place in the starting line-up for our next two games – 4-0 and 1-0 wins over Finland and Albania respectively. I played on the left wing in those games, with Gareth Barry at left-back. We developed a really good understanding. He was brilliant on the ball and frequently made good overlapping runs.

Howard Wilkinson stepped down as manager in the summer of 2001 and his replacement was David Platt, who'd worked with Howard before. I was really pleased to be named in the starting line-up for Platt's first game, which was a 4-0 victory over the Netherlands. The Dutch had Rafael van der Vaart and Arjen Robben in their side, so it was a great result.

On 31 August 2001, we beat Germany 2-1 thanks to Francis Jeffers's stoppage-time goal. I didn't have the best game, but it was special to beat the Germans in their own backyard.

A few days later, we beat Albania 5-0 at the Riverside Stadium, Middlesbrough. I'd got a bit above my station by then and spent the game coming out of position to get on the ball because I wanted to show everyone how good I was. I got subbed and didn't receive a particularly good reception from the manager or coaching staff.

My performances in training hadn't been very good. It didn't happen very often in my career, but my attitude was really poor. I saw younger players like Jermaine Pennant called up to the squad and resented the fact that he was playing instead of me. Jermaine did a fantastic job, and then Shaun Wright-Phillips came along. Although I was named in Platt's next three squads, I was an unused substitute and never played for England again.

I always harboured ambitions of playing for the senior squad, but as soon as I realised that I wouldn't have a long-term future at United, I knew that the chances of me actually receiving a call-up were slim. But although I never won a full cap, I'm incredibly proud that I had the opportunity to represent my country playing the game that I love.

A family holiday with my mum and dad, and brother Carl.

Sporting my Cambridge United tracksuit, playing in the back garden of our house in Meldreth.

Signing for Manchester United was a dream come true.

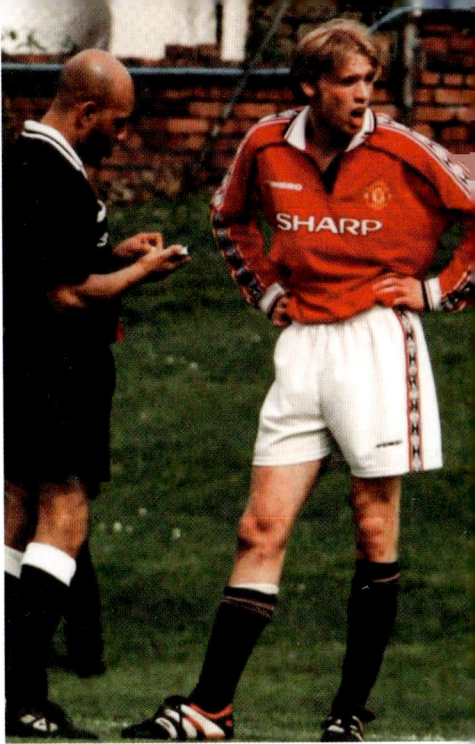

Getting a talking to by the ref during a youth team match for United.

I made my Manchester United debut against Aston Villa in 1999.

David Beckham assisted my first United goal to give us a 3-0 win over Bradford City.

Skipping past future World Cup winner Xavi for England under 21s against Spain.

I set up Paul Scholes's last-minute equaliser on my Champions League debut against Panathinaikos.

I began the 2001/02 season on loan at Antwerp and finished it holding aloft the Premier League trophy.

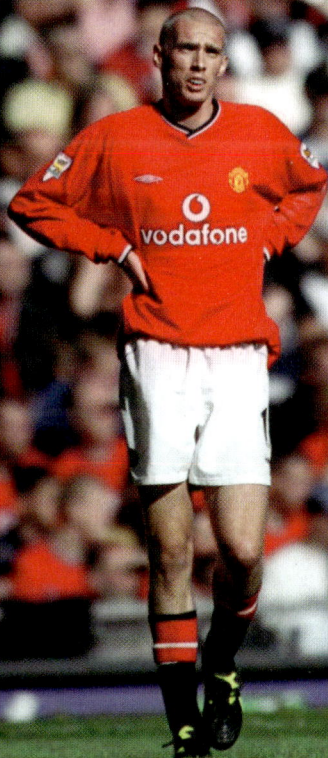

I suffered with mental health issues during my time at Old Trafford. At times, I felt completely isolated.

I gained a new lease of life during my loan spell at Reading during the 2002/03 season.

Chapter 12

Not the Same Player

I RETURNED to first-team action on 6 January 2002 in an FA Cup tie at Villa Park. It was an absolute nightmare. I began the match on the subs' bench and replaced the injured Nicky Butt midway through the first half. I was playing quite well, although I missed a couple of very good chances, including a one-on-one with former Manchester United goalkeeper Peter Schmeichel that I should really have scored.

Aston Villa went 2-0 up and then I suffered the ultimate humiliation for a footballer – I was sub-subbed. Ruud van Nistelrooy took my place and scored two goals, which helped us to a 3-2 victory, it was a fantastic comeback and everyone was buzzing afterwards. Everyone but me. The game was shown live on BBC (the same channel that broadcast *They Think It's All Over*, of course) and I felt hugely embarrassed. It was a real kick in the balls.

That's it, I'm finished at United now. I need to move, I thought to myself on the coach back to Manchester while I was surrounded by my jubilant team-mates. That night I lay awake for hours pondering my future. I eventually fell asleep having made a decision – I was going to ask for a transfer.

So, the next morning I surprised myself by plucking up the courage to knock on the manager's door. Sir Alex greeted me with a wry smile. I'm sure he knew exactly what I was going to say.

'Boss, I came on last night as a substitute and then you took me off again. I don't think it's going to work out for me here, so I'd like a move,' I said.

He was incredibly supportive. 'I understand why you're disappointed, Luke, but we needed to get back into the game and I decided to throw on another striker. We won. It was the right decision,' he replied, before adding, 'You're a valued member of my squad and you're going nowhere.'

Sir Alex had a knack of knowing the right thing to say. I'd gone into his office feeling at rock bottom and came out feeling ten feet tall. Still, I left his office with mixed feelings. On the one hand, it's fantastic when the greatest manager in the world tells you he wants you to stay at the biggest club in the world. On the other, I honestly felt that I needed to leave in order to play regular first-team football and make a career for myself. But I was never going to argue with Sir Alex!

The manager told me I'd be starting in the next round of the FA Cup, away at Middlesbrough. The night before the match, I was chilling in my hotel room when I heard a pounding on my door. I opened it and saw Laurent and Fabien standing there.

'Have you got any cigarettes?' Laurent asked.

'No, sorry. I don't smoke,' I replied.

They looked at me with puzzled expressions because I'd clearly smoked with them on an earlier night out. I saw one of the coaches walking down the corridor and didn't want to get into trouble, so I closed the door and assumed they'd gone back to their rooms. About 20 minutes later there was a knock on my window. It was Laurent and Fabien again. They'd got hold of some cigarettes – I've no idea how – and they asked if I wanted to climb out of the window to join them. It was hilarious. We were preparing for an FA Cup match and here were two legends of the game sneaking around to have a sneaky fag! I politely declined, but it was kind of them to offer.

I didn't play well against Middlesbrough. I'd lost so much confidence by then and it affected my performance. I was again replaced by Ruud, but this time the Dutchman couldn't prevent us from going out of the cup.

I went to see a specialist the following week because of the problems that I'd been having with my pelvis and hips. I was experiencing discomfort when I first noticed it, but it had become more and more painful. I wasn't moving as freely as before because of the pain, and this was another reason for my poor performances.

After going for a scan, the specialist told me that my muscle was rubbing against the bone and that was what was causing the pain. There were two options: the first was to have complete rest for two months, followed by a further month of building back up to full fitness; the second was to have an operation, which could mean I'd be out for the rest of the season. The specialist's advice was to try the first option, and that's what I did. Surgery was often the very last resort.

It was the first significant injury that I'd suffered, and it was a tough period of my life. My daily routine was so mundane: I'd go into Carrington for a little bit of treatment, be back home for lunchtime, plonk myself on the sofa and spend the rest of the day watching TV. That was it. That was my life.

You can feel very isolated as an injured footballer, but I isolated myself even more. I didn't go to United's games that often, even though we were supposed to attend the home matches. I didn't like people speaking to me because all everyone asks when you're injured is when you're coming back, and I had no idea. I didn't even eat at the club with the lads after they'd finished training. Hayley would pick me up and we'd get a Burger King or something from a different fast-food restaurant. My diet was awful, but I didn't care. I began to question whether I still wanted to be a footballer.

My confidence had deserted me anyway because of the abuse I was receiving about my appearance on TV, and football had always been my release, my way of dealing with challenges. I felt guilty because I wasn't able to do what the club was paying me to do. Without football, I realised that I didn't have a lot else going on in my life. I was never interested in fame or money. I had no ambitions to drive a fast car or live in a big house. I just wanted to play football. I was desperate to run around and kick a ball. But I couldn't and I found myself going stir-crazy with nothing to do. My mind started to wander into dark territories. *Is it worth it? Is this really what I want my life to be like?*

Although I discussed, with my mum and Hayley, quitting the game and finding a new pathway, the thoughts weren't quite strong enough for me to seriously want to retire at such an early age. The only positive for me was that, because I wasn't featuring in the first team, I was out of the public eye, and this was when *They Think It's All Over* forgot about me and moved on to someone else.

After an agonisingly frustrating three months, I finally returned to first-team action at the end of April 2002, starting and playing the majority of the Premier League game against Ipswich. It was good to be back, and I played quite well – Sir Alex gave me some positive feedback – but I recognised straight after the match that the problems with my hip and pelvis remained. Adrenaline had got me through the game but, once that had worn off, the pain returned. My season was over.

United came third in the league, ten points behind champions Arsenal, and we finished without a trophy for the first time in four years. The only piece of good news was that Sir Alex had changed his mind about retiring, signing a new three-year contract instead.

I met with the specialist again and he told me that I needed to have the operation after all. I was devastated. I was fortunate that the operation was only a small keyhole procedure that involved the surgeon cutting away some of the muscle that had been rubbing against the bone and causing me pain.

After a short period of rest, I spent the majority of the summer at Carrington, undertaking a rehab programme and rebuilding my fitness. By the time we reported for pre-season, I was raring to go mentally, although not physically.

It didn't take me long to realise that the op, particularly where it was, meant that my movement patterns and the way that I ran would never be the same as before. I lost some of my pace, and pace was an essential part of my game. My biggest strength had always been my ability to run fast, with and without the ball. Don't get me wrong, it wasn't that I couldn't run, I just didn't quite have the same speed off the mark that I'd enjoyed previously. At the highest levels, these fine margins make all the difference.

My whole game was built around pace; I was someone who'd dribble past defenders, run with the ball and excite fans. I'm sure it was noticeable to everyone watching that I wasn't beating players as easily as I had done before my injury. It was incredibly frustrating that my body wasn't doing what I wanted it to do, what it had been doing forever. The pain, although not as bad as before, was still there.

During one session I broke down and thought I'd sustained the same injury. All I'd done was take a left-footed shot, and I was in sheer agony. I couldn't walk so the physio sent on a little golf buggy to cart me off. Luckily a subsequent scan showed that I'd just torn some scar tissue, and after a couple of days of rest I returned to training.

By that stage, Sir Alex had made one of his greatest-ever signings, acquiring England international defender Rio Ferdinand from our rivals Leeds United. Rio was a huge character and from day one looked like he'd been born to play for Manchester United. I tried to get past Rio in training a few times and failed miserably. He was strong and quick, and his passing was up there with the best midfielders in the Premier League – Rio was world class. No disrespect to Laurent Blanc, but we'd finally found a replacement for Jaap Stam.

Despite Rio's arrival, we didn't make a great start to the 2002/03 season, winning just one of our first five league games. Often an unused substitute, I didn't make my first appearance of the season until 14 September 2002 when I came off the bench in a tough match against Leeds. Elland Road was a cauldron that day, with most of the almost 40,000 in attendance taking every opportunity to boo and jeer Rio. The game was played with such pace and ferocity, and I found it hard to get into it.

The last time I'd played here I'd scored and had one of my best performances for United. This time, I cost us the game. I gave the Leeds left-back Ian Harte too much space and he was able to cut inside and cross the ball in for Harry Kewell to head home the only goal of the match. I was gutted and felt that I'd let down the club, my team-mates and the fans.

A month went by before I got my next opportunity, again coming off the bench for the last 30 minutes, this time in a Champions League game against Olympiacos. We were 2-0 up at the time, courtesy of goals from Laurent Blanc and Seba Verón. But ten minutes later the Greeks had pulled it back to 2-2. A late Paul Scholes wonder strike salvaged three vital points.

Afterwards, Roy Keane overheard me telling the physio that my hip and groin were still painful. Roy came over to me and said, 'Sometimes as a footballer, you just have to get through it and play, even when you're injured.'

I didn't feel that I could 'get through it' because I was in so much pain, but as my career progressed, I took on board Roy's feedback and often played through the pain barrier. At the time, though, Roy's comments, although intended to help, were another reminder that I was letting people down. I felt guilty that I wasn't performing, and I could feel myself slipping further and further from becoming a first-team regular.

I just wanted to play football and contribute to the team, and with the realisation that I wasn't the same player I had been, I approached Sir Alex and asked for a loan move so I could get some game time. The manager reiterated that I was still part of his plans but, as 2002 became 2003, I'd made just three further appearances. My performances hadn't improved, and I think Sir Alex had realised that I perhaps wasn't going to reach the heights he'd predicted two years earlier. The next crop of youngsters, including Kieran Richardson and Darren Fletcher, were on the fringes of the first team and we all knew that my time at Old Trafford was coming to an end.

This time I didn't have to knock on the manager's door asking for a move. Sir Alex came to me. 'I'm sorry, Luke, but you're not going to have a career at Manchester United.' And that was it. I was on the lookout for a new adventure.

Chapter 13

You See What Happens

THE ONLY way is down when you leave Manchester United. That was fine with me, though, because I didn't ever see myself becoming a proper member of the first team at Old Trafford. Playing week in, week out was far more important to me than sitting on the bench at United. I was actually quite excited to try something different and become a valuable part of a team.

At the end of January 2003, not long after Sir Alex told me that I could leave, I was selected for a reserve-team match against Manchester City in the Manchester Senior Cup. We played at Ewen Fields, home of non-league Hyde United. There was a pretty big crowd there because, although it was a second-string match, it was still a Manchester derby. Sitting among the supporters were several scouts (including one from Scottish giants Rangers, who were apparently interested in signing me), so it was a good opportunity to go out there and put myself in the shop window.

My evening didn't quite go to plan, though. We lost 3-0 and I had an absolute stinker. It was probably the worst performance of my career. My confidence ebbed away with each mistake I made, and when our manager, Brian McClair, took me off in the second half I knew that I'd let myself down. I sat on the bench with my head in my hands, thinking that it couldn't get any worse. Then I heard the City fans sitting behind our dugout start to give me a load of stick. I expected it, to be honest, because I was a first-team squad member who'd played terribly for the reserves, but then it turned personal, some nasty insults hurled in my direction, mainly about my appearance. It was relentless and I felt so powerless. The abuse became so bad that McClair eventually turned around and had a go at the Manchester City fans. That was probably the lowest point of my United career.

The next day, Sir Alex told me that he wasn't at all happy with how I'd performed. 'A player who's been involved with the first team should be performing much better than you did last night,' he said.

He was right. It had got to the stage where I was desperate to leave Manchester and start again somewhere else. I still had two years of my contract remaining and United wanted a fee for me, so the idea was to find me a loan move to help secure a permanent transfer in the summer.

I soon received word of interest from Reading, which I was quite excited about. The Royals had been promoted to the Championship the season before and were doing quite well. They had an outside chance of winning promotion to the Premier League. Hayley was eight months pregnant, and we were both keen on a move back down south so we could be closer to our families. Reading ticked all the boxes. Well, almost all of them. The only box it didn't tick was the one that read 'manager's approval'.

Sir Alex was good friends with Cardiff City manager Lennie Lawrence, and he wanted me to go to the Welsh club. Cardiff, in League One at the time (they won promotion that season), are a fantastic club with passionate fans and it would have been a good move, but it was too far away from Cambridge for me to commute and I didn't want to go.

Sir Alex gave Lennie my phone number and he kept calling the flat. When I was in, I just didn't answer the phone. Hayley's parents were staying with us, helping her during the final stages of pregnancy. My mother-in-law spoke to Lennie a couple of times, and although she passed on the messages for me to call him back, I never did. I wasn't ignoring him to be rude, it was because I didn't like saying no to people.

At the training ground later that week, Sir Alex asked me why I hadn't been answering Lennie's calls. I made up an excuse about not being at home, but I was stalling for time until I knew for certain that Reading were going to make a formal bid for me.

Finally, I was invited to the Madejski Stadium to meet the manager Alan Pardew and discuss a potential move. Sir Alex was unaware of Reading's interest, so I thought the best thing to do was to go to Carrington early the following day, before anyone else arrived, tell the manager that I was going to join Reading, then head down south and make it official.

So, first thing in the morning, Hayley drove me to the training ground. I saw the manager as I was walking down the corridor to his office, and my heart sank. He didn't look happy with me to start with, so I knew it was going to be a difficult conversation.

'I've spoken to Reading. They want me to join so I'm going down there today to sign for them,' I said, trying to sound assertive, even though I was shitting myself. It was the first time I'd ever gone against the manager's wishes.

'No, you're not,' Sir Alex replied. 'You're going to Cardiff.'

'Sorry, Boss, but I'm going to Reading. That's where I want to play.'

'Do what you fucking want then. You just see what happens when you get down there,' he said.

That didn't quite go to plan, I thought as I walked out of his office, and back to the car, where Hayley was waiting patiently. During the four-hour journey to Berkshire, I couldn't stop wondering what he meant by 'you just see what happens'.

As soon as I caught a glimpse of the modern 26,000-seater Madejski Stadium, I turned to Hayley and told her that this was the club for me. Alan Pardew was waiting for me in reception. He introduced himself and he led me to his office to talk about his vision for the football club. We'd barely sat down when his assistant knocked on the door with a message for Pards – Sir Alex Ferguson wanted to speak to him.

I remained in his office while Pardew called Manchester United. Within seconds, Pardew's face had turned as white as a penalty spot. I didn't need a speakerphone to realise that Sir Alex wasn't happy – I'm sure the people in the next room could tell that! I couldn't hear every word, but I knew that he was having a pop at Pardew for inviting me to Reading without his consent.

After a couple of minutes, Pards put the phone down and said, 'Well, it's not great news. Sir Alex has said that you can do what you want but Manchester United aren't going to pay you a penny of your wages if you come here.'

He asked how much I was on at United (around £12,500 by then, a lot more than most Championship players) and told me that Reading could only offer me £6,000 a week. With

United refusing to make up the shortfall, I'd have to forfeit the rest. I did a quick calculation in my head and realised that I'd be losing out on around £100,000 if I signed for Reading instead of Cardiff. I was way too scared to speak to Sir Alex myself and ask him to reconsider, but it wasn't about the money – it never was during my entire career – I just wanted to play regular first-team football and be near our families for when the baby came along. Reading could offer me that, so I signed a loan contract until the end of the season. Although it probably wasn't the best decision financially, I have no regrets from a footballing or personal point of view. I couldn't wait to get started.

Before my first training session, I felt the usual nerves about meeting new people and I had some nagging doubts about my ability because of my recent poor performances, but that anxiousness quickly evaporated.

Reading were in a transitional period and didn't yet have a permanent training ground when I joined. The lads got changed at the Madejski and then travelled by coach to a private school where we'd train on the playing fields. I loved it, even though it was a world away from the top-spec training facilities I was used to at Carrington. I even had to take my own training kit home and wash it myself. For Hayley to wash, I mean!

Instead of going to the stadium, I travelled straight to the school from Cambridge, already wearing my training kit and more often than not I was the first one to arrive. There were no staff there and the equipment travelled down with the team, so I was alone in the middle of a huge field. I always kept a football in the boot of my car, so I'd do keepie-uppies or kick a ball against the wall until the lads arrived.

I soon realised that I was one of the better players in the group. During small-sided games, I was able to get past my man with ease, just like I had a few seasons earlier. I instantly felt my confidence come rushing back.

At United, training sessions were intense; they often felt like you were in the middle of a war zone, with the win-at-all-costs mentality. Reading were in a position in the league that no one had expected, so there was less pressure, and the general day-to-day environment was much more relaxed. That's a testament to Alan Pardew, who'd created a fantastic dressing room atmosphere. Team morale was so high and I'm sure that must have been one of the contributing factors to the previous season's promotion and the good campaign Reading were enjoying.

Pards was a completely different character to me. He was an extrovert, really out there, and someone who courted attention. The lads joked openly that he loved himself. This was his first managerial role, and he was still learning his trade. Before becoming the manager, Pardew had been Reading's coach and he still had quite a pally approach with us – he was one of the lads. It was unusual for a manager, but it worked, and he was able to get the best out of the players at his disposal. Everything that he did was first class, and I could tell that he'd eventually become a Premier League manager.

I never felt any pressure because I'd come from Manchester United. The fact that I've played for United is always brought up by the fans and the media, but I didn't ever think that I was better than anyone else because of my background. I mucked in with the lads and found it easy to settle in wherever I went. The only time it was mentioned at Reading was during my first week when we were practising set pieces. Everyone assumed that I'd be good at taking corners because I was a winger, but I hated them. James Harper was our usual corner taker, but Pards asked him to take a break to give me a chance to take some. I took ten corners, each more dismal than the last.

'Fucking hell, Luke,' the manager shouted. 'You're a Manchester United player and you can't even take corners.'

'To be fair, Becks takes them at United,' I replied. The lads were howling with laughter, absolutely buzzing with my response. It won't surprise you to read that I didn't take a set piece for Reading.

We had a very strong squad with some fantastic players, a mixture of experienced pros and exciting youngsters. Everyone was pulling in the same direction. It was a good dressing room with excellent team spirit.

Steve Brown and Ady Williams, our centre-backs, were vastly experienced and gave a solid foundation to the team. Nicky Shorey was a young, gifted left-back who went on to be capped by England. Graeme Murty was the club captain and my roommate. A really good, experienced pro. A consistent performer and strong leader. Behind them in goal was Marcus Hahnemann, an American international. A brilliant shotstopper and a top bloke, although Pards gave him a hard time on a couple of occasions.

On the left wing was former England international John Salako. John was a great character. I rented a flat from him in the centre of Reading, where I stayed occasionally. He had a couple of properties dotted about and I'm sure he had a few quid stashed away, but he didn't give me any cheap mates rates! In the heart of our midfield was Steve Sidwell, who'd joined Reading from Arsenal a few weeks before me. A fantastic young player who went on to have a great career in the Premier League with Chelsea, Aston Villa and Stoke City. His midfield partner was James Harper. James and I had played together as kids with East Anglia Boys. It was strange but nice to meet up with him again, and quite surreal to play together in the Championship.

Glen Little was on loan from Burnley. Another winger, Glen was a bubbly character with a great sense of humour and kept everyone entertained. Andy Hughes played in the attacking midfielder role. One of the best blokes that I've met in my life. He was brilliant at helping me to settle in by showing me the ropes. Andy was a fantastic guy in the dressing room, always looking out for others. I played with him again later in my career. We had Nicky Forster up top. A hard worker and a prolific goalscorer at Championship level. Waiting in the wings were Darius Henderson and Nathan Tyson, two talented youngsters just breaking into the side.

The lads were all so welcoming and made me feel part of the team from day one. I felt more comfortable knowing that I was going to be a first-team regular. I wasn't just there to make up the numbers; I was there to play. I think the other players recognised that I had the ability to have an impact on games and help the team.

I was pleasantly surprised that I didn't have to go through any new-signing initiations. Come to think of it, I got away with it at every club I played for – apart from Fun and Games at United, of course. The most common initiation is singing a song in front of your new team-mates. If I'd had to sing one, I'd probably have gone with 'Angels' by Robbie Williams. That's a nice little karaoke song, although I may not have done it justice!

I made my debut on 10 February 2003, in a home match against Gillingham. It couldn't have gone any better. Just 13 minutes into the game, I came inside on my left foot, caught a glimpse of the goal, and shot. The ball took a deflection off the defender, wrong-footed the keeper and hit the back of the net. To score in any game is great, to do it on my debut was a dream come true. I ran to celebrate with the jubilant supporters, one arm held aloft. Nothing too over the top, but inside I felt a huge release of emotion. *Oh, how I've missed this feeling.* It's amazing what a difference a goal can make. It helped endear me to the fans, my nerves were settled and I felt at ease in my new environment.

John Salako added a second late in the second half to give us a 2-1 win. It was quite a tough game. Gillingham were struggling towards the bottom of the table and battled well, but we managed to scrape through. Our supporters were fantastic and cheered us off the pitch at the end.

Sitting in the dressing room after the game I felt delighted. For the first time in a long time, I knew that I'd contributed to the team's success. *You can still do this,* I thought to myself. *Just because it won't happen for you at United doesn't mean there isn't still a future for you as a footballer.*

A few days into my loan spell, I picked up the Sunday papers and read with astonishment a story about a post-match argument between David Beckham and Sir Alex that had left Becks with a cut on his head. I phoned John O'Shea to find out what had happened. The manager had lost his temper after a defeat to Arsenal and kicked a boot that had hit Becks, studs side up, in the head. It wasn't intentional but obviously the newspapers made a big deal of it. I know Sir Alex has a reputation for the hairdryer, but I can't really remember him blowing his top like that. I've heard lots of stories of the Sir Alex of old and I can only conclude that he'd mellowed by the time I'd broken into the first team.

We beat Millwall away in my second game and then travelled to high-flying Sheffield United. We won 3-1 with a brace from Nicky Forster, either side of a rare Ady Williams goal. We were outstanding that day and that's when people started to sit up and take note. There was a strong belief within the squad that we could make the play-offs, and that became our aim.

The two standout teams in the Championship that season were Portsmouth and Leicester City. Portsmouth, under the leadership of Harry Redknapp, had a strong, experienced squad that featured the likes of Shaka Hislop, Steve Stone, Tim Sherwood, Paul Merson and two future Premier League managers, Eddie Howe and Gary O'Neil. Leicester had been relegated from the top flight the season before and had managed to keep hold of most of their players. So, with the two automatic promotion spots pretty much in the bag for Portsmouth and Leicester, we set our sights on reaching the play-offs.

I loved my first experience of the Championship and felt more comfortable at that level. It wasn't the Premier League, it wasn't the Champions League, but the standard was still extremely high, and I found myself playing against fantastic players each week.

Off the pitch, I was delighted to become a father for the first time, on 23 February 2003, when Hayley gave birth to a healthy baby boy, Louis. Fortunately, by then I'd passed my driving test (on the second attempt), so I was able to drive her to the hospital when she went into labour. With a newborn baby, I should have gone for something practical, a car with plenty of boot space for a pushchair and all the other paraphernalia babies seem to need. But, of course, I went for something flash instead. I bought a BMW 325Ci convertible. It was a soft top but also had a hard top you could put on in the winter.

Despite the way things had been left with Sir Alex, I was delighted when we received a huge bouquet from Manchester United and a card congratulating us. Such a lovely gesture that was typical of the club.

Once Louis was born, I'd drive to training and back on the same day to make sure I was home early to spend as much time as I could with my family. The quickest, most logical route from Cambridge to Reading was along the A1 and M25, both notoriously busy roads. I was a nervous driver and didn't want to drive on the motorway, so I plotted a route that meant I could avoid the main roads. Satnavs weren't commonplace back then, so I studied a map and wrote down the route I needed to take. I was quite proud of myself, although it probably stuck another half an hour onto each leg of my journey.

I'd get up at 5am when Louis woke, drive to Reading and arrive around 7am, have a couple of hours' sleep in the flat, and then head off to training. It was exhausting, especially with the sleep deprivation that comes with a newborn. It was an unusual set-up, but you learn to make adjustments when you have kids. It was worth it to make sure I didn't miss out on watching him grow up, although, to be honest, babies are a bit boring and don't do much, so I could probably have done with a bit more time away from him to catch up on sleep!

On 21 April 2003, we played the champions Portsmouth at Fratton Park. They tore us apart and ran out 3-0 winners.

Early in the second half, I saw that Pardew was going to make a change. I was shocked when I realised that I was the man coming off. Okay, I wasn't having a great game, but I'd been no worse than anyone else. I felt my anger build as I reluctantly trudged off the pitch. *How dare he sub me. I'm a Premier League player.* I slapped hands with Darius Henderson, my replacement, but refused to make eye contact with the manager. 'Fuck off,' I mouthed in his direction. I immediately regretted it.

The following day, Pardew called me into the boot room at the Madejski Stadium and read me the riot act. I'd got a bit above my station, and he soon brought me right back down to earth. I apologised and played the full 90 minutes in our next match, a 2-1 win at home to Grimsby Town.

We lost 1-0 away at Stoke in our final league game of the campaign and finished in fourth place in the league table. That meant we'd be facing Wolverhampton Wanderers in the two-legged play-off semi-final. The fact that we'd finished one position higher than Wolves meant nothing. When the season ends, the league table goes out of the window and a new competition begins. It's not uncommon for a team that has sneaked into the final play-off spot to win promotion.

At the start of the season, I'm sure everyone would have been delighted to make the play-offs, so it was a fantastic achievement for the club. A few of the lads had been involved in Reading's play-off final defeat to Walsall in 2001, but it was a whole new experience for me. We had to make sure that we didn't get too carried away. I wasn't thinking about the possibility of playing at the Millennium Stadium in the final, it was just a case of playing these two games and seeing what we could do.

Wolves had a very strong side, with Joleon Lescott and my former United team-mate Denis Irwin at the back, my future manager and assistant manager, Paul Ince and Alex Rae marshalling the midfield, and Kenny Miller partnering Dean Sturridge up front.

We surprised them in the first leg, held at Molineux, with the way we came out of the blocks to attack. Nicky Forster gave us a deserved lead in the 25th minute but, although I think we were the better team on the day, their quality and experience shone through. Wolves scored twice in the final quarter of an hour to take a 2-1 lead into the second leg.

I picked up a knee injury in training so had to settle for a place on the bench when Wolves visited the Madejski four days later. Nicky Forster, our top scorer, was also out injured, which was a huge blow. The Wolves keeper Matt Murray was outstanding, and we just couldn't put the ball in the back of the net. Eight minutes from time, Alex Rae put the tie beyond all doubt when he fired home from 15 yards. Wolves went on to beat Sheffield United in the final to gain promotion, although that was scant consolation to us.

The dressing room after the match was a hard place to be. It was full of disappointment, but there were so many positives too. We'd exceeded expectations and proved we could compete with the best teams in the division. On a personal note, I'd been a regular starter and finally had my confidence back. The big question I asked myself as I went away for the summer break was: where would I be next year?

Manchester United had reclaimed the Premier League title and I knew it would be very difficult to get back into the reckoning at Old Trafford. Even though Beckham was sold to

Real Madrid, Sir Alex went out and signed a replacement – a young Portuguese by the name of Cristiano Ronaldo!

I had my heart set on a permanent move to Reading. Hayley and I had even started looking for houses in the area. Then I received a letter from Alan Pardew, a nice handwritten one that thanked me for what I'd done for him but, because of the financial constraints the club was under, he wouldn't be able to sign me. I was gutted and felt a little bit in limbo.

So, after having an operation to correct my jaw, I returned to Manchester United for the start of pre-season training, wondering what 2003/04 had in store for me.

Chapter 14

Fish and Chips and WKD

I DECIDED to have the operation on my jaw at the end of the 2002/03 season and spent the rest of the summer recovering. When I returned to Carrington for pre-season training, I was quite worried about seeing Sir Alex again because I hadn't heard from him since I'd defied the manager by signing for Reading. But when I bumped into him on my first day back, I was pleasantly surprised that he was happy to see me. Sir Alex said that he'd been impressed with my form while out on loan and that Alan Pardew had been giving him regular feedback on my progress. Sir Alex also told me how much he respected my decision to sign for Reading, even though it meant taking a huge pay cut.

Hayley, Louis and I had moved back into our flat in Sale, although there was still uncertainty about where I'd be playing. I knew that I wouldn't be content with reserve-team football and the odd cameo for the first team so that meant I needed to find another new club.

Within days of returning to Carrington, the manager called me into his office and explained that Stan Ternent was desperate for me to join Championship club Burnley on loan for the entire season. Sir Alex was big mates with Stan. 'We'll make sure you'll get all your money this year,' he joked.

I was keen on the move, even though I'd be staying in the north-west, instead of moving down south. Burnley was well within commuting distance of Manchester, so we could stay in the flat, and my mate Lee Roche had just joined them on a free transfer. I felt wanted by Burnley and was ready to pick up where I'd left off with Reading.

Burnley is an old mill town in Lancashire. The football club is one of the oldest professional clubs in the world and a founder member of the Football League. There are only five clubs to have been crowned champions of all four divisions in England – Burnley is one. Despite a rich history, Burnley was suffering financially when I joined. Like a lot of clubs, it had been hugely impacted by the collapse of ITV Digital, a broadcaster that had agreed on a massive TV deal with Football League clubs. When ITV Digital folded, the football clubs got nothing, which caused many to go into administration. Burnley managed to avoid that but still had to balance the books, so were forced to sell strikers Gareth Taylor and Dimitrios Papadopoulos for £500,000 and £200,000 respectively, while a host of big earners were given free transfers. There was no money to spend on new players, so Stan had to rely on loans and frees.

The facilities at Burnley were very different to Reading, let alone Manchester United. Our training ground was at Gawthorpe Hall. The River Calder ran alongside the training pitches and when it rained the river overflowed and the pitches became flooded. Our changing rooms were located in an old building that was freezing in the winter. The showers weren't great, and they didn't put food on either. It was just a case of getting in, getting changed and making your way to the pitches.

When we lost, Stan made us do the factory run, which was a horrible three-mile run through the woods by the factories. It was all very old-school, and that phrase also sums up our manager Stan Ternent. Stan is a Burnley legend. A former player, he became manager in 1998 when the club was languishing in League Two. Within a few years, he'd taken them to the Championship, and he did it on a shoestring budget. Stan had cultivated an environment that was so much fun, with a fantastic team spirit. I loved my time at Burnley.

I felt comfortable straight away and went into an environment that was very different from Reading. It was a very lively dressing room with some big characters. For the first time in my career, I felt fully integrated within the squad, joining in with the stuff that happens off the pitch – the banter and practical jokes. Every Friday we'd have a kangaroo court where you could bring up charges against anyone. If you were found guilty by Stan or his coaching staff – the judges – you had to pay a £2 fine. People would make up the most ridiculous allegations, like driving without wearing a seat belt, and then you'd wait and see if you'd be found guilty.

There weren't too many youngsters at the club. Richard Chaplow was an excellent young player, and Robbie Blake was as good a finisher as anyone at that level. But what we lacked in youth, we more than made up for with experience, including my old mate David May. Maysy was someone I'd spent a huge amount of time with when playing for United's reserves and we got on really well. Glen Little had returned to Burnley following his loan spell at Reading and it was good to link with him again.

Our season began at Turf Moor against Crystal Palace. Although we lost 3-2, I played really well and was named man of the match. But that paled into insignificance when Rochey and I were given the devastating news that our former Manchester United team-mate Jimmy Davis had died in a car accident.

Jimmy was a year younger than me, so we weren't close friends, but we'd played together for the youth teams, reserves and first team, and I knew him well. He was an incredibly talented footballer. I remember when he arrived at The Cliff for his first day as a YTS; over the summer his body shape had changed from slim to muscular – he'd become a man.

Jimmy's passing affected me badly. Death is always horrible to deal with, but when someone so young and full of potential is taken, it's even harder. I was overcome with grief and spent the next few days crying. It was an awful time, and I can't even begin to imagine how terrible it must have been for his friends and family.

It shows how highly Jimmy was regarded that the entire United squad, including Sir Alex and his coaching staff, travelled to Birmingham to attend his funeral. I was asked to be one of his pallbearers, which was a huge honour, but I couldn't do it. It was too much.

At the end of the season, Manchester United won the FA Cup, and when captain Roy Keane was presented with the trophy, he along with the rest of the United players wore shirts bearing Jimmy's name and squad number, 'Davis 36', on the back of their shirts, which was a lovely tribute.

Sadly, I lost another friend in a car accident the following summer. I'd grown up with Ian 'Gibbo' Gibson. He'd come to the Lowry with me to celebrate United's title win in

2001. Gibbo was a great lad taken too soon and he's still missed today.

* * *

We lost to West Brom (4-1) and Wigan (2-0) in our next two games and that's when I realised that things would be very different on the pitch at Burnley. I was used to playing for teams who were challenging at the top of the table, but it was clear that there was a big gap between us and the others, and I knew it would be a tough season. The plan was to be as close to the play-offs as possible – I think that's the case for every team in the Championship, given how tight the division is – but realistically we just needed to avoid relegation.

At the end of August, we travelled down to Gillingham, desperate for a victory. The game was played on a Monday night, which meant that we had our pre-match meal in a hotel in Gillingham. At United, everything ran like clockwork, but this was so disorganised. The whole squad was gathered in reception but none of the hotel staff knew where we were supposed to be eating.

Maysy ended up sorting us out. He led us to a carvery, and we helped ourselves to the biggest roast dinners you could imagine, followed by unlimited helpings from the dessert trolley. It was a sports nutritionist's worst nightmare, but we went on to win 3-0, so maybe we should have tried it more often!

I scored my first Burnley goal on 6 September against Stoke City, and it turned out to be the winner. I'd played at the Britannia Stadium for United's reserves, so I knew their fans were passionate, but I didn't realise how hostile the environment was for opposition players until that day.

David May opened the scoring early in the first half, and I doubled our lead nine minutes later. Graham Branch set me up with a great bit of play. I ran to the corner to celebrate in front of the fans – and then realised I'd run to the Stoke supporters! I stood and stared at them until they began throwing objects at me. I was quite surprised, to be honest, as I didn't realise that they'd be so partisan in what was really a mid- to lower-level Championship match. My Burnley career had got off to a really good start and it was nice to grab my first goal.

A strong Norwich City ended our winning run, although I was irate that the referee didn't give a blatant penalty that could have given us the lead. Darren Huckerby and Peter Crouch were outstanding for the Canaries, who ran away with the league that year.

We lost our next game too, at home to Nottingham Forest. Even though we'd been well beaten, I actually thought I'd played well, so I was surprised when I was dug out by Ronnie Jepson, Stan's assistant, after the game. Jeps had been a no-nonsense centre-forward in his day and was now a no-nonsense coach. He told me that I should have smashed their keeper. I disagreed and, armed with my newfound confidence, told him that he was wrong. It was a little childish on my part, to be fair to Jeps.

Stan was fuming by the manner of our defeat and made us come into training the following morning as punishment. We were doing two-v-two drills. The ball was knocked out to two attackers who started near the halfway line and had to try to score, with the two defenders trying to win the ball back. I was sulking because I was tired from the previous day's game and thought that the whole additional training thing was a shambles, so whenever the ball came to me, I just took a shot, even if I was 40 yards away. I'd done it four times when I suddenly heard Stan yell, 'What the fuck is he doing?' There was a little bridge between the changing rooms and the training pitches, and I hadn't realised the manager had walked across. 'Fuck off inside, Luke,' he yelled. He had the right hump with me that day.

A few days later I scored two goals in a 4-0 win over Bradford City. Maybe all that long-range shooting helped! It was a really important result as we were starting to slip down the table.

We made history when we played Wimbledon at the National Hockey Stadium, their first-ever game in Milton Keynes. There was a weird atmosphere inside the ground. There were only 5,000 there, most of whom were curious locals because the majority of the Dons fans had boycotted the match in protest of the relocation of their club. Wimbledon had lost their last seven games and had gone into administration, so it was a game that we were expected to win. Robbie Blake scored two goals in the first half, but they came back to draw 2-2, which was really disappointing.

I scored a couple more goals over the next few weeks and felt so confident every time I stepped onto the pitch. I'd had my jaw operation by then and wasn't receiving as much abuse about my appearance as before, so I felt good. I knew by then that it was unlikely that I'd be returning to Manchester United, but my rich vein of scoring led me to believe that it was only a matter of time before a Premier League club snapped me up.

But then I got a little injury that caused me problems for the rest of the season. My toe swelled up like a balloon and, although an X-ray showed that it wasn't broken, it was incredibly painful, and I was out of action for a couple of weeks. It was a real blow that knocked me back at a time when I was flying.

I returned to action on 18 October 2003 in an away game against West Ham United. My old manager Alan Pardew had just been appointed as manager of the Hammers, although it was Trevor Brooking in the dugout that day. Before the game, I spoke to Michael Carrick and Jermain Defoe, my former Under-21 team-mates, and they told me that Pards was speaking favourably about me.

We played well and really should have won, but it finished 2-2, with the Hammers scoring a late equaliser. I had a great chance to win the game, but David James made a good save to deny me. I bumped into Pards afterwards. He asked how I was doing and hinted that a move to East London might be on the cards later on down the line, which really excited me.

Just before Christmas, we lost 5-3 to Preston North End, with my old United team-mate David Healy scoring their fifth. Dave is a great guy, a fantastic finisher and we played against each other quite a few times over the years for our various clubs. He's now manager of Linfield, where he's enjoying a lot of success.

Stan lost his temper during that match, with Glen Little the target. Glen gave as good as he got and it was quite a sight, seeing Glen arguing with the manager during the middle of the game. Afterwards, the manager turned his attention to David May. After a big row, Stan threw his phone at Maysy, which resulted in the pair squaring up. Fortunately, they were separated before they came to blows. As Maysy stormed out, Stan shouted, 'You're finished here. You'll never play for the club again.'

We didn't see David for a week or so, and then one Thursday he strolled into training with no explanation. Stan even made him captain for our next match! We were all pleased to see Maysy return. Not only was he a top-quality centre-back, but he was also a legend off the pitch. After a 0-0 draw away against Crystal Palace in January 2004, the coach driver stopped at an off-licence, not far from Selhurst Park, so we could get some refreshments for the long drive back up north.

Maysy went inside and came out with some beers for the lads, bottles of wine for the manager and coaching staff, and some blue WKD for yours truly. The alcohol went straight to my head, and I decided to ask Stan why he'd substituted me in the match.

'Oi, Stan,' I shouted from the back of the coach. 'Why did you take me off?'

Stan looked at me, took the fag out of his mouth, turned to Ronnie Jepson, and said loudly, 'What the fuck is he drinking? Meths?'

Win, lose or draw, it was always fun on the bus ride to and from away games. On every trip, we'd be served a soup – pea and ham, or tomato – with a bread roll, and sometimes we'd stop for fish and chips on the way home.

We didn't start 2004 very well. We were struggling and there was little cohesion. We had a talented squad, and we should really have been much higher up the table. The manager liked us to play an entertaining style of football, which meant we were good going forward but that sometimes left us a little exposed in defence.

By March we'd been dragged into a relegation battle, so the manager decided to take us to Marbella for a four-day team-bonding session. We flew out to Spain on 7 March 2004, and stayed in a beautiful hotel that was a 20-minute taxi ride from the lively Puerto Banus. After checking into our rooms, Stan gave us the itinerary for the four days. 'Every day is the same. We'll meet on the beach at 8am for a 30-minute jog. The rest of the day is yours.'

It turned into a free-for-all; it was carnage. We'd be in Puerto Banus by midday, drinking in the bars all afternoon and dancing in the nightclubs until the early hours of the morning. The next day, after a 30-minute run, we did it all over again.

We flew back to England on the Wednesday and it's fair to say that our training session the following day was an absolute shambles. To say we looked like Sunday league footballers is disrespectful to Sunday league players.

I'm sure most of us were still hungover when we arrived at Highfield Road on 13 March for our league game against Coventry. I was named as a substitute and watched on from the bench as Coventry battered us. We were 3-0 down at half-time, with Julian Joachim tearing us apart, particularly David May. In the dressing room during the interval, Stan lost his head. He was effing and blinding and throwing cups of tea all over the place. He had a right go at Brian Jensen, our goalkeeper, and had to be talked out of subbing him. I just sat there, thinking, *Thank God I ain't part of this.*

Things didn't improve in the second half. I was desperate for the toilet and, when Coventry added a fourth in the 78th minute, I decided to run back to the dressing rooms. During the minute or two that I was gone, Stan had decided to bring me on, but when he turned round to tell me to get ready, he saw that I wasn't there. He was fuming. I didn't know this at the time, and when I returned from the toilet, nothing was said.

It was easily one of our worst performances of the season and I was so grateful to have played no part. I felt quite relaxed in the dressing room, wondering who was going to be in the firing line. I was shocked when Stan proceeded to give me the biggest bollocking I've ever received in my life! For ten minutes he yelled at me for not being where I should have been.

It was very tight at the bottom of the table, but back-to-back wins over Wimbledon and Derby County at the end of April were enough for us to stave off relegation and remain in the division.

We finished the season with a home match against Sunderland. The big story was that it was Stan's last match in charge of the club. Despite what he'd achieved during his six years at the helm, his contract wasn't being renewed.

It was also my last game for Burnley.

We lost 2-1 to a good Sunderland side that had already qualified for the play-offs. I was fairly pleased with my season. It had started really well, before tailing off after my injury. After the game, I was desperate to get away and start my summer. The problem was that the lads had hidden all my gear, so I had nothing to wear! I was raging because I was in such a rush to get home, but it was typical of the banter that I'd enjoyed over the last year. I had such a great time at Burnley and the camaraderie we enjoyed is something that I'll never forget.

I eventually cobbled together some clothes, shook hands with the lads and drove home, wondering where I'd be the following season. I'd instructed my agent to find me a club down south. Although I still had another year left on my contract with Manchester United, I knew that I wouldn't be returning to Carrington again. Or so I thought.

Chapter 15

Next Stop – Hammer Time

AFTER SPENDING the previous two close seasons under the knife, it was a relief to finally have a summer holiday. Hayley and I left Louis with my mother-in-law, and we travelled to Antwerp for a short break. When we returned from Belgium, I set my sights on securing a permanent move away from Old Trafford.

I'd given my agent, a great guy called Chris Lomas, the remit of finding me a new club based down south. I wasn't too bothered about which division I'd be playing in, but I was realistic enough to know that my most likely destination would be a Championship club, rather than a Premier League one. Ipswich Town and Norwich City were both on my radar because of their close proximity to Cambridge, but neither club had made an approach.

Manchester United had agreed that I could leave on a free transfer, so I didn't think it would be long before someone snapped me up. But when pre-season began there hadn't been a single offer, so I reported back to Carrington. As strange as it sounds, I was incredibly disappointed. No disrespect to United because I loved the club and they always treated me well, but I knew I had no future there and I needed a fresh start.

On that first day of pre-season, I sat in my car outside the United training ground, wondering what I was going to do. When I eventually walked into the familiar dressing room, it felt strange, although it was nice to bump into friends I'd known for years. I was surprised to find out that I'd be training with the first team. I'd assumed I'd be with the reserves because I wouldn't be there for long, but the lads who'd played at Euro 2004 had been given extended leave, so I was there to make up the numbers.

I was even more surprised when I was selected to go on the pre-season tour of America. In contrast to my first tour with the club, this time I was gutted because it meant that there was still no interest in me. That was a big blow to my ego. *Surely someone wants me*, I thought. I briefly wondered how things could play out if I remained at Old Trafford and fought for my place, but with Ryan Giggs and Cristiano Ronaldo as the two main wide men, and some great young players like Chris Eagles, Kieran Richardson and Darren Fletcher next in line, I had to accept the reality that I wouldn't be getting anywhere near the first team. Being a bit-part player didn't interest me at all; I wanted to be a regular somewhere.

By now I was prepared to go anywhere. I felt desperate and rang my agent just before we flew to the States. 'Listen, Chris, I need a new club. What else can I do?'

'At this stage of pre-season, there isn't really any interest. The only offer we've had is from Swindon Town, who want to take you on a season-long loan. However, they are a League One club and it's unlikely they will be able to afford your wages.'

I'd have preferred to join a Championship club, but if League One was all that was on the table, I didn't really have a choice. 'I'll go there. I don't care how much they offer me, I'll take it,' I said.

'I strongly advise you not to do that,' Chris replied. 'Be patient and sit tight. A lot of clubs leave it until the end of the transfer window before doing any business. Go out to America, enjoy it and we'll see what happens.'

So, I went on the tour and, although I didn't appreciate it at the time because I didn't want to go, it was an incredible experience. We used the Philadelphia Eagles' training facility and that was unbelievable. Everything was state-of-the-art and the changing rooms were huge because of the size of the American football squads. Philadelphia was an amazing city and we got to see some of the sights before travelling to Chicago for a friendly against Bayern Munich. The Germans lined up with Oliver Kahn, Sammy Kuffour, Michael Ballack and Owen Hargreaves, and we did well to earn a 0-0 draw in front of 60,000 fans. Three days later we returned to Philadelphia and played Celtic at the Lincoln Financial Field, home to the Philadelphia Eagles. The 55,000 in attendance created an amazing atmosphere. I got some unexpected game time in both matches, although I don't think I was particularly good or effective in either.

A couple of days after the Celtic game, Ryan Giggs, who was good friends with my agent, told me that Chris had been trying to get hold of me. I phoned him immediately.

'Good news, Luke. West Ham United have made an offer,' he said.

I was absolutely buzzing. West Ham is a massive club, Alan Pardew was the manager and I'd be able to commute from Cambridge. The only downside was the wages. By then I was earning £14,000 a week at United and the offer from West Ham was £2,000. Still a lot of money, of course, but a huge pay cut. I thought that West Ham could have afforded to pay me a bit more, with the size of the club, but the offer was take-it-or-leave-it, so I had to make a quick decision. I discussed it with Sir Alex, and he advised against the move, telling me that I should be commanding a bigger wage.

A lot of people probably would have turned it down, but money wasn't the driver for me and the opportunity to play for the Hammers felt too great, so I accepted it. I told Sir Alex that I'd made my decision, and he wished me all the best and reminded me that I could contact him in the future if there was ever anything he could do. Such a great gesture but nothing less than expected from an incredible man.

I flew straight back to England, signed for West Ham and joined my team-mates just a few days before the Championship season kicked off. After weeks of waiting, everything happened so quickly.

The Hammers were relegated from the Premier League at the end of 2002/03 and had been expected to bounce straight back up the following year, but they'd been defeated by Crystal Palace in the play-off final. Determined to go one better in 2004/05, Alan Pardew strengthened the side by bringing in Ukrainian international Serhiy Rebrov and my former team-mate Teddy Sheringham on free transfers.

While playing alongside Andriy Shevchenko for Dynamo Kyiv and the Ukrainian national team, Serhiy had garnered a reputation as one of Europe's deadliest goalscorers. He signed for Tottenham Hotspur in May 2000 but struggled to adapt to the pace of the Premier League. He joined West Ham to great fanfare but sadly he didn't really have the impact that everyone expected. Serhiy was a lovely fellow who got on well with everyone, even though he spoke little English. You could see his undoubted quality in training – sometimes he'd do something that would make us all go 'wow' – but we didn't see enough of that on the pitch.

Teddy was 38 when he joined the team he'd supported as a boy, but age was no barrier because of the way he played. Teddy's game was never about pace and power, he was such a clever player and was no different to the Teddy I'd played with at United all those years earlier. I'm lucky to have played alongside so many world-class players, but if I had to pick my favourite team-mate, I'd choose Teddy. He made the game look so easy and made everyone around him look better because he knew exactly where you wanted the ball. Teddy scored over 20 goals for West Ham that season and was named Championship player of the season.

Serhiy and Teddy joined a vastly experienced squad that included fellow internationals Steve Lomas, Chris Powell, Don Hutchison and Christian Dailly.

West Ham has always been renowned for its youth academy, with Bobby Moore, Geoff Hurst, Trevor Brooking, Frank Lampard, Joe Cole and Rio Ferdinand just some of the incredible players the club has produced over the years. In 2004, the standout youngsters were Michael Carrick, Anton Ferdinand, Mark Noble and Chris Cohen. I'd played with Michael for the Under-21s and knew he was a hugely gifted midfielder. Unfortunately, he was sold to Spurs before the season began so I missed out on the chance to link up with him again. Anton, a central defender like his brother Rio, was a great guy and a talented player looking to establish himself in the first team.

Mark, now a West Ham legend with over 500 appearances for the club, was on the fringes of the team at the start of the season. A local lad with a great affinity for the Hammers, Mark had bags of energy and put everything into every single training session. He was an all-action midfielder back then, but over the years his game evolved, and he became more of a holding midfielder. It didn't surprise me to see the incredible effect that he had on the football club.

I take a bit of credit for Mark's stellar career because it was my ineffective performance for West Ham against Southend United in the League Cup that led to him making his Hammers debut on 24 August 2004, when he replaced me for the final 20 minutes.

Chris was another shining light from the youth team and, although it didn't work out for him at Upton Park, he enjoyed a great career at Nottingham Forest.

In addition to the highly experienced pros and hungry youngsters, we had a talented group of players in their early to late 20s who made up the rest of the squad. In goal, we had Stephen Bywater, who was also my roommate. He was a great character. A typical goalkeeper, Stephen was as mad as a hatter and a very entertaining man to share a room with. Tomáš Řepka lined up at right-back. He was an incredibly aggressive player and sometimes that aggression spilled over, resulting in yellow or red cards. He joined the Hammers in 2001 and was sent off twice in his first three games. He received a staggering 20 red cards during his career! Off the pitch, Tomáš was a lovely guy; quite laid-back and placid. But when he stepped over that white line, something inside him changed. The left-back berth was held by Powell, while Ferdinand, Dailly, Malky Mackay and Elliott Ward, another product of the youth team, shared the two centre-back positions. Ferdinand and Ward both excelled in what can be a challenging position for youngsters.

Matty Etherington played on the left wing and created and assisted a lot of the goals that we scored. Carl Fletcher, Hayden Mullins, Nigel Reo-Coker and Steve Lomas provided the engine in the centre of midfield, with yours truly playing on the right wing. And providing the firepower up front, alongside Teddy and Serhiy, were Marlon Harewood and Bobby Zamora. Marlon was quick, strong and great at getting behind the defence. His pace also gave me the option of playing him down the channel. Bobby was a fantastic finisher with a really good personality. He went through some real challenges that season, where things didn't always come off for him, but he kept working hard and that paid off when he became the hero in Cardiff. But we'll come to that later.

Alan Pardew was still the same character that I knew from Reading, but he wasn't as close to the lads at West Ham. He kept his distance, but everyone loved him. We nicknamed him Chocolate because he'd eat himself if he could. Pards had a huge amount of self-confidence and that aided his ability to manage people and achieve success. He certainly wasn't afraid to make some tough choices. As the season progressed, the manager made some brave decisions, phasing out some of the elder statesmen and introducing the younger players.

No disrespect to Burnley but moving to West Ham was a big step up for me. The dressing room was strong, with everyone pulling in the same direction, and there was a certain element of professionalism that you get with the big clubs. Expectations were high – anything less than promotion was unacceptable – and the fans made sure we never forgot that.

What the Hammers supporters wanted from the players was 100 per cent commitment. If you put the effort in, you'll earn their support. No matter who you are, if you're not playing well, the fans will tell you in no uncertain terms. I recognised that more at West Ham than at any other club. When you're winning games and performing well, the supporters are incredible. The night games, under the lights, produced probably the most electric atmosphere I've experienced. Upton Park, so compact that it felt that the fans were almost on the pitch, was an amazing arena to play in. The passion they have for their club spreads to the players on the pitch and I found them a wonderful crowd to play in front of. Obviously, it's the team's responsibility to get the fans going by giving them the performance – and results – that they demand.

I missed the season opener (a 0-0 draw against Leicester City that was memorable only for Rufus Brevett and Leicester's Dion Dublin having a scrap that resulted in both players receiving red cards) as I'd only arrived at the club a few days earlier.

After scoring in a reserve game against Norwich, I was named on the bench for our home match against Reading on 10 August 2004. The fans were in full voice, and I was desperate to get on the pitch and get my Hammers career started. Finally, with 15 minutes on the clock, Pards brought me on. I made an immediate impact, crossing for Teddy to stroke home his first goal of the season. Upton Park erupted. Sheringham's strike proved to be the only goal of the game and I was delighted to have made an impact on my debut.

I was expecting to start the next game, against Wigan, but had to settle for a place on the bench. We lost the game 3-1 and Pards was getting pelters from the fans, who were shouting to him to send me on. Boos rang around Upton Park when the referee blew the final whistle, and that was my first glimpse of the West Ham fans showing their displeasure at the team.

I was named in the starting line-up for our next match, against Crewe. I played well and once again assisted Teddy when he finished my cutback. It was a tighter game than it needed to be and, although we ran out 3-2 winners, their young striker Dean Ashton caused our defence lots of problems. Rufus Brevett, of all people, scored the winner with an absolute worldy, a volley from the edge of the box.

Next up was Burnley at home. I had quite an ineffective performance in our 1-0 victory. After the game, I went on the Burnley team coach to have a bit of banter with my former team-mates, although I declined their offer of a bowl of ham and pea soup!

After a fairly promising start, our form stuttered and we struggled for consistency. We hadn't really clicked and weren't playing well in terms of our shape. On paper, we had a really strong team with a Premier League-quality manager, but I wonder whether the strength in depth was actually a weakness. Maybe there were too many options for Pards because the team was rotated frequently as he tried to find the right combination.

In the middle of October, we lost to Queens Park Rangers at Loftus Road, a defeat that meant we dropped out of the play-off places. We received a lot of stick from our supporters in the car park on the way to the team coach.

'It's not acceptable.'

'It's not good enough.'

With a few other choice words thrown in too! There wasn't a lot that we could say because they were right. We should have beaten QPR. With the players we had we should have been competing for the title.

After a good start, my form declined. Although I was playing regularly, I wanted to be playing well. It didn't matter if the fans said I was rubbish or if my team-mates didn't rate me, the most important thing for me was to be assured in my mind that I was doing everything I could. I was honest enough to admit that I was struggling and the confidence that had come with the move and a fresh start quickly dissipated.

The problem was that I wasn't as quick as I used to be, and I was in the process of changing the way that I played. I was transitioning from someone who ran with the ball all the time to a player who was perhaps a little cleverer, looking for little pockets of space to exploit. I was caught in the middle of that change, still trying to figure out how I could be more effective when out on that pitch.

My form picked up by the time we played the return fixture against QPR on 6 November. I was very nearly injured in that match when Kevin Gallen absolutely wiped me out, but I managed to run it off. I went back to basics, making sure I did everything I could out of possession. I really put in a shift that day and was rewarded with a much better performance – and a vital three points as we won 2-1.

We played Millwall at The Den two weeks later. A local derby; a huge game with bragging rights on the line. This was possibly my best performance in a West Ham shirt. I had a running battle with Dennis Wise, and I came out on top against the former England man. I managed to time my tackles to perfection and smashed him up in the air three or four times, which he wasn't too happy about. Our fans loved it, though! The atmosphere was intense, and they got the better of us, with Danny Dichio scoring the only goal of the game.

Losing to our local rivals led to speculation that Alan Pardew would be facing the sack unless things improved. The players were fully behind the manager and that was demonstrated in our next game when we came back from 2-0 down to beat Watford 3-2. That was a huge victory and we followed that up with a 2-0 victory against Sunderland. I always seemed to do quite well against Sunderland and assisted Marlon Harewood's opening goal. I felt that my form was returning.

During the match, I got involved in a bit of a scuffle with Steven Caldwell that saw the Sunderland man sent off. Peter Grant, who was Pardew's assistant, was big mates with Sunderland's manager Mick McCarthy. Granty approached me after the game and asked if I'd be prepared to attend a tribunal and tell them that Caldwell hadn't touched me. I was happy to do so, but Pards told me not to because Sunderland were our promotion rivals, and they'd be weakened if Caldwell was suspended.

On Friday, 10 December 2004, we played Leeds United at Upton Park. The match was broadcast on Sky Sports, and I always loved playing in front of the TV cameras. I scored my first goal for the Hammers, just after half-time. I'd love to say it was a wonder strike, but it was more of a poacher's goal; Harewood's header was blocked, the ball fell to me and I smashed it home. My hips and groin felt sore during the game, so I came off not long after my goal and was sitting in the dressing room getting iced up when I heard the cheers from the Leeds fans. My old mate David Healy had scored a 90th-minute equaliser with a penalty that I think he dived for.

As we entered 2005, Pards received the dreaded vote of confidence from the board. We'd improved since the Millwall game, only losing once in seven matches, but automatic promotion looked out of our grasp and there was fierce competition for the play-off spots.

During our first training session of the new year, I was presented with an award for the best trainer of 2004. It was a strange award, a bit like the clubman-of-the-year trophies that are given out to the kids who don't play, and the lads gave me a load of stick. It was snowing at the time and, when I was presented with the award, Bobby Zamora threw a snowball that hit and smashed the trophy! Pards wasn't very happy because he saw the award as a serious thing.

I must have been doing something right because as well as the now broken trophy, I was also awarded with a new two-and-a-half-year contract. My wages increased from £2,000 a week to £3,500, although I didn't negotiate a further increase in the event we won promotion.

After beating Ipswich on New Year's Day, we lost three games in a row. The last of these was a 2-1 home defeat to Derby County. Boos rang out after the final whistle, and it was clear that we'd lost the fans by then. Pards called us in for crisis talks the next day, demanding that we turn our fortunes around.

Next up in the league was another home match, this time against Cardiff City, who'd beaten us 4-1 in the corresponding fixture earlier in the season. It was a make-or-break game, and we knew that if we lost, it was likely that Pardew would be sacked. We left it very late, but Carl Fletcher scored an 89th-minute header to give us a 1-0 win. Pards lived to fight another day.

I pulled my hamstring on 13 February and was told that I'd be out for six to eight weeks. I was gutted as I was playing quite well by then and wanted to help the team turn things around. The only positive for me was that the club allowed me to have a week off, so I went to Dubai with Hayley, Louis and Hayley's mum, which was nice. I'm not sure if it was the warm weather or the rest, but when I returned to England my hamstring felt much better and I was back in the squad for the trip to my old club Reading. I came off the bench at half-time but didn't really make much of an impact. Dave Kitson absolutely tore us apart, scoring a hat-trick and condemning us to another defeat. The Reading supporters loved it as they hadn't forgiven Pardew for leaving them to take up the hot seat at West Ham.

The West Ham fans were constantly on Pardew's back, and everyone thought it was just a matter of time before he was relieved of his duties. During those difficult days, one thing he never lost was the dressing room; we were all behind him 100 per cent. I've never seen a manager under that much pressure able to stick with it and turn things around.

But that's exactly what happened. After the Reading debacle, we went on an eight-match unbeaten run that gave us a fighting chance of making the play-offs. Unfortunately, my hamstring flared up again and I missed a few matches during the run-in.

On the final day of the season, we beat Watford 2-1 to sneak into the play-offs – at Reading's expense. The Hammers had reached the play-offs the year before, losing to Crystal Palace in the final. This year we were determined to go one step further.

Ironically, we took on Ipswich in the semi-final, the same opponents as the previous year. And just as before, we saw them off over the two legs to set up a final against Preston North End.

My inability to stay fit at the business end of the season meant that I was seen as a risk, so I wasn't named in the squad for the trip to Cardiff's Millennium Stadium. It didn't come as a huge surprise because I'd been in and out of the side during that incredible run-in, but I was still disappointed. Everyone wants to play in the big games, and I was no different.

I watched on from the stands as Bobby Zamora became an absolute West Ham legend, with his second-half strike proving to be the winner. The Hammers were back in the Premier League. I was delighted for the supporters, the lads and especially the manager, who'd done such an incredible job to achieve promotion from what at times seemed like an impossible position.

As is customary, I went out onto the pitch in my suit after the game to congratulate my team-mates and join in the celebrations with the fans. It was all a little awkward for me; I never felt comfortable in those situations, but even less so when I hadn't even played in the final.

After the match, we flew from Cardiff to Stansted. The club had booked a hotel near to the airport where we met our partners and continued the celebrations long into the early hours. Pards was absolutely buzzing, and when he spotted me he came over and we embraced. 'Back where you belong now, Luke. Back in the Premier League,' he said. 'It'll be great to have you as part of our squad.'

I distinctly remember that conversation because not long after the words had been spoken, I discovered that I was surplus to requirements.

Chapter 16

Don't Mess with Bywater

I LOVED playing football, but by the end of each season I was ready to get away for a few weeks to recharge my batteries, both mentally and physically. With West Ham winning promotion, the club had organised an open-top bus parade so the fans could celebrate with us. As I've mentioned, I always felt awkward celebrating team achievements and I didn't want to go. As far as I was concerned, the season had finished and all I wanted to do was enjoy some time with my family.

I racked my brains and came up with a cunning plan that I shared with Stephen Bywater the day before the parade. 'I'm going to phone the reception in the morning and tell them that my tyre has burst, so I can't make it.'

A couple of hours later I received a call from the club. 'We're looking forward to seeing you tomorrow, Luke. Make sure your tyres are fully inflated. You don't want to get a puncture!' Bywater had grassed me up!

So, I ended up going on the bus and I'm so glad I did because it was a fantastic experience. The supporters were out in force; tens of thousands lined the streets around Upton Park, singing and enjoying themselves. Hayley and Louis (who, now aged two, was starting to develop an affinity for football) joined me on the bus and it was lovely to share the special occasion with them.

I returned for pre-season ready for another crack at the Premier League. I asked Alan Pardew if I could wear the No.36 shirt because that had been my number at United the last time that I played in the top flight. Pards said no because he wanted to keep the squad numbers close together. It was a short, sharp conversation but I didn't really mind. I was never too bothered about what number I wore.

We flew out to Sweden and played several friendlies against Scandinavian opponents. Matty Etherington was injured so I deputised for him on the left wing. Throughout my career, I'd played predominantly on the right, and I enjoyed the change of scenery. Although it's technically the same role (a winger), swapping sides is very different because the pitch looks inverted, but it allows you to do new things. For example, instead of cutting inside on my left foot, when playing on the left I could cut inside and be on my stronger right foot. Paul Konchesky, a solid left-back I'd played with for the Under-21s, had joined us by then and we developed a good partnership down the left-hand side. I was flying and felt I was one of the better players on the tour.

From Sweden, we travelled to Germany to play 1860 Munich in a match to commemorate the 40th anniversary of West Ham's European Cup Winners' Cup win over the Germans in 1965. The match took place in the brand-new Allianz Arena. It was an incredible venue, a brilliant place to play football, and the two sides battled to a 1-1 draw in an entertaining game for the spectators.

Following a few weeks of intense training and several friendlies, our preparation for the new campaign was progressing nicely and Pards allowed us to have a night out in Munich. Stephen Bywater (my roommate) and I arranged to go out with Carl Fletcher and Gavin Williams. We had a team meal in the hotel restaurant and then returned to our rooms to get ready. When we walked into our room, we discovered it had been absolutely trashed; the sheets had been removed and chucked in a pile, our clothes were scattered all over the place. It was a mess. Bywater did a bit of digging and identified the culprits – Carl and Gavin.

When it was time to meet them in the hotel reception to call a taxi, Stephen told me to go alone and keep them talking so he could grab their room key and deliver some revenge. I told Carl and Gavin that Stephen would be joining us shortly, and he appeared ten minutes later.

'You should see what I've done to their room,' Bywater whispered to me with a mischievous grin on his face.

We got a cab into the centre of Munich and enjoyed a few beers in the Bavarian capital. When we returned to the hotel later that evening, we decided to go to Carl and Gavin's room for one final drink. When the door opened, we all froze. I'd never seen anything like it in my life. The mattresses and bedding had been thrown out the window. The bed frames were lying on their sides. If our room had been trashed, theirs had been obliterated. Carl and Gavin had to go down into the car park to retrieve their mattresses and pillows and drag them back to their room. It was hilarious.

I returned to England with a real spring in my step. I was confident that the hamstring injury that had kept me out of the play-offs was behind me. I was playing with freedom and felt I had a chance of becoming one of the key members of the squad. Everything felt right.

And then it didn't.

We'd scraped into the play-offs and Pards was astute enough to realise that we needed to strengthen the squad if we were to remain in the Premier League. In addition to Konchesky, we also signed defenders Danny Gabbidon and James Collins from Cardiff City, goalkeepers Roy Carroll and Shaka Hislop, and an Israeli international by the name of Yossi Benayoun. I didn't know too much about him and, when he first walked into the dressing room, I couldn't see him being much of a threat to me. He was so slight, there was no way he'd have much of an impact in the Premier League. Then I saw him on the training pitch, and I thought, *Oh shit.*

Yossi was on another level, an absolutely brilliant player. I soon realised that when Matty was fit again, he'd be the first choice on the left and Yossi would be the first choice on the right. I'd gone from thinking I'd be one of the better players in the team to realising I'd be a back-up. Still, if I continued to work hard and made sure I was ready when my chance came, I knew I could force my way back into the side.

Then, completely out of the blue, on 3 August 2005, Peter Grant, Pardew's assistant, phoned me and said, 'Stoke City have made a loan offer for you. We want you to go there, play some matches and see what happens. There won't be any game time for you here, so this is a good opportunity to play regularly.'

I was shocked, to be honest, because I felt I still had something to offer the Hammers, even if it was as a squad member. I could have dug my heels in and rejected the move but the way I saw it was that Stoke wanted me and West Ham didn't. I hadn't been part of a Premier League team for a few years, so dropping back into the Championship wasn't a huge wrench. I just wanted to play football.

My only real concern was geography. One of the reasons I'd joined West Ham was because they were within commuting distance of Cambridge. Stoke was more than 80 miles away and, to add to the challenge, Hayley was pregnant with our second child.

I didn't really have any time to digest it and consider my options, though. Stoke wanted me to join them for training the following day because I'd be in the starting line-up for the season opener in just three days' time.

The two clubs and my agent sorted out the financials. My only request was to wear the No.10 shirt, and Stoke agreed. I'm not sure why I asked because, as I've mentioned, I was never really bothered about the number on my back. Maybe it was my way of exerting some control over the situation.

Everything happened so quickly, such is the life of a professional footballer.

Chapter 17

The Dutch Experiment

STOKE CITY was a club in a transitional period when I joined in August 2005. Popular manager Tony Pulis had been sacked two months earlier by the club's Icelandic owners, and his replacement was former Netherlands international Johan Boskamp.

The Dutchman had a great pedigree. During his playing career as a talented midfielder, he won multiple trophies, including three Dutch championships and one UEFA Cup, and he was a member of the famous Dutch 'Total Football' team that reached the World Cup Final in 1978. Johan's most successful spell as a manager was winning three back-to-back Belgian titles with Anderlecht. His extensive knowledge of Belgian football meant that I was already on his radar.

Johan was a huge guy, an absolute lunatic in terms of how he was and how he spoke, but I enjoyed working with him and we got on well. His remit was to change Stoke's style of play from the direct approach that Pulis had utilised to a more European passing game. To do that, Boskamp had to revamp the side and bring in his own players. No fewer than four players were signed from Belgian clubs, including Carl Hoefkens, a very good centre-back, and record signing Sambégou Bangoura.

The core of our squad was British: Gerry Taggart, Michael Duberry, Steve Simonsen, Dave Brammer, Peter Sweeney and John Halls, and I could tell that the dressing room was divided into cliques. The manager was multilingual and spoke different languages to different players, which didn't really help the foreign lads integrate, although no one fell out with anyone.

The manager and the board's expectations were for us to reach the play-offs, but it became clear very quickly that it was going to be a tough season because of the size of the transition. At that time, a lot of Championship teams were looking overseas for signings, trying to unearth a new gem, because they could represent better value than their British counterparts, but it wasn't without risk. A lot of the players found it hard to adapt from the slower-paced, less physical Continental game to the frenetic Championship where you're usually playing twice a week, often at a million miles an hour. I think Boskamp found it tough to find the right blend of experience, youth, English and foreign, and what he tried to do was possibly too much too soon.

The season began with a 0-0 draw at home to Sheffield Wednesday. Gerry Taggart was sent off early in the first half. It was tough playing against an extra man and we were pleased with the result.

From day one I loved the Stoke fans. The atmosphere that they generated was incredible – especially when they sang their version of Tom Jones's 'Delilah'. Sadly, the stadium wasn't ever at full capacity while I was there but, nevertheless, I loved playing for those passionate supporters. They took to me too. I think I was quite popular because I worked hard and sometimes

I'd do something to get them out of their seats. I could feel their excitement when I received the ball; they inspired me.

One of Stoke's most famous fans is Nick Hancock of *They Think It's All Over* fame. I bumped into him once and signed a couple of autographs for his kids. It was a little strange, seeing him so soon after my 'appearances' on the show, but there was no animosity at all, and I was happy to sign.

The Britannia Stadium did have one downside – it's without a doubt the windiest stadium I've ever played at. It seems to be located on the top of a hill and was built without corners, so there was a swirling wind around the pitch more or less every game.

In our second game of the campaign, we lost 4-2 to a top Leicester City team. Despite the defeat, I played really well, and for the first time in my career I was moved inside and lined up in the centre of midfield. I put in a real shift and my improved fitness allowed me to play my second full 90-minute game in a row.

Our first win of the season came away at Millwall. John Halls scored his first of the season to earn us three points and again I thought I'd played well. I always used to buy the newspapers on a Sunday to read the match report and see what rating I'd been given out of ten. One paper had given me a five, which shocked me. *I thought I'd done alright. I wasn't that bad, was I?* The next newspaper gave me a nine! That was when I realised that the people who gave the markings probably hadn't even watched the game, so I stopped buying the papers.

My old mate from Burnley, Tony Grant, came to Millwall with us as he was on trial with Stoke. We were great mates, and I was buzzing at the prospect of him joining us, but unfortunately the move didn't materialise and he went to Bristol City instead.

We ended August with a stunning 3-1 win at home to Norwich City, who'd been relegated from the Premier League. During the match, I went into a tackle with Youssef Safri, Norwich's Moroccan defender, and he stamped on me as he was getting up, leaving a nasty mark on the inside of my leg. *What a horrible, horrible man*, I thought. I later played with him, and it turns out that he's a lovely guy, one of the nicest blokes I've ever met!

My season began incredibly well; I was by far and away the best player on the team. I had a fantastic relationship with the fans, my team-mates respected me and the manager valued me for my contributions on the pitch. Everything was going so well. And then it got even better.

On Monday, 12 September 2005, I'd just opened the front door to drive up to Stoke to meet with the lads, and travel to Humberside for our game against Hull City the following day, when Hayley shouted, 'My waters have broken.' If it had happened ten minutes later, I'd have been on the road behind the wheel and able to play in the match. Instead, I stayed with Hayley and our second son Liam was born the following morning – the day of the game. Both were healthy so I decided to drive up to Hull and make myself available for the match. My head was all over the place because I hadn't slept, and John Rudge – Stoke's director of football and an absolute legend of the game – rang me and told me to stay at home and spend some time with the baby.

In my absence, we beat Hull and, although I was back in the team for the following game, a televised victory away at Preston,

I was subbed at half-time because I was so ineffective. To this day I still blame Liam for my temporary loss of form!

After the win at Preston, we went on a terrible run, losing four in a row. One of those games was an away match at Plymouth, a game that was memorable to me for two reasons. The first was that I opened my account for Stoke, giving us the lead just after half-time, although the hosts fought back to win 2-1. The second was the incredibly long drive back from Plymouth to Cambridge. As Hayley was pregnant when I signed for Stoke, and my move was only a loan, we'd decided not to move house. I'd stay in a hotel in Stoke on a Thursday and Friday, return to Cambridge after the game on a Saturday, and then commute the rest of the time.

Liam was only a couple of weeks old when we played Plymouth, so I decided to ask the kit man to drive my car down there so I could go straight home after the game, instead of travelling back to Stoke on the coach with the rest of the lads. I had a Range Rover, and the kit man had never driven one before, so he had a practice in the car park before taking it on the long journey down south. His driving was so bad that I honestly thought he was taking the piss when he was practising! I was a bit concerned that my car might not arrive in Plymouth in one piece, but I had no choice because I wouldn't be able to get home after the match without it.

Somehow, he managed to drive the Range Rover to Plymouth without it getting so much as a scratch. After getting changed I collected my keys and began the 300-mile trip to Cambridge. It was a nightmare. I was stuck in traffic in Plymouth city centre for ages and decided to speed up my journey by driving in the bus lane. Even though I only hit a top speed of ten miles per hour, at least I was moving. I eventually arrived home in the early hours of the morning and ended up sleeping most of the day. The following week I received 12 different fines from Plymouth County Council for various driving offences!

The commuting was really taking its toll on me and often when I got to the stadium I'd just lie on the treatment table, have a massage and sleep, instead of actually taking part in the training. Rudgey would come into the physio's room and see me lying on the treatment table. 'Are you fit or are we at full strength today?' he'd ask, taking the piss.

By now we were really struggling, so the manager initiated a team night out. He booked a table at an all-you-can-eat Chinese restaurant called Charlie Chans. He told us that after the meal we could do what we wanted. The restaurant was quite nice. I'd been there with the lads a few times before. On this occasion, we were over-excited because we weren't paying for the food and drink, and a few of us – me included – had a few too many beers. At the end of the meal, the hot towels came out and we had a bit of fun throwing them at each other.

The alcohol I'd consumed gave me a little Dutch courage and I screwed up my towel and launched it towards the coaches' table. It was the perfect storm because Johan was taking a sip of his wine at the exact moment that my towel reached his table. The towel hit his glass and the drink went everywhere. The manager lost his temper and demanded to know who the culprit was. He was going crazy, demanding someone own up. There was no way I was going to admit it was me, not with the size of him, so I kept my mouth shut and hoped no one would grass me up. I was quite surprised that the lads remained silent, and I managed to get away with it. But the incident put a dampener on the evening, and it ended on a sour note. The team-building exercise hadn't really worked out as Johan had intended, although we did enjoy a good little run after that – I take full credit for that!

To be fair, one of the main reasons for our change in fortune was Sammy Bangoura, who hit a purple patch, scoring eight goals in ten games. Sammy started like a house on fire and became a fans' favourite, although that changed pretty quickly.

He was a complete maverick, with a questionable attitude. I've never seen anyone have a spring like Sammy; it was incredible how high he could jump. He was a great player with undoubted quality, but when the going got tough he downed tools. He also told us that he couldn't speak a word of English and was lazy about interacting with us, but I'm convinced that he could understand a lot more than he let on.

At the time, Sammy was Stoke's record signing, but his debut had been delayed because of issues with his visa. It took three weeks from him signing before he was allowed into the country, and even then he was arrested for allegedly attempting to bring an illegal immigrant through East Midlands Airport. It was all a bit bizarre. He had a house in Trentham that was always full of people. I'm not sure if they were family, friends or strangers, but it was very strange.

Sammy was named in Guinea's squad for the 2006 Africa Cup of Nations, held in January and February 2006. He helped his country reach the quarter-final, where they were defeated by Senegal. After Guinea's elimination, Sammy was expected to return to Stoke but he didn't come back. He wasn't the most dedicated of professionals and I think he fancied spending a little longer at home than he should have done. We missed his goals.

When he eventually returned, he wasn't the same player. He'd lost some hunger for the game. Sammy also claimed that he didn't like the climate in Stoke-on-Trent, yet he'd spent his entire career in Belgium, which isn't that much different. We used to chuckle when he'd walk out onto the training pitch wearing three or four layers to keep warm!

Johan didn't suffer fools gladly and there was one occasion where he pinned Sammy up against the wall! The manager was very hands-on and there were times when he'd grab you by the scruff of your neck to wind you up ahead of a game.

Boskamp was a very emotional guy capable of losing his temper very quickly. After one match against Coventry, he argued with his assistant manager, Jan de Koning, and they had a huge falling-out. It was a strange situation because the club couldn't sack either of them because of their contracts, so they continued to work together without speaking to each other. The situation became so bad that Gerry Taggart even took charge of one game while Boskamp was meeting the board of directors. There was never a dull moment at Stoke, that's for sure!

There was another unusual situation after our match against QPR in December 2005. We lost 2-1, although should have drawn. Mamady Sidibé missed an absolute sitter from my cross. Despite that miss, Mamady was one of the hardest-working players in the side, and a great guy. Anyway, when the referee blew the full-time whistle, one of our fans jumped over the barriers, onto the pitch, and tried to attack QPR's goalkeeper Simon Royce. I was the closest player to Royce, and I remember thinking, *What is he doing? I need to stop this.* So, I ran towards the scuffle and, as I got closer, my thoughts changed to, *What am I doing? Surely the police or stewards should be sorting this out, not me!* I arrived on the scene and gave the assailant a half-hearted tug, and then big Danny Shittu, an absolute man mountain, turned up and ripped the guy off of Royce's back.

In January 2005, Stoke made an offer of £100,000 to West Ham to make my move permanent. The Hammers were flying in the Premier League and Peter Grant made it clear that there wasn't a future for me at Upton Park, so I told Johan that I'd sign a permanent deal. But before I put pen to paper, Watford made an approach. I was really interested because Watford is closer to Cambridge than Stoke, and I'd had enough of the commute by then. Aidy Boothroyd, Watford's manager, offered me more money than Stoke did, but I'd already promised Johan that I'd stay, so I turned down Watford and signed a two-and-a-half-year contract. Watford won promotion that season, so it would have been a good move for me, but I'm a firm believer that everything happens for a reason.

Just ten days after rejecting Watford we played them at Vicarage Road. With Sammy away at the Africa Cup of Nations, I lined up as a striker. We lost 1-0 and, after the game, an FA charge was made against me. I have no recollections of the incident – it doesn't even sound like something I'd do – but apparently, near the end of the game, I told a ball boy to 'give me the fucking ball'. Someone – I've no idea who – reported me to the FA. I had several meetings with the club solicitor and eventually the charge was dropped. A strange situation.

We were really struggling at this stage and things got even worse in the FA Cup. The draw for the third round had been kind to us, non-league Tamworth at home. We had several chances and should have won it, but they defended stoutly and held us to a 0-0 draw. The replay took place ten days later. On the coach down there, I had the hump because I'd been promised a £5,000 relocation fee when I signed permanently, and I hadn't received it. I was really annoyed and told the lads that if the money wasn't in my bank by the time we arrived at Tamworth's ground, I wouldn't be playing. I didn't receive the money for a few more days, but I played anyway. It was a really tough match and we edged through on penalties, which was a huge relief. I didn't take a spot kick in the penalty shoot-out, and it's probably a good job because, up to that point, I'd never taken one during my professional career. But that changed in our next match against Hull City on 21 January 2005.

We'd gone seven matches without a win when we faced Hull at the Britannia Stadium. The fans were beginning to get on our backs. Hull took an early lead and were leading 1-0 at half-time. Shortly after the interval, the normally reliable Paul Gallagher missed a penalty. Jon Parkin – who was a real handful – added Hull's second and then we won another spot kick.

Right, I'm taking this one, I thought. I placed the ball on the spot and decided to go straight down the middle, hoping the goalkeeper would dive. He didn't. He just stood there and caught the ball with ease. It was one of the worst penalties you could ever see. The fans, who were fuming when we missed the first, were absolutely raging by now. I ran back to my position on the right wing, wanting the ground to swallow me up. It was a hugely embarrassing moment.

I made amends by scoring a worldy the following week against Walsall in the FA Cup. Four minutes after Mamady Sidibé had opened the scoring, I played a one-two with Gallagher, cut inside from the right and bent it into the top corner with my left foot from 20 yards out. It's one of the best goals I've ever scored and an important one too, as it proved to be the winner.

Premier League Birmingham City knocked us out of the cup in the next round. We actually played quite well and made it hard for the Blues, but their quality helped them to edge through. After the match, I swapped shirts with Nicky Butt. I wasn't really one for exchanging shirts, but I'd always got on really well with Nicky and it was good to catch up with him.

On 25 February 2006, we finally ended our nine-match winless run in the league, coming from behind to beat Millwall 2-1. Those three points meant that we weren't going to be relegated, but barring a miracle we wouldn't be promoted either. It was the first time during my career that there wasn't really anything left to play for, other than pride, of course. And my pride took a bit of a battering when we played Norwich away on 4 March.

As Norwich is so close to Cambridge, I knew I'd be home for a decent time after the match, so Hayley and I arranged to meet some friends that evening at a nightclub called De Niro's in Newmarket. Two days before the game, Hayley went out to have her nails done and bought herself a tube of fake tan. 'If there's any left, can you do it on me too?' I asked while she was applying the tan. She did and it was a disaster – I went so orange it was mad.

The next day in training I was getting absolutely battered by the lads. Even Johan joined in. 'Luke, what have you done to yourself?' he asked. No one would go anywhere near me in the showers because the tan was running down me and gathering on the floor.

I still looked orange by the time we played Norwich. My former Reading team-mate Andy Hughes lined up for the Canaries and he spent most of the game taking the piss out of me! We lost 2-1 and then went out as planned, where the dim lighting inside De Niro's masked the orangeness of my skin. I never bothered with fake tan again.

I picked up a little knock against Wolves on 7 March and couldn't really shake it. To be honest, I was ready for the season to end by then and didn't do as much as I could have done to get back. The expectation for injured players was to report to the Britannia Stadium each morning, where we'd be given a training programme that we'd be expected to follow at the nearby David Lloyd gym.

Peter Sweeney and I were both injured and, after receiving our programmes, we'd get in my new car – a top-of-the-range Audi A8, complete with TV screens – drive the 500 metres or so to the gym, recline the seats and watch movies. After a couple of hours, we'd return to the stadium and tell the physio we'd followed their programme to the letter. Awful professionalism, I know, but it's very easy to become lazy when the season is almost over and you're struggling to get fit. I found treadmills and exercise bikes boring; the fun bit for me was getting out on the grass with a football.

We finished the season in 13th place, which was a fair reflection of our campaign. It was always going to be tough with so many changes and an influx of players from abroad who, although incredibly talented, didn't really know what the Championship was about. With the exception of Mamady Sidibé (who'd been signed by Tony Pulis) and Carl Hoefkens, the foreigners didn't turn into the signings Johan would have expected.

It was a really entertaining year, though. I started well, playing some fantastic football, and I was beginning to find my feet in a slightly different role. But then I picked up a few niggling injuries and my form tailed off towards the back end of the season.

I was delighted to see my old mates at West Ham reach the FA Cup Final, although they were beaten by Liverpool. I was particularly pleased for Alan Pardew, even though he'd let me go. There was never a point where I thought that I'd missed out, though, and wondered what if. In fact, when I look back, the majority of the clubs I played for went on to achieve success not long after I left. I'm not sure what that says about me!

Anyway, with the season over, I had a big reason to be excited – Hayley and I were getting married. But first, there was the small matter of my stag do.

Chapter 18

Happily Ever After

THE SPANISH island of Ibiza was the chosen destination for my stag do, and 36 of my closest friends joined me in Europe's party capital. Most of the trip is a blur, to be honest, but I can remember one night when we came out of a nightclub at some ungodly hour. I was standing with my mates, talking to a group of girls in Spanish. Well, when I say Spanish, that's not true – I couldn't speak a word of the language (except *cerveza*), so I was just making weird noises that I thought sounded Spanish. My friends thought it was hilarious, but the girls didn't. And neither did the men they were with. One of them took exception and gave me a shove. I was a bit tipsy, so I lost my balance and fell backwards. When I stood back up, my mates were staring at me in horror. I'd landed on some broken glass and blood was trickling down my face. I soon sobered up and headed back to the hotel to painstakingly remove shards of glass from my face, careful to ensure none of it went into my eyes. Fortunately, the damage was superficial, and the cuts had healed by the time I walked down the aisle.

* * *

Hayley and I were at school together, although I was in the year above, so we didn't really have any contact. In 1998, we bumped into each other at Barrington Social Club, got chatting and the rest is history. On 17 June 2006, at the church in Barrington, we became man and wife.

Forget playing in front of 70,000 people and millions more watching around the world on TV, my wedding day was the most nerve-racking experience of my life. I spent the night before the wedding with Carl and two of my closest friends: Shane Iles (nicknamed Lurch) and Gareth Hopwood (nicknamed Barnes because he was a massive fan of John Barnes when we were kids). Lurch and Barnes were my ushers and Carl was my best man. I had a couple of drinks that night to try to settle the nerves, but it didn't really work. The nerves were because Hayley had done a huge amount of organisation, and I wanted it to be perfect for her.

And it was. The weather was glorious, and we had a brilliant day surrounded by close friends and family. Everyone always says that you never see your wife as beautiful as the moment you see her walking down the aisle, and that was certainly the case for me. She looked absolutely stunning.

The wedding breakfast was held at the Cambridge Motel, five miles from the church. I mumbled my way through my speech before my father-in-law delivered his. Last, but not least, Carl, who was a little worse for wear, gave a humorous speech that everyone seemed to enjoy. It was an incredible day.

Then it was time for our honeymoon. We flew to Capri, a beautiful island in the Gulf of Naples. We stayed in an amazing five-star hotel with a Michelin-starred restaurant. The food was unbelievable, with 11 courses of delicious cuisine, but it was very different from what we were used to, so we sneaked out a couple of times to look for a little pizza and pasta place. The one downside was that the hotel bar didn't have a big screen, so we had to hunker down in our bedroom to watch the 2006 World Cup. I'm sure the guests wondered what was going on when we cheered and celebrated Joe Cole's wonder strike against Sweden!

It's hard to be a footballer's girlfriend or wife. Football is such a short career and has to come first. In the eight years that we'd been together, we'd lived in Antwerp, Manchester, Cambridge, Manchester again, Cambridge again and Stoke. Every time I joined a new club, I was surrounded by people of a similar age, so it was easy for me to make friends, but Hayley had to keep starting again, and it's not easy to meet people when you're new to the area and have two young children.

So, when we returned to England to begin our married life, I made the decision to leave Stoke City. We'd been renting a nice house in the village of Alton, near Alton Towers, but we wanted to put roots down. A huge factor was how I'd been as a child. The thought of having to move from school to school filled me with dread, and it was important to us that the boys had somewhere they could call home before they started primary school. There aren't many things more important than football but, for me, family is one.

I thought I'd played my last game for the club, but when I returned to tell Johan Boskamp that I wanted to leave, I was in for a shock. Johan had been sacked and replaced by former manager Tony Pulis. And Tony saw me as a key member of his squad.

Chapter 19

In the Wars

I DON'T think many people were surprised when Johan Boskamp was relieved of his duties. I really liked him, but it had been a turbulent year, and our results just weren't good enough.

There were changes in the boardroom too. The Icelandic owners sold the club back to Peter Coates and one of Peter's first tasks was to reappoint Tony Pulis, who'd left Stoke just a year earlier. Tony is a great guy and up there as one of the best managers I've ever played for. He brought some much-needed positivity to the club. He'd tried to sign me before I joined Reading, but I'd already given Alan Pardew my word.

So, it was really difficult for me to tell Tony that I wanted to leave before I'd even kicked a single ball for him. Nigel Worthington, the Norwich City manager, had made an offer and I was keen to join the Canaries to reduce my commute. That was the only reason I wanted to leave Stoke.

One of Tony's strengths is that he makes the conversation about you. He shows empathy and is a real genuine man. That's why I felt so guilty. I was probably one of the better players in the group and he didn't want to lose me. Tony explained that he couldn't let me go because the fans had taken to me, and he didn't want to upset them. Instead, he asked me to give him my all for a few months while he looked for a replacement. He gave me his word that he'd let me go at a later date if that was still what I wanted. I thought that was fair enough and agreed to do my best for him.

It was another transitional summer for the club as we moved away from the Continental feel back to old-school British football. Pulis brought in Dave Kemp as his coach. A great fella who loved the banter. Sam Ellis was another addition to the backroom staff. He'd been Stan Ternent's assistant at Burnley, a fantastic football man. He actually knew my nan and grandpa, and I was buzzing when I saw him at training.

There were changes on the playing front too; a lot of Boskamp's signings departed and were replaced by players who had experience of the English game. Central defender Danny Higginbotham was one of the first to come in. I'd played alongside Danny for Manchester United Reserves, so I knew he possessed a lot of quality. But he was also a fantastic character, and we needed his personality to bring the dressing room together. He became club captain later in the season.

Next in was Ricardo Fuller – an absolute player. From day one you could see he was Premier League quality, who, for one reason or another, had dropped down to the Championship. He was incredibly gifted and became a fan favourite at the Britannia Stadium. With a big chunk of the transfer kitty spent on Danny and Ricardo, Tony turned to the loan market to bolster the squad. Former Stoke left-back Andy Griffin returned to us on loan from Portsmouth. Andy was from the Stoke area and had spent the last eight seasons in the Premier League with

Newcastle and Pompey. He slotted straight back in as if he'd never been away.

Pre-season training was tough. Tony wants his players to be as fit as they possibly can be, and he loves making them run. He had us running up and down the hills at Lilleshall, before moving us on to a picturesque place in Austria that was in the middle of nowhere. It was intense and exhausting, but Pulis was the kind of manager who made you want to run for him.

During our pre-season friendlies, I realised that our style of play was going to be very different to what I'd been used to. It was much more direct in comparison to Boskamp's pass and move, and the wide men had probably the hardest jobs in the team in terms of what was expected of them in and out of possession.

Sports science was in its infancy, but Tony was keen to explore it, and we were offered various supplements to give us more energy. It was completely optional, but I decided to give it a go.

Our season began away at Southend on Saturday, 5 August 2006. In the hotel the night before the game I took my supplements after dinner as usual. In my room later that evening I began to throw up – and worse, I got the shits. It was horrendous. I think my body disagreed with one of the supplements I'd taken.

The following day I was named in the starting line-up. It was one of the hottest days of the year and my face had turned purple because of the heat. That was before we'd even kicked off! During the first half, people kept asking if I was alright. I was asked again at half-time. I felt fine (apart from the heat) but I obviously wasn't, because of what happened next.

I remember kicking off the second half and then ... I was coming round in the back of an ambulance on the way to Southend General Hospital. I didn't have a clue what was going on. The paramedic told me that I'd passed out during the game and was being taken to hospital so they could perform some tests. My team-mate Peter Sweeney was in the ambulance too, because he'd injured his wrist and needed an X-ray. He was really worried; he probably thought I was going to pop my clogs. I've never seen any footage, but I can imagine it was very scary for my team-mates, opponents, family and people watching.

Fortunately, the tests came back clear, and the diagnosis was that I'd suffered severe dehydration, likely caused by losing all the fluids from the sickness and diarrhoea episode the night before. The doctors were concerned because people who collapse with dehydration usually come round fairly quickly, but I'd been out for the count for 40-odd minutes, so I was kept in overnight for observation.

Hayley collected me from the hospital on Sunday and drove me back to Cambridge. Tony Pulis rang me on the Monday morning and asked me if I'd be able to play against Derby County the following night. The doctor had advised me not to play but I felt okay and agreed to travel up to Stoke. Tony was a bit like Sir Alex Ferguson; you didn't want to disappoint him.

So, three days after collapsing on the pitch, I was named in the starting line-up and had a really good game. Carl Hoefkens played behind me at right-back and we doubled up on Derby's Ryan Smith, a talented young winger on loan from Arsenal.

During the first half, I caught an elbow, which cut my head open, and I had to have four stitches at half-time. I was certainly in the wars, but I carried on and helped the team to a 2-0 victory. If there were any doubts about my commitment to Pulis before, there weren't any after those two games.

After drawing 0-0 with Birmingham City – a good result considering they'd only just been relegated from the Premier League – we played Luton Town at Kenilworth Road. I've already mentioned that I didn't like taking corners. Alan Pardew had given me stick while I was at Reading, and on the few occasions where I'd practised them at Stoke, I inevitably messed them up, causing Pulis to shout, 'Fuck off, Chadders!'

For some reason, I was put on set pieces for the Luton game and every single one was unbelievable. I set up Peter Sweeney for our opener from a set play, and I hit the bar from another one. For the first time ever, everything I tried came off. I nicked the equaliser too, although that was with a header. Afterwards, I thought that I'd added a new string to my bow, but I was taken off set pieces for the next game and never took another one for the club!

On 26 August 2006, we drew 1-1 at home to Plymouth in what was a poor team performance. The supporters weren't happy and made their feelings known at the end. It got even worse the following week away at Barnsley. Clint Hill gave us the lead in the third minute, and I grabbed our second 20 minutes later with a decent finish from ten yards. The three points should have been in the bag, but we let our two-goal lead slip and had to settle for a point. The tunnel at Oakwell is behind one of the goals near the visiting fans. As we walked past, we all received a load of stick from the Stoke fans. Tony took the brunt of it.

We travelled back up to Yorkshire three days later and got another draw, this time against Sheffield Wednesday. Martin

Paterson, a bubbly young striker, scored our goal. My car was at Hillsborough because I wanted to travel straight back home after the game, and that was the moment I knew I couldn't keep on like this. I was driving from Sheffield to Cambridge on a Tuesday night, and likely wouldn't get home until 2am. I'd be like a zombie the next day, and then have to drive back to Stoke on the Thursday morning. I was spending more time on the motorway than I was with my family. But I'd given my word to Tony and knew I wouldn't leave until he'd found my replacement.

By the end of September we'd won just one of our opening ten league games. The fans weren't happy, and the manager was under immense pressure. It was a strange situation because, although Pulis was popular with the supporters, most of them felt underwhelmed when he returned to the club. The appointment of Johan Boskamp was supposed to move the club forward, so when that didn't work and the previous manager returned, some sceptical fans saw it as a backward step. Tony had a vision, though, and the owners knew that he needed some time to bring in his own players, those who could play his specific brand of football.

Just before a difficult away match against Leeds United, Tony brought in two new players, and everything clicked into place. Lee Hendrie was an exciting signing from Aston Villa. Lee had burst onto the scene at Villa Park but was going through a tough time, and a loan move was just what he needed. He made an instant impact at Stoke. Lee and I had played together for the England Under-21s so we knew each other, but he was surprised when he saw me again. I'd grown up quite a bit since then and was no longer the shy, introverted player he'd known. Lee is a good guy and I still see him every so often because, for some reason, he turns out for the Manchester United veteran's team.

The signing who perhaps had the biggest impact on the club, although not during the 2006/07 season, was Rory Delap, who came in on loan from Sunderland in October 2006. Rory changed everything with his long throw, literally propelling the club into the Premier League in 2008 and to the FA Cup Final in 2011.

For the Leeds game, Lee slotted in on the left wing and Rory played on the right, which meant that I was relegated to the bench. Elland Road is always a difficult place to go, but we put in a stellar performance and battered them 4-0, with goals from Hendrie, Griffin, Higginbotham and Fuller – all four players had been signed by Pulis. I came on for a five-minute cameo, but we were already 3-0 up at that point so I can't take any credit for our victory.

I was on the bench again for our next match, which was at home to Sunderland. I bumped into Roy Keane before kick-off, and we said hello, which was nice as I hadn't seen him since I left Manchester United. Despite being dropped, I was feeling quite pleased because I knew that if Rory continued to play well, I'd be allowed to leave.

However, just 11 minutes into the match against his parent club, Rory suffered a terrible leg break. I was gutted for him. I came on as a substitute and helped us to a deserved 2-1 win. During the game, I went in for a 50/50 with another former team-mate, Dwight Yorke. I won the ball and earned a big cheer from the Stoke fans. Unfortunately, during the challenge my shoulder popped out of its socket, causing incredible pain, and I had to see a specialist after the match.

The first time I'd dislocated my shoulder was during a YTS game, years earlier. By the time I'd joined Stoke, it seemed to be happening more frequently and, although I could pop my shoulder back into the socket, I felt that it was getting weaker every time it happened.

So, the day after the Sunderland game, I went to the hospital and a scan showed a serious issue. There was a small fracture within the shoulder and the muscle around it had torn. From the specialist's point of view, I couldn't play and needed an operation. From the club's point of view, I could play because they needed me to. Regardless of what the club or specialist wanted me to do, I always listened to my own body when deciding if I was okay to play.

It all harks back to that night in Greece when Roy Keane said, 'Sometimes you need to play when you're injured.' I took that advice on board, and it stuck with me throughout my career. If I ever had any chance of playing, even if it could potentially make the injury worse, I'd play. The only time I made myself unavailable is if I couldn't physically run and kick a ball.

While I was in the hospital, I visited Rory. He was devastated. It was touch and go whether he'd get back to the same level as before, but he obviously did – and then some. It was great to see Rory become a key component in Stoke's later success.

I only missed one game because of my shoulder, and I was back in the starting line-up for the visit of Norwich on 28 October 2006. Nigel Worthington, the man who'd tried to sign me, had left by then, but his replacement was someone I knew very well – Peter Grant, who'd been Alan Pardew's assistant during my time at West Ham. I knew Granty liked me as a player and the agents had been speaking, and as I walked out of the tunnel for the kick-off, I thought, *This wouldn't be a bad game to play well in.*

Norwich had been relegated from the Premier League just 15 months earlier and had promotion aspirations, but we blew them away with a stunning performance. Lee Hendrie and Ricardo Fuller both scored to give us a 2-0 lead at half-time. In the second half, I was brought down in the box by the Norwich keeper, who was sent off, and Danny Higginbotham put the resultant spot kick in the back of the net. A few minutes later, I twisted and turned in the box before smashing the ball into the bottom right with my left foot to make it 4-0. The rout was completed in stoppage time when my right-footed cross was headed clear to Darel Russell, who hammered home our fifth from 20 yards. It was an incredible result, and I was so pleased for Tony.

After the win against Norwich, Stoke lost just once in the next eight games and finished the season in eighth place, narrowly missing out on the play-offs. I wasn't at the club by then, though.

My last game for Stoke came on 11 November 2006, a 1-0 win against Crystal Palace. By then Pulis had signed Liam Lawrence from Sunderland and that meant that I was free to leave. Norwich made an offer for my services (a loan initially, but it was agreed that it would become permanent in January), and Tony, true to his word, accepted it. After the game, I said my goodbyes to the lads and received a lovely phone call from the manager thanking me for my efforts and for not spitting my dummy out when he first rejected my transfer request. He finished the call by telling me that I was a credit to the game, which made me feel ten feet tall.

I left Stoke with mixed emotions. I loved playing for the fans and the manager, and I thoroughly enjoyed my time at the club. I wished I could have played under Tony for longer, but I had to do what was right for my family. So, I joined Norwich and prepared for my debut against Ipswich Town. It was a match that I'll never forget.

Chapter 20

Dream to Despair

AFTER YEARS of living a nomadic football lifestyle, transferring to a new team every 12 to 18 months, I was hopeful that I could finally settle at Norwich. I was ready for a long, successful spell at the club. Norwich were aiming to win promotion back to the Premier League. We were ninth in the league table when I joined in November 2006, but with the players that Peter Grant had at his disposal, we should have been sitting in the play-off places. We were underachieving.

Peter was taking his first steps on the managerial ladder, having been Alan Pardew's assistant at Reading and West Ham. Granty had spent two years at Carrow Road as a player and was popular with the fans. He felt like the right fit, but it never really clicked for him.

A former Scotland international midfielder, Peter had spent the bulk of his career at Celtic, winning trophies galore. He was still a very good player and often joined in the small-sided games. On my first day of training, we played on the same team, and I kept forgetting to call him Gaffer, shouting Granty instead. The lads thought this was hilarious because the manager is always known as Boss or Gaffer.

I also had to change the way I addressed club owners, who were usually known as Mr, Mrs or Sir. Norwich were owned by Delia Smith and her husband, Michael Wynn-Jones. They were lovely people – Norwich through and through – and both did a lot for the club. They were around the training ground quite a bit and I found it quite strange that the lads were on first-name terms with them. That took a bit of getting used to as I only knew Delia from her cooking programmes on the TV.

Having a celebrity chef as the owner certainly had its perks; the food in the canteen was superb. It was like eating at a posh restaurant. Our chef, Terry, came on the bus with us for away trips. At other clubs, you'd have microwave meals or pizzas (or pea and ham soup at Burnley, of course). At Norwich, Terry cooked our meals on the coach: a starter and a couple of selections for the main. Delia certainly did us proud with the quality of food.

There was plenty of quality within the squad too. It was nice to link up with my old Reading team-mate Andy Hughes again. Andy was a great lad and helped me to settle in. Darren Huckerby was the main man. Hucks is an absolute Norwich legend, a brilliant player. He wasn't the best defensively, but more than made up for that with his attacking prowess. He'd get fans out of their seats, carried the ball extremely well and scored some fantastic goals. The supporters loved him, and he was a popular figure within the dressing room too. I'd played against Hucks a few times in the past when he tore us to pieces, so it was nice to be on the same side this time!

Granty's plan was for us to play three up top: Huckerby on the left, me on the right and Welsh international Robert Earnshaw in the middle. Robbie scored a lot of goals for us, but I don't think our shape really suited him. Earnshaw was an incredible finisher around the box – probably the best in the division – but in the No.9 role he was expected to drop in, whereas he preferred to get in behind the defence. Local lad Chris Martin gave us another option up front because he was a little bit different to Robbie. He did a brilliant job as a young player and was linked with several Premier League clubs.

Our captain was Adam Drury. He'd grown up in Cambridgeshire, although he was a couple of years older than me, so I don't think we'd played against each other as kids. Adam has been inducted into the Norwich Hall of Fame, and rightly so. He was a very loyal and consistent player. Adam was usually partnered at the back by Jason Shackell, a young player who'd progressed through the ranks.

Equally able at playing centre-back or right-back was Gary Doherty, a good, strong defender, who attacked the ball well. He got a bit of stick from the fans at times, but Gary was a great lad. One year we had an end-of-season trip to Las Vegas, which was brilliant. We spent a day at a pool party in one of the big hotels and we all had way too much to drink, Gary especially. We were standing at a taxi rank, waiting to go back to our hotel, and Gary – who was bare-chested – was told he needed to put a top on before getting into the cab. He was so drunk that he was struggling to put his vest on. In the end, an old lady came over, told him to put his hands in the air and put his top on over his head. It was hilarious watching him being dressed like a small child. That was a great holiday.

My roommate was Lee Croft, another right-winger. We were vying for the same position but there was never any animosity. In fact, we couldn't have got on much better. Every time we stayed somewhere overnight, Lee would order room service, but he'd have it delivered to the room next door so that the club didn't know it was him. As soon as he heard the trolley, he'd run out to the corridor to collect his food from the waiting staff.

And then there was Dion Dublin – my hero as a kid. I'd made my debut against him, of course, and I was absolutely buzzing to get to know him in the dressing room and find out what a brilliant human being he was. I think I bored him to tears, bending his ear every day talking about the old days at Cambridge United. I probably made him feel a little bit old because I was just a boy when he was scoring all those goals. I asked him to sign a couple of my old Cambridge shirts, and he duly obliged.

Dion had a great personality, but I never thought he'd become a television presenter. At that stage I thought he'd become a manager. When he spoke, everyone listened, and he could hold the attention of the group – which is certainly no mean feat in a football dressing room! He was a real leader on the pitch, but Dion knew how to enjoy himself too. He was like Peter Pan; he didn't act like the elder statesman and was always in and among the banter. He always came out with us for a night out, enjoying a pint of real ale. An absolute legend of a bloke. Despite the fact I played with him for a couple of years, I was always in awe of him. I still am.

I trained with my new team-mates on 16 November 2006 and Granty told me that I'd be making my debut three days later against big rivals Ipswich Town at Portman Road. The East Anglian derby isn't considered one of the big ones, but it really is a massive game for the two clubs. The local media were hyping it up all week. The fans were talking of nothing else. It was a great opportunity for me to show the Norwich fans what I could do.

A few days before the game, I went out with some friends for a low-key evening to celebrate my 26th birthday. It wasn't a great night because I had to go home early due to a bug I'd picked up. I couldn't stop throwing up. *How is this happening?* I spent the next day in bed, drinking lots of water and, fortunately, I was fine by the time I arrived at Colney (Norwich's training ground) for training on the eve of the game.

My first game for Norwich couldn't have started any better. And couldn't have finished any worse.

With 26 minutes on the clock, Ipswich's Matt Richards made a mistake, the ball fell to me and I rolled it under the keeper to give us the lead. I was absolutely buzzing and ran over to the Norwich fans to celebrate. Our goal was probably against the run of play, and Ipswich scored an equaliser just before half-time. We were under the cosh again in the second half, being forced deeper and deeper by a strong Ipswich side.

And then disaster. I was shielding the ball, letting it go out of play, when Ipswich defender Matthew Bates, a really good player who eventually came on loan to Norwich, charged into the back of me. I went flying off the pitch and collided with one of those furry microphones that Sky have dotted around the pitch. My immediate reaction as I was lying on the ground hunched over was that I was winded. That's a horrible feeling and I was trying to catch my breath. Then I realised that my shoulder had popped out again and that was causing further pain. I was battling to put it back into its socket when Adam Drury came over to check if I was okay. His face turned white, and he said, 'Don't look down.'

So, obviously, I looked down. I wish I hadn't. There was a gaping hole in my kneecap. It was so deep that you could see the bone. I managed to sort my shoulder out and then, as I lay waiting for the stretcher, I felt sheer agony surging through my body. When the physios arrived, they were shocked because blood was pouring out of the wound, and I mean pouring. I think one of them held a bandage on my knee to try to stem the bleeding, and then I was loaded onto a stretcher and carried round the pitch. I'd got injured near the Norwich fans and they gave me a nice round of applause. Then we turned a corner and I saw a sea of blue. The Ipswich fans gave me a load of stick and the stretcher bearers almost dropped me. I had to grip the sides to stop myself falling out!

I was taken to the treatment room at Portman Road and that's when the pain really hit me. My knee felt like it was hanging off. Our club doctor tried to stitch it up, putting the needle into the flesh on either side of my kneecap. But the cut was too big, and he had to keep starting again. I felt like I was being tortured and I begged him to stop. It was agony and I began to cry my eyes out. Luckily, someone gave me some gas and air and the pain started to dissipate.

Ipswich midfielder Gavin Williams, my old West Ham team-mate, came in to try to cheer me up but the gas and air was kicking in by then and I was pretty out of it. The next thing I remember is lying in the back of an ambulance on my way to Ipswich hospital. The biggest concern to the doctors was the risk of infection, so they cleaned my knee, and a couple of hours later I was taken to the operating theatre where they stitched it back up. I spent the next few days in Ipswich hospital for observation. It wasn't a great place for a newly signed Norwich player, but the staff treated me extremely well and even gave me my own room.

Although the pain had subsided by the time I returned home, my knee had swollen to the size of a football. I thought that I'd be out for six to eight weeks, but the swelling wouldn't go down. I was concerned because I was only on loan at Norwich, but I spoke to Peter Grant and he reassured me that the club would honour the agreement to sign me in January. That was huge. They could easily have cancelled the transfer, but they stuck to their word, and I'll always respect Norwich for that. It was one less thing for me to have to worry about.

While I was recovering, I was contacted by some lawyers asking if I wanted to sue Sky Sports for the injury, but I decided not to do that. It wasn't anyone's fault. It was just one of those things.

This was without a doubt the most challenging injury I ever had. There's normally a set timeframe around injuries, a standard rehab protocol that you just follow, but I couldn't do anything until the swelling reduced. At times, I wondered whether it could be the end of my career because you can't play with a hugely swollen knee. No matter what we tried, we just couldn't reduce the swelling and I was becoming incredibly frustrated. There wasn't a huge amount of pain, it was more discomfort because it was twice the size of my other knee, and that affected the way I moved. I told the doctors that I was ready to come back, but there was no way they could let me play.

The first six weeks were tough. It was obviously nice to be at home and spend some time with Hayley and the kids because we'd been like ships in the night at times when I'd been at

Stoke, but at the same time I wanted to be running around and kicking a ball. I couldn't really do a lot, so I bought myself a La-Z-Boy chair and spent my days sitting in that, drinking beer and watching TV. For the first time in my football career, I put on a bit of weight and developed a little belly. I was turning into Jim Royle from *The Royle Family*!

I began my rehab in January 2007, and it was a bit of a shock to my system. I was used to getting my own way and taking it easy when I was injured. At Norwich, they expected me in for 9am each morning and they worked me hard for the entire day. There was a lot of swimming involved because it's low impact. I hated swimming, though.

The worst part of being injured was the knowledge that I was letting people down. The manager had shown faith in me, my team-mates needed me and the owners were paying me really good money to essentially do nothing. The fans wanted me back too because we were struggling on the pitch and there was a real possibility that we could go down, although I never really feared relegation. Not with the players that we had. But I still felt guilty. I'm not sure how different our results might have been with me in the line-up, but at least I'd have been helping the club and doing something.

After months of hard work and frustration, I was named on the substitutes' bench for an away match against Barnsley on 3 March 2007. I wasn't really fit and had no chance of playing, but I think Granty picked me to help keep me sane, to show me what I was working towards. A week later I played a practice game against Cambridge United at Colney. It was strange to be lining up against my boyhood team, but great to be back on the pitch.

I made my long-awaited comeback against Birmingham on 13 March. I received a great reception from the fans inside Carrow Road, many of whom had probably forgotten who I was! Hucks scored a really good goal to give us a 1-0 win.

I played again in our next game, again at Carrow Road, against Stoke City. Huckerby scored the only goal of the game. It was good to see some of my old team-mates, but even better to be part of a team who'd claimed back-to-back victories. In my head I was convinced that our turn in fortune was down to my return to action, but in reality I didn't really do a lot in the two games.

A fortnight later I made my fourth appearance wearing the yellow-and-green shirt in a 3-0 defeat to Colchester. Their striker Jamie Cureton caused chaos that day. I only came on for the last half an hour, but during that time I managed to pull my quad muscle, an injury that had been caused by a weakness in the muscle of my injured leg. So, after valiantly fighting back to fitness, my season was over. I was absolutely gutted.

To make matters worse, I had to have a tonsillectomy during the summer because I kept catching all the bugs Louis and Liam were picking up from school and nursery. It was a nightmare first season at Norwich.

Things could only get better, right?

Chapter 21

The Nightmare Continues

HAVING MY tonsils removed was painful and left me feeling uncomfortable, but strangely it also gave me loads of energy. I returned for pre-season full of hope and optimism that my injury woes were behind me. I was ready to work hard and get back into the team.

We went on tour to the Netherlands and, although the coaches worked us hard, we were allowed one night out to let our hair down. There wasn't a great deal to do in the area we were staying in, so Gary Doherty, Chris Brown, Jon Otsemobor (who'd signed from Crewe) and I decided to find somewhere a bit livelier. We rang for a cab and asked the driver to take us to Amsterdam, not realising that the famous city was over an hour-and-a-half drive away!

We enjoyed a few beers and then hailed another taxi to take us back to our hotel. The weather was awful, torrential rain, and while driving back in the early hours of the morning, the taxi spun off the road. Luckily no one was hurt. We didn't get back to our rooms until the following morning and we all felt the worse for wear at training a few hours later. I don't think I was the only one wondering why we'd bothered to go out in the first place.

I was desperate to start repaying the manager for the faith he'd shown in me, and I did really well during the pre-season friendlies, playing in a more central role. There were quite a few changes that summer as we lost several key players, including Dickson Etuhu and Youssef Safri. They were a good combination in the middle of the park, and they were a big miss. The biggest blow was the departure of Robbie Earnshaw, who joined Derby County for £3.5m.

There were some good players coming in, including Scottish goalkeeper David Marshall and former Norwich players Darel Russell and Jamie Cureton.

My hard work paid off and I was delighted to be named in the starting line-up as part of a midfield three for the opening game of the season away at Preston North End. Granty was trying something different, and we lined up in a formation that we didn't truly understand. Normally when you play three in the middle, you have two sitting and one ahead, or one sitter and two higher up, but we were a flat three and it didn't really work. We battled to a 0-0 draw, which was a decent result.

We won two and lost two of the next four games and only scraped through in the League Cup by beating Rochdale on penalties. Performances, both individually and collectively, weren't good enough. When you begin a new season, you hope you'll be able to turn over a new leaf and start again, but we encountered the same issues that we had the previous year. We weren't clicking as a team and the fans were becoming restless. It was the beginning of the end for Peter Grant.

On 2 October 2007, we lost 1-0 away to QPR and fell into the bottom three. On the bus ride back to East Anglia, the news spread that Granty had gone. The next day we went into Colney and Peter said goodbye to us. It was quite emotional because we all respected him and, despite the rumours, he hadn't lost the dressing room.

Granty's assistant, Jim Duffy, was appointed as caretaker manager. Jim was a proper football man, quite dour and deadpan in the way that he spoke. He'd managed Falkirk, Dundee and Hibs north of the border, and I think he was keen to take the role on a permanent basis. But we lost his three games in charge, so he was never really in contention.

One of those matches was against Burnley. A 2-1 defeat saw us drop to the bottom of the table, and to make matters worse the coach broke down on the motorway on the way home. We had to wait for hours for a replacement bus. It was a freezing cold Tuesday evening and we all lay on the floor under our seats, trying to keep warm and get some sleep. We eventually arrived back at the training ground at 6am.

I think Delia and Michael wanted a fresh start and, at the end of October 2007, Glenn Roeder was announced as our new manager. A central defender during his 20-year playing career, Roeder was an experienced manager who'd enjoyed spells with West Ham and Newcastle United. He'd also coached the England national team during Glenn Hoddle's reign.

You only get one chance to make a good first impression, and Roeder messed his up. When he addressed the group to introduce himself, he tried to make his presence felt straight away. He was quite critical of the team – and rightly so because our league position was unacceptable – and told us that he wasn't going to stand for it. He was clearly trying to stamp his authority, but it all seemed a bit forced, an unnatural approach, and when he walked out of the room he'd lost most of the lads already. He didn't get off on the right foot.

The atmosphere around the club changed instantly. Glenn got rid of most of the existing coaching staff and brought in his own people. Lee Clark and Paul Stephenson, who'd been with him at Newcastle, came in, and they were good lads who joined in the banter. But Roeder distanced himself and created a barrier between the players and manager. An unnecessary one, in my opinion.

To be fair to Roeder, we needed a complete change, and he made it clear that everyone had a clean slate. I performed well in training and was pleased to find myself named in his first line-up – a home match against bitter rivals Ipswich Town. We were 2-0 down at half-time. I don't think I was alone in thinking, *Here we go again*. But we fought back to earn a draw. I actually thought we were the better team on the day and were unlucky not to win.

Despite losing the next two matches, I still wasn't worried about relegation because of the players we had. We were struggling, but I knew we'd be okay. We just needed a win to kick-start our season.

We got that much-needed victory on 24 November 2007, beating Coventry City 2-0. I opened the scoring with a really good goal ten minutes before half-time, and Jamie Cureton wrapped up the points in the second half.

We followed that up with a 3-1 win over Blackpool. I was doing pretty well, and I think Roeder saw me as a key player, but once again an injury hampered my season. The story of my career. The problems with my shoulder had worsened and it had got to the point where I was suffering dislocations on a daily basis. It just wasn't sustainable, and I was advised that without surgery I'd be causing long-term damage. The team needed me, and I was desperate to help the club get out of the mire, so we agreed that I'd rest for a couple of weeks and then we'd review the situation.

After our first back-to-back wins of the season, we took on Stoke City at the Britannia Stadium. My old club was flying and on their way to automatic promotion. I wasn't part of the squad, but I travelled up to support the lads. Around 15 minutes before kick-off I bumped into Tony Pulis. We swapped pleasantries and then he asked me what the Norwich shape was going to be. It put me in a really difficult position because I didn't want to give away secrets, but Tony had looked after me and I didn't want to disappoint him. We were lining up in a slightly different formation, with Gary Doherty playing at right-back. He'd find out in a few minutes anyway, so I couldn't see what damage it could do, so I told him that Doherty was playing right-back.

Stoke went on to beat us 2-1, although I thought Gary did quite well in his new role. I'm not 100 per cent sure, but I believe that my conversation with Tony got back to the manager and his coaching staff because the way they treated me changed after that match.

I never really had a relationship with Glenn. He was the type of manager who focused on the players who were fit and able to help him, and I felt a bit out in the cold while I was injured. I had my doubts whether I liked it at Norwich, whether I actually enjoyed playing for him. I'd been doing quite well since Roeder came in, but I never felt settled or comfortable during his tenure at the club. It was the first time during my career that I didn't like the environment. I'm not the only one who thought that either.

After the defeat at the Britannia Stadium, we went on a 13-game unbeaten run and moved out of the relegation zone. We'd finally turned a corner, although we were very much still in a relegation battle. I can't take any credit for that run, though, because my shoulder hadn't improved, and in January 2008 I finally went in for surgery.

I couldn't do a huge amount in the aftermath of my operation. The physios told me not to run because they didn't want me to be pounding my shoulder while I was still in a sling, so I returned to my La-Z-Boy and became Jim Royle again for a few weeks.

When I was finally able to get rid of the sling and begin jogging, I went out to Tenerife with Hayley, the boys, my mum and my brother Carl. The holiday got off to a bad start and I found myself in Hayley's bad books on the day we landed. There were too many of us to fit in one taxi, so Carl and I caught one cab and the others got into another. When we arrived at the hotel, Carl and I got caught up in the excitement and ran straight inside to check in. We'd completely forgotten that Hayley's suitcase was in the back of the taxi! The driver went to on to collect his next fare and the luggage was lost forever. To say she wasn't impressed with me is an understatement!

My aim was to get fit and fight my way back into the starting XI. Despite my doubts, I still wanted to be at Norwich, although I was beginning to wonder whether it was a poisoned chalice, with injury after injury.

My road to recovery began in Tenerife. I knew that I had to do everything I could to get myself as fit as I could possibly be. I was 27, no longer a kid, so I had to kick on with my career and play as many games as I could. I had to work my socks off and it began on that holiday. Every morning I went for a run, and it felt so good.

My hard work paid off. On 19 April 2008, I made my long-awaited return to action in a 2-1 defeat against West Brom – the eventual champions. I received a fantastic reception from the Carrow Road faithful, which was nice. The Norwich fans were always great to me, although I'm sure they were frustrated. I was perceived as a decent Championship player when I signed for them, but they'd only seen me in action on a handful of occasions.

Although our form had picked up during the second half of the season, we were still embroiled in a relegation battle. A week later we played QPR at home in a must-win game. Ched Evans, who'd joined the club on loan from Manchester City, scored an early goal to settle the nerves. Mark Fotheringham doubled our lead ten minutes into the second half. I came on for the last half an hour and played really well. Darel Russell scored our third goal seven minutes from time to give us a 3-0 win that secured our Championships status for another season.

Our final game of the season was against Sheffield Wednesday at Hillsborough. Wednesday needed a win to avoid relegation. Darren Huckerby put us in front in the ninth minute, but the Owls fought back to win 4-1. I was an unused sub for that match, but I remember it well because it was Dion Dublin's last appearance as a professional. At 39, he'd decided to hang up his boots at the end of his 20th season. With 25 minutes remaining, Dion was substituted and left the pitch to a standing ovation from all four sides of Hillsborough. It was an emotional moment, and I'm honoured to have been part of the squad for the final game of Dion's outstanding career.

The end of the season came at the wrong time for me. By May I was usually ready for a rest to recharge my batteries, but this time I felt in fantastic shape and was raring to go. The summer was typically a six-week period where I wouldn't do a great deal, but that year I did more work than I'd ever done before. As a result, I was in the shape of my life, buzzing to return for pre-season. I still didn't have a relationship with the manager but, if I could stay fit, I knew I could become a big part of the team.

It was a good job I'd worked hard during the summer months because Roeder brought in Alan Pearson to be our new strength and conditioning coach. Alan was an ex-rugby player, a great guy with a big personality. He ran us into the ground and was a big advocate of ice baths for recovery, something that my team-mates and I weren't too keen on initially.

We went out to Sweden for our pre-season tour, and I thought I did okay in the two friendlies I played in. However, towards the end of the tour we were doing a crossing and shooting session. I put in a couple of poor crosses and Roeder completely lost his head with me. He'd never spoken to me like that before. I wasn't the sort of player that managers usually shouted at because I always worked hard, so I was shocked. Immediately after that session I realised that I didn't want to play for him anymore. I'm sure it all went back to the Stoke City game and the conversation I'd had with Tony Pulis.

As soon as I got back to my room, I phoned my agent. 'I can't stand it here and need to get away. I don't want to leave the area and I've always wanted to play for Cambridge. What do you think?' I asked, floating the idea.

'Cambridge is a non-league club, Luke. You're at the peak of your powers and can't play at that level,' he said.

'I'm not moving house and I don't want a long commute. What about MK Dons?' I suggested.

'Okay. Leave it with me,' he said.

When we returned to England, I told Glenn Roeder that I wanted to leave. He surprised me by saying that I was part of his plans, but he agreed to let me go if I could sort a move out. I felt guilty because Norwich had been great to me and I'd done very little in return, but I needed a fresh start. I wasn't even named on the bench for the season opener away at Coventry City, and I knew then that I'd played my last game for the club.

Ironically, Norwich played MK Dons in the League Cup on 12 August 2008 and, although I wasn't in the squad, I went to watch the game. I looked around the newly built Stadium MK and felt quite excited at the prospect of playing there. The Dons played in League One, but I didn't really see it as dropping down a level.

The talks dragged on but finally, on 1 October 2008, I joined MK Dons on a three-month loan. It turned out to be one of the best decisions of my life.

I spent an enjoyable 2003/04 season on loan at Burnley working with the legendary Stan Ternent.

Teddy Sheringham is one of the best players I've played with. I was delighted to reunite with him at West Ham during our 2004/05 promotion-winning season.

I have so many happy memories from my time at Stoke City, including scoring one of the best goals of my career against Walsall.

Family is everything to me. Here I am with Liam and Louis.

I was more nervous on my wedding day than I was before any game, but it was an incredible day.

My Norwich City debut against rivals Ipswich Town began with a goal and ended with the worst injury of my career.

I played the best football of my career during my six years with MK Dons. My only regret is that I didn't get chance to say a proper goodbye to their magnificent supporters.

Taking the ball from Shaun Wright-Phillips. I always loved a tackle.

Playing for Cambridge United fulfilled a lifelong dream.

Winning promotion at Wembley with Cambridge is one of my career highlights.

My last start as a professional footballer came in the FA Cup at Old Trafford against Manchester United. I left the pitch to an unexpected standing ovation. Not a bad way to sign off!

I am proud of the men Liam and Louis have become. Both are still involved in the game.

With James Cutting and Jonny Martin, co-founders of the Football Fun Factory.

Cheers to my wonderful wife Hayley who has been a constant source of support throughout my career.

I regularly bump into ex-team-mates while working as a pundit for MUTV. Here I am with Wes Brown and Mark Sullivan, the presenter.

Chapter 22

More Painful than Childbirth

FOUNDED IN 2004 when Wimbledon controversially relocated from their South London home to Buckinghamshire, MK Dons took the former FA Cup winners' place in League One. The Dons struggled during their inaugural year, only achieving survival on the final day of the season. Relegation followed, before MK Dons, under the leadership of Paul Ince, were promoted as champions at the end of the 2007/08 campaign.

The club was still very much in a transitional period when I joined in October 2008. MK Dons played their home games in the stunning new Stadium MK, which had opened in 2007, but the training facilities were a world away from the all-singing, all-dancing set-up at Norwich. Lunch was chicken nuggets and chips from a little hut, as opposed to Delia Smith's restaurant-quality cuisine that I'd enjoyed at Colney. None of that bothered me, though. I embraced the fact that we had to do things for ourselves.

After winning the League Two title, Paul Ince had joined Premier League club Blackburn Rovers, with former Chelsea midfielder Roberto Di Matteo named as his successor. It was

Robbie's first managerial role and he got off to a mixed start: winning four, losing four of his first eight league games. People outside the club were suggesting a mid-table finish would be deemed a successful campaign, but internally we felt we were capable of aiming for a play-off place at the very least.

Robbie was as cool as a cucumber. He had all the gear, with the stylish Italian-made suits he wore and his flash car. We all had huge respect for him because of what he'd achieved in the game and the way he went about his business. A very quiet manager, Robbie was tactically astute, and he left most of the coaching to Eddie Newton, his assistant. Eddie's training sessions were very structured, with a lot of shape work as we adapted to the attractive style of play that they wanted us to adopt.

I was looking forward to getting my career back on track. I didn't know any of the MK Dons players, but I was comfortable building relationships by then and my new team-mates were excited to have a Championship player joining them.

The squad was full of great lads, on and off the pitch. Kevin Gallen, who'd had a brilliant career at QPR, had bags of experience up front, and the younger strikers learned a lot from him. Sam Baldock was the first player to progress from the youth academy and become a regular starter. He scored some vital goals for us over the years. Aaron Wilbraham was a really bubbly guy who brought everyone together. Aaron was a prolific striker who spent six years with the Dons and is currently second on the club's list of all-time goalscorers.

I can't talk about my team-mates without mentioning Dean Lewington – Mr MK Dons. Dean joined the Dons from Wimbledon back in 2004 and, at the time of writing, he's still there. In fact, I don't think he'll ever leave! Lewy, a strong left-back, was the club captain and I didn't realise how good he was until that first day of training. We played out from the back, and he was crucial to our system because he could spot a pass through the lines. A lot of our attacks were started by Lewy. Alongside Dean at the back was Sean O'Hanlon, another very good defender.

Looking around the dressing room after my first day of training, promotion should definitely have been the aim. There was nothing for us to be fearful of. There was a real opportunity to try to achieve a second successive promotion.

It certainly wasn't going to be easy because there were some big clubs in the division – including Leicester City and Leeds United, two teams with recent Premier League history, whereas we were a brand-new club. We were the underdogs going into most games, but that was a good thing as it took the pressure off. It can weigh quite heavily when you're playing for a bigger club in a lower division than the supporters are used to, and it doesn't take much for the fans to become restless and for the pressure to increase. From my perspective, it didn't matter whether we were playing Leeds United or Hereford United, we were all League One players, regardless of the history of our respective clubs.

I made my debut on 4 October 2008 in a 4-0 win away at Millwall. I played wide left, got an assist and thought I played quite well. The New Den isn't an easy place to go, and Millwall were doing okay, so it was a great result. On the journey back to Milton Keynes, I was shocked when the coach stopped off at a McDonald's and someone ran out to get us some Big Macs as our post-match meal!

Three days later I made my home debut against Bournemouth in the Football League Trophy. We lost 1-0, but no one was too disappointed because the league was our priority. I played a more central role, lining up against Darren Anderton, who I'd watched play for Spurs and England when I was a kid.

I loved playing at Stadium MK. The facilities were fantastic, and the fans took to me immediately. It was great for my family too. The boys were getting older and were beginning to get into football, so Hayley regularly brought them to watch me play.

I got off the mark for my new club in my fourth game, scoring an equaliser towards the end of the match against Crewe. It wasn't a spectacular goal, just a tap-in, but the supporters went wild and started to sing my name. I wouldn't say that League One was easy, but I was having more of an effect on games and felt confident that I was capable of making a difference.

A week or so later, I scored a brace away at Leyton Orient. By now I was playing in the No.10 role and managed to find some fantastic pockets of space. That first half was probably the best half of football I've ever played. I combined with Peter Leven, a clever player who always seemed to know where I wanted it, to give us the lead. My second was the most outrageous backheel you've ever seen. I still can't believe it actually went in. But it did and it proved to be the winner.

So far, so good. I was earning rave reviews, but with Norwich struggling I was a little worried that they might recall me. My hope was to make the move to MK Dons a permanent one. I felt proud that I'd engineered a transfer to a club playing the type of football I wanted to play. But I was also conscious that I'd enjoyed good starts with other clubs before my form tailed off. I wanted to maintain some consistency. But just as everything was going well, I inevitably got injured.

In the middle of November, we were playing a small-sided game in training. A legacy from my time at Manchester United was that I always trained how I played. I wasn't hugely competitive, but I'd run my socks off doing everything I could to win. Even though I was a skinny winger, I loved a tackle and I often upset my team-mates when running around like a madman, smashing people. On this occasion I went in for a tackle with Dean Lewington and I ended up with his full weight on my knee. I immediately knew that I'd done some damage, but I didn't know the full extent. I limped off the pitch and painfully drove back to Stadium MK, which is where we got changed. The physio iced my knee and then I took a shower, thinking that I'd be alright to travel up to Hartlepool, our next opponents, the following day. I stupidly tried to squat down, and my knee gave way. I could barely stand, and realised then that the injury was quite serious.

I was still technically a Norwich player, so I travelled to Norwich General Hospital the following day for a scan. By now my knee had swollen to the size of a football, so Hayley had to drive. Afterwards, to try to kill some time while the physios analysed the scan, we went to Great Yarmouth and sat on the seafront, eating fish and chips, watching the waves.

An hour or so later, I was in the physio's office, braced for the bad news. 'You've ruptured your medial ligament,' the physio told me. 'That's the one on the inside of your knee. There are still some fibres holding it together, which means we don't need to operate, so it's good news.'

I was pleased that it wasn't my cruciate ligament, but I knew I'd be out for a minimum of eight weeks, possibly even 16. I did the calculations in my head and knew that, either way, my loan spell would be over before I could play again.

I spent the next ten days feeling sorry for myself and then I began the arduous road to recovery. It was a strange situation because I did my rehab with Norwich, even though I was desperate to leave them.

In the middle of December, Robbie told me that he still wanted to sign me, which was a huge relief. I went to London with the MK Dons physios for a scan so they could assess a likely return date. The results looked good, and the two clubs began negotiating a permanent deal for me.

By now, Glenn Roeder had been sacked, as Norwich were in a relegation battle. Bryan Gunn, an absolute legend, stepped in as interim manager, but there was never any talk of me staying with the Canaries. Norwich is a fantastic club, with great people. It just wasn't the right club for me.

On 1 January 2009, I signed a three-year contract with MK Dons on £3,300 a week, £700 less than I was earning at Norwich. I didn't hesitate to take a pay cut. Money was never a driver for me. I was quite a boring fellow with inexpensive tastes, so I was in a fortunate position that had allowed me to save and invest a decent chunk.

At the beginning of my career, I'd started banking with the prestigious Coutts, but it never really worked out. Their clients included the royal family and billionaires, and they weren't too bothered about a young footballer, so I went elsewhere.

I was never really a risk-taker, although I did, like a lot of footballers, invest in the infamous film schemes that were sold as a tax shelter. The idea was that you could invest money in a film and claim your tax back. It was a no-brainer. Or so we thought. HMRC eventually changed the rules and investors had to repay their tax. Some of the big hitters had put millions in and got stung hard. I managed to get out before the loophole was closed and, although I didn't make a penny, I didn't lose anything.

So, my wages didn't really matter. My priority was finding somewhere I could be happy, and I felt that place was MK Dons. The lads had played brilliantly while I'd been injured. We were exceeding expectations and very much in the hunt for an automatic promotion spot.

I made my long-awaited return to action on 20 January 2009 against promotion rivals Peterborough United. As a Cambridge United fan, I can't stand Peterborough. I still had some stiffness in my knee, but I didn't tell the physio because I was so keen to play. I came on as a second-half substitute in a tight game that finished 0-0. It was a decent point away from home.

I was back in the starting line-up a week later in our home match against Leyton Orient and I gave us an early lead in a game we were expected to win. Orient went 2-1 in front and our young striker Sam Baldock missed a last-minute penalty that would have given us an equaliser.

It was a disappointing result, but we put it behind us and got back to winning ways in the following game against Cheltenham Town. It was goals galore, with Cheltenham's Danny Spencer and our Aaron Wilbraham both bagging hat-tricks in our 5-3 victory. Out of the eight goals, the pick of the bunch was scored by Jemal Johnson. It was one of the best goals I've ever seen. He picked up the ball in his own area, ran past several defenders, before smashing the ball into the top corner. JJ was such a talented player, but he didn't have the best attitude, and that probably prevented him from playing at a higher level.

We followed that victory up with wins over Stockport and Hartlepool, but then we only won one of the next nine games. Although we only lost twice, we had six draws, which wasn't good enough. That's ultimately what cost us an automatic promotion spot. If we'd turned just one of those draws into a win, we'd have gone up in second place. But it's all ifs, buts and maybes.

Everyone was pulling in the same direction and, when we realised that we'd be entering the play-off lottery, we had to get our heads in the right place. I'd experienced both sides of the emotional rollercoaster that's the play-offs; at Reading we fell short in the semi-final; at West Ham we won promotion. I was hoping my experience would help the team but, unfortunately, I suffered yet another injury.

Just before the penultimate game of the season, away at Northampton, someone stood on my foot in training and my little toe was in agony. I went for an X-ray and discovered that it was broken. I lost my head, thinking that I was going to miss the play-offs. I was struggling to walk and was in no condition to train. It was one of the most painful injuries I've ever had. The only way that I could play was to have a pain-killing injection before each game, but that was easier said than done.

The doctor had to put a needle into my little toe and, because there was no meat or flesh there, it was the most excruciating thing I've ever felt. I always tell Hayley that it was 100 per cent more painful than childbirth, and I stand by that. It was crazy, because within seconds the pain had subsided and my toe was completely numb, which allowed me to play. After the game, when the injection had worn off, my toe would start throbbing and I'd struggle to walk. If it had happened earlier in the season, I'd have rested it until it was fully recovered, but there was no way I wasn't going to be involved in the play-offs.

We beat Hereford United 1-0 on the last game of the season. Edgar Street is a strange stadium that looks different to the other grounds I've played at. The stands are very close to the pitch, and you can hear everything the crowd say. At one stage, the ball went out of play, and I ran after it to take the throw-in. A bloke on the lower tier shouted, 'You're shit, Chadwick.' Then I heard a voice coming from the second tier saying, 'And you're bald too!' I still had a bit of hair, but I have to admit that it was beginning to thin. I looked up and chuckled when I saw that my heckler was a little old lady who must have been in her 70s.

We finished the season in third place on 87 points. If we'd achieved that points haul the season before or after, we'd have gone up automatically, but it wasn't to be. Peterborough (it had to be them, didn't it?) finished one point ahead of us.

Scunthorpe were our opponents in the two-legged play-off semi-final. The first leg, at Glanford Park, finished 1-1 and we were confident that we had enough to get a win back at our place. Unfortunately, we just couldn't find a breakthrough and the match finished 0-0. There wasn't an away-goals rule, so the game went to a penalty shoot-out. My injection was starting to wear off by then, so our fitness coach spoke to the fourth official and I was taken off the list. To be honest, I'd have taken one, because the adrenaline would have masked the pain, but with my record of taking penalties I doubt it would have changed the outcome. We lost 7-6 in the shoot-out. It was heartbreaking.

The lads were devastated to miss out on a trip to Wembley and, more importantly, the chance of promotion. But what was even more disappointing was that we lost our manager. Roberto Di Matteo joined Premier League club West Brom and later went on to win the Champions League with Chelsea. I was gutted because he'd signed me and put his trust in me when I was injured. When a manager leaves a club, there's always uncertainty among the squad as you wonder whether you'll feature in the new man's plans.

Some of the lads went away to Las Vegas for the summer, but I stayed at home with my family, resting my toe and working on my fitness. By the time pre-season came around I was in good physical condition. We went to Albufeira, in Portugal, for our pre-season training camp. It was a place that Robbie and his coaching staff had booked and, as we didn't have a manager, it was a bit of a free-for-all. Paul Mitchell, a former MK Dons player who's now doing incredible things in the player recruitment world, and our youth coach, Mike Dove, were running things.

I was always grumpy when I was away from home and there didn't seem to be any authority or discipline on the trip. It felt like we were wasting our time. We'd start each day with a run, then do some ball work, before finishing with a game. As the week progressed, my grumpiness intensified and I took it out on Mike, who was often the referee. Finally, on the last day, Mike had enough and told me to fuck off. I don't blame him, although I'm surprised that he didn't say it earlier!

We managed to have one night out, but it was difficult because the chairman's son, Bobby Winkelman, who worked in the recruitment team, was in Portugal with us. We had to climb over the hotel walls when we wanted to venture out. When we came back worse for wear at 4am, we had to pull Danny Swailes up and over the wall. Danny was coming back from a snapped Achilles tendon, and I remember panicking that I was going to drop him. I thought we'd avoided detection, but Bobby had texted Aaron asking him why I was climbing over a wall in the early hours of the morning! It was a memorable trip, but probably not the best preparation for the new season.

Within days of returning to England, we were introduced to our new manager. Or should I say *former* manager?

Chapter 23

Smashing the Guvnor

I WAS over the moon when I heard that Paul Ince was to be our new manager. As a Manchester United fan, I loved Ince as a player, with his heart-on-the-sleeve performances. I'd had the privilege of playing against him and his assistant Alex Rae numerous times and had always enjoyed the battles.

During Ince's previous spell as MK Dons boss, they'd been crowned champions of League Two and he also won the club's first piece of silverware, the Johnstone's Paint Trophy. Following that successful season, Ince became manager of Blackburn Rovers, but his spell at Ewood Park lasted just six months.

The plan was for us to challenge for promotion again, but it can be difficult to maintain momentum when there's a change at the top. Incey was a different type of manager to Di Matteo. Paul was very vocal and a motivator, like he had been as a player. His philosophy was to outwork and outfight our opponents, whereas Robbie had been more tactical. I'm not sure everyone bought into Incey's style. If he liked you, he liked you, but if he didn't, you got left behind.

The one similarity between the managers was that they both left the coaching to their coaches. In addition to Alex Rae,

Incey brought with him in a young coach called Karl Robinson. More about him later.

Paul was still a fantastic player – head and shoulders above the rest of us in training – even though he was in his 40s and long retired. At times he became frustrated because the lads weren't at his level, and he couldn't understand that they couldn't do what he could. We played little tournaments at the end of his first training session and Paul joined in. I was in a team playing against him. Incey chopped past one player, and I came out of nowhere and went straight through him. Absolutely ruined him. He lay crumpled in a heap holding his ankle, and I thought, *Oh shit. What have I done?*

I went over to apologise, terrified that I'd injured my new boss. Paul turned over with a massive grin on his face and said, 'I fucking love that.' That's how we'd trained at United and that's how he wanted us to train at MK Dons. You train how you play. On Fridays, typically the day before a game, we'd finish training with a game that was dubbed Death Ball. Alex Rae was on one team, Paul on the other, and they'd go around flying into tackles and smashing people. Some of the lads worried that they'd pick up an injury, but I loved it.

There were several new arrivals by the time the 2009/10 season began. Paul signed mainly British and Irish lads who had experience of the lower leagues of English football. Jabo Ibehre was a lovely fellow. A big strong striker, he'd caused us problems when he'd played against us for Walsall the previous season. Jermaine Easter was another good attacker who came in and scored some important goals. Richie Partridge was an Irish lad who'd begun his career at Liverpool. We were a similar age and had played against each other several times. Richie was an incredibly gifted winger, but he'd suffered some serious injuries that hampered his career. When his playing days were over, he rejoined his former club Liverpool as a physio. Sol Davis, a left-back, came in from Luton Town. Big character, aggressive, he was the epitome of a Paul Ince player.

Later on in the season we signed Nigel Quashie, a vastly experienced player, who'd spent the bulk of his career at the top level. His impressive car collection showed that he'd played in the Premier League. His motors were very different to the ones the other lads were driving, that's for sure! He was a great player and did well for us during his short spell.

Another notable signing was a young, flying winger called Andros Townsend, who came in on a two-month loan from Spurs. We'd played against him when he'd been on loan at Leyton Orient, and he was outstanding. Andros excited fans with his positive play. He'd get the ball and run with it, beating three or four players. You could tell that he was going to go right to the top.

Our season began with two 0-0 draws, against Hartlepool and Swindon. It was a bit of an anticlimax because, if you're going for promotion, they're the kind of games you should be winning. Our form picked up and we won five of our next six games, including a brilliant 2-1 victory against Norwich City live on Sky. My performance was decent, but no more than that.

We then lost six league games in a row, including a 5-1 defeat at Charlton, and a 4-3 home defeat against Carlisle where I scored a brace and should really have got a hat-trick. We were underperforming and the fans became restless.

We struggled for consistency for the rest of the campaign and there were few highlights. The main one was our performances in the Johnstone's Paint Trophy. We saw off Dagenham and Redbridge, Southend United, Northampton Town and Hereford United (the old lady who'd reminded me of my receding hairline didn't seem to be there that day!) to reach the area final, where we faced Southampton. The Saints were an incredibly strong side, with Jose Fonte, Morgan Schneiderlin, Rickie Lambert, Adam Lallana and Michail Antonio in their line-up. The prospect of a place at Wembley was enticing, but unfortunately Southampton were much better than us over the two legs and we lost 4-1 on aggregate.

I bumped into Southampton's manager, Alan Pardew, after the game. We exchanged pleasantries and had a nice little catch-up, but he didn't explain why he'd sold me five years earlier!

We played the Saints again, at Stadium MK in March 2010 and once again they were too strong for us. Rickie Lambert scored a hat-trick; one of them was an absolute worldy. As is custom, with around ten minutes remaining on the clock, the stadium announcer named the man of the match: 'Today's man of the match is Luke Chadwick.' The announcer couldn't have picked a worse time as Lambert had just stuck one in the top corner from 30 yards. A loud 'boo' rang out from the away fans who, quite rightly, felt their hat-trick hero should have won it. I felt awkward, but they always give the man-of-the-match award to a member of the home team.

I was named man of the match for most of our games that season. It became a running joke with the lads that I'd win yet another bottle of champagne. Maybe the sponsors liked me because the man of the match had to go into the lounge after the game and do a little speech, which, of course, I was never too keen on. After the game I just wanted to get straight in the motor and head home.

I hadn't been able to drive at all during the first part of the season, though, because I'd lost my licence. I'd accumulated too many points during all those hours spent commuting, and received a letter summoning me to Bedford Court. I spoke to Incey and told him it would be a nightmare for me to get to and from training if I couldn't drive. He assured me that it wouldn't be a problem because he knew a solicitor who could sort it out. *Happy days*, I thought.

I phoned the solicitor to explain the situation, and he told me that I'd be alright. When I arrived at the court for my hearing, I met my legal counsel for the first time. 'Don't worry about a thing. You won't have to do anything. You won't have to say anything. Just sit there and I'll take care of this,' he said. Within about ten seconds, one of the magistrates asked me to approach the stand to answer the charge. I turned to my solicitor for guidance, but he was staring at the floor. He didn't say a single word during the hearing. Three minutes later, I was handed a six-month driving ban. The expensive lawyer closed his briefcase and walked out of the court, and we never spoke again!

It was a challenging six months, particularly for Hayley, who often drove me to training. One of Paul's coaches gave me a lift home when it was cold and wet, but when the weather was nice he went for a round of golf after training, and I was left stranded. The kit man was the next to act as my chauffeur. I'm sure it was the last thing he wanted to be doing. It was a long six months, but I certainly learned my lesson.

When my ban was lifted, I ditched my Audi A6 and bought a Smart car. I've wasted so much money on flash cars over the years – all purchased out of ego – but the Smart was one of the best cars I've ever driven. Very difficult to speed, very easy to park. I got a bit of banter from the lads, but I was never the coolest guy in the world and the Smart car suited me down to the ground.

A week after the Southampton game, we travelled to Gillingham for a league match. The day began with the team coach breaking down, so we had to drive our own cars to Gillingham's Priestfield Stadium. Things didn't get any better.

During the pre-match meal, my phone was going crazy. I read the first text message, from my former team-mate Lee Croft:

Oh my God. What's your missus going to say about that?

I had no idea what he was talking about, so I read some of the others. There was a television programme on Sky on Saturday mornings called *Soccer AM*. Each week they featured a Soccerette, an attractive girl wearing a football shirt. On this occasion the Soccerette told the presenters that I'd chatted her up in the players' lounge after a game. Everyone was buzzing off me, but it was complete rubbish because I always went straight home after a match. I didn't get into any trouble with Hayley because she knew that I was one of the most antisocial people around and never went into the lounges.

I was pissed off when we took to the pitch but felt a little better when we took a 2-1 lead. Gillingham went down to ten men and came back to equalise. Jermaine Easter had a chance to win the game for us late on but missed a sitter and it finished 2-2. The gaffer had the right hump. In the dressing room, he had a go at Jermaine. He was relentless, getting right in his face. 'My daughter could have scored that,' he said several times.

Eventually Jermaine, who was quite a feisty lad, snapped. 'Well, get her in then. Pick her in the line-up.'

Incey lost it. 'Right, fuck off, you lot,' he shouted. We had to leave the dressing room and stand in the corridor, still wearing our dirty kit, while the gaffer had a shower and got changed.

Dressing room rows are a part of the game, but they're usually quickly forgotten about. At the training ground the following Monday, the kit man had hung a kid's-sized shirt with 'Ince 8' on Jermaine's peg!

We didn't win any of our final 11 games and, on 16 April 2010, Paul Ince announced that he'd be leaving the club at the end of the season, blaming budget cuts. To be fair, the squad was pretty thin on the ground. We were so short of players that our 40-year-old assistant manager Alex Rae, who'd retired almost six years earlier, dusted down his boots and made four appearances for us during the latter part of the season.

We finished in a disappointing 12th place, 20 points adrift of the play-offs. On a personal level, I made 47 appearances in all competitions – the most I'd ever played in a season. After my injury hell at Norwich, I'd worked harder than ever before and was in the shape of my life. I'd even taken up yoga, which helped with my flexibility, and I'm sure prevented injuries.

I was also delighted to be named MK Dons player of the season by both the fans and my team-mates. It was nice to be recognised individually, but I felt a little awkward having to collect the trophies, one of which was huge!

My performances had been noticed by people outside the club, and a couple of the lads told me that their agents had been asking about me. I didn't have an agent at the time, but I told the lads I wasn't interested in speaking to anyone. I was settled at the club, the kids were happy in their schools and I had no interest in leaving. I wanted to stay at MK Dons as long as they wanted me.

I liked playing for Paul and was sad to see him go, but that's football. I had to move on and throw my support behind the new gaffer. Incey's replacement was our coach, Karl Robinson, who at 29 years of age became the youngest manager in the Football League. Robinson's appointment was seen as a gamble by many outside the club, but he proved them wrong and went on to become one of MK Dons' greatest-ever managers.

Chapter 24

Here's to You, Mr Robinson

KARL MAY have been seen as an unknown by the supporters, but within the game he was a highly regarded progressive coach. Exactly what our visionary chairman, Pete Winkelman, was looking for.

In contrast to his high-profile predecessors, Roberto Di Matteo and Paul Ince, Karl had never been a professional footballer. As a teenager, he'd played for Liverpool's famed academy until injury prematurely ended his promising career before it had even begun. Robinson joined Liverpool's academy as a coach and combined his coaching duties with a non-league playing career, before becoming a full-time coach at MK Dons under Martin Allen in 2006. Karl had a spell as coach at Blackburn and then followed Paul Ince back to the Dons in 2010.

Robinson was a good talker with big plans and a strong focus on developing youth. He didn't need a big budget, which I'm sure was music to the chairman's ears! He had his own philosophy of how the game should be played: playing out from the back, sharp movements, different patterns. He wanted us to play through the thirds, no long balls, and give the fans really good, entertaining football to watch.

In his coaching role, Karl had acted as the bridge between the players and the manager, and we'd seen him as one of the lads. He wanted to get the senior players on board so, just after his appointment, he held a meeting with Sean O'Hanlon, Aaron Wilbraham, Dean Lewington and me to outline his vision. I was really impressed with his plans and was more than happy to support him.

John Gorman, the former England assistant manager, came in to be Karl's number two. That was an incredible appointment. John is up there with the best people I've ever met. Obviously, he had a wealth of experience, but he was also a lovely guy.

Damien Doyle was brought in to be our strength and conditioning coach. Damo was tasked with whipping us into shape during our pre-season training camp in a picturesque training facility on the coast of Ireland. Every session felt structured and organised, and we all felt fully prepared by the time the 2010/11 season began.

There were some new arrivals on the playing side as Karl brought in players capable of playing his expansive brand of football. Lewis Guy, a midfielder who'd played really well against us for Oldham the previous season, was the first arrival. Next in was Champions League winner Didi Hamann. Didi openly admitted that his legs weren't what they once were and he didn't train every day, but he did a fantastic job holding the middle of the pitch. His presence had a huge impact on the younger players, who learned a lot just by watching him every day in training. Mind you, he didn't lead the healthiest of lifestyles off the pitch. He pulled his hamstring early doors during one match. When I walked into the dressing room at half-time, he was sitting on the treatment table icing his leg, smoking a cigarette! You couldn't really argue with him, though, after the career he had.

Karl liked to surround himself with experienced people who'd achieved a lot in the game, and Didi certainly fell into that category. There were times when Robbie Fowler and David Thompson, Karl's mates from his Liverpool days, would come in and train with us. Arsenal legend Ian Wright was with us quite a bit too. It gave the lads a real buzz to be around those guys, hear their stories and receive their feedback. It was all good stuff and helped to increase the club's profile.

Continuing with the Liverpool connection, one of Karl's most important signings was goalkeeper David Martin. David was really comfortable with the ball at his feet. He'd pass through the lines rather than put the ball down and smash it up the pitch like most other keepers in those days.

Our season began on 7 August 2010 at the Bescot Stadium. A 2-1 victory over Walsall was the perfect start to life under Karl. It was a sign of things to come that the first goal under his leadership was scored by Sam Baldock, a product of the youth academy. Sam had made his debut under Danny Wilson back in 2005 and had been mainly used as a rotation player under Di Matteo and Ince. But Karl decided that Sam would be his main striker. He excelled and went on to have a fantastic campaign.

After losing to Carlisle, we beat Premier League Blackpool 4-3 in the League Cup. A great result, and an important one in terms of confidence. To beat a side two divisions higher than us gave us and the coaches the belief in our new style of play. Unfortunately, we went out of the cup in the next round, losing 3-1 to Birmingham, another Premier League side. We gave a good account of ourselves, but we weren't quite strong enough.

After wins over Swindon and Hartlepool, we travelled to the south coast to take on promotion favourites Brighton, managed by Gus Poyet. We stayed overnight in the Royal Hotel, a huge white building on the seafront. Hampshire cricket club were staying there too. I got in a lift with the Australian legend Shane Warne, which was very surreal. Brighton played an attractive passing game and I'm sure it was a great match for those watching. The Seagulls, with Glenn Murray and Ashley Barnes up front, edged it slightly on the day, beating us 2-1.

We picked ourselves up to beat Southampton 2-0 at home in our next match. The Saints were a very strong side and lined up with Alex Oxlade-Chamberlain, who was in his breakthrough season, but we played really well and deserved the three points.

The season had started well, which wasn't surprising to us. The way we played was different to most of the other sides in the division; we'd often have possession for long periods, and opponents found it difficult to play against us. Our starting 11 was as good as anyone's, but we didn't have the strength in depth that the bigger clubs with larger budgets had.

After a great start, we then embarked on a poor run that included defeat away at Peterborough. I missed a one-on-one, putting the ball over the bar when I should have scored. During my time at MK Dons, we enjoyed some great battles against the Posh. The games were always evenly contested, but they tended to get the better of us in the important ones.

We then struggled for consistency, winning one, losing the next. Karl made it clear that he was sticking to his principles and, despite the results, we were going to keep playing the way he wanted us to. It was a long-term project. The supporters could see what we were trying to do and remained patient.

At the end of October, we lost 4-2 to Tranmere. Their young winger Dale Jennings tore us apart; we couldn't deal with his pace. Didi Hamann was so impressed with Jennings's performance that he recommended him to his former club – Bayern Munich. After a short spell with the German champions, Dale returned to English football, and later made a handful of appearances for MK Dons.

A few days after the Tranmere game, we played Yeovil at home. With just two wins from our last eight games, we desperately needed a victory to kick-start our season. With three minutes remaining on the clock, the score was tied at 2-2. I received the ball and ran into the Yeovil penalty area. I knocked the ball past the advancing defender, but overhit it and the ball was running out of play. To this day I don't know why I did what I did next. There was no contact from the defender but I went down anyway. It was instinctive. It was a dive. To my absolute shock, the referee blew his whistle and pointed to the spot. Peter Leven scored the penalty and we won 3-2.

After the game, Yeovil's manager and players were giving me a load of stick, and rightly so. I couldn't defend myself, because I'd cheated, so I retreated to the sanctuary of our dressing room as quickly as I could. The lads were all celebrating the much-needed victory, but I felt incredibly guilty at what I'd done. That was the only time in my career that I've ever dived. Yeovil got their own back a couple of months later, beating us 1-0 at their place. Karma, I guess.

Three weeks after diving for the first time, I experienced another first – an own goal! Sheffield Wednesday were on fire when they visited Stadium MK on 20 November. Darren Potter, who later played for us, orchestrated the game in the middle of the park, and Neil Mellor helped himself to three of Wednesday's four goals. I, of course, scored their fourth.

It was a strange feeling, scoring an own goal, although there wasn't really a lot I could have done about it. The ball hit my leg and wrong-footed our keeper, so it wasn't a howler, but I still felt that I'd let everyone down. It was made worse because the game was shown live on Sky Sports.

After the Wednesday game I found myself on the bench as Karl opted for Lewis Guy in the No.10 role. I was disappointed, obviously, but the manager was right. I hadn't played particularly well for the last few weeks. I got my head down, did well when I came off the bench and soon found myself back in the starting line-up.

In January 2011, we sold Jermaine Easter and Aaron Wilbraham. Jermaine had scored 20 goals in his first season at the club, but struggled to get into the side when Karl came in. He joined Crystal Palace. Aaron had been an excellent player for MK Dons. A great target man, strong in the air and good at holding the ball up, but he wasn't as integral to the side under Karl as he had been when Ince and Di Matteo had been in charge. Aaron moved to Norwich City, which was a good move for him.

The emergence of Daniel Powell was one of the reasons why Karl was able to let Aaron leave. Powelly, another product of our youth academy, was a powerful boy, naturally athletic and lightning fast. He wasn't always the easiest on the eye, but he could beat players and made some fantastic runs in behind the defence. Powelly chipped in with a decent number of goals too.

After losing to Plymouth on 18 January, everything clicked and we went on a fantastic run, losing just one of 13 games. One of those was against Leyton Orient, who had a certain Harry Kane in attack. I could see that Kane was a talented player, but I honestly didn't think he'd go on to achieve the incredible things he has. He's unique in the way that he leads the line, and he had a different route to the top than many others. He had several loan spells at clubs outside the Premier League. It can be difficult for young strikers playing in those physical leagues when you've got a big centre-half going through you, but Kane seemed to take it all in his stride.

Another memorable game during that run was a 1-0 victory over Brighton, who went on to become champions. Karl was really into analysis, and he developed some tactics to stop the Seagulls. Brighton had a holding midfielder called Liam Bridcutt, and everything seemed to go through him. Gordon Greer was their centre-back and he was the link between defence and midfield. I played in the No.10 role, with Baldock as No.9, and our jobs were to press and win the ball high up the pitch. Karl's tactics were spot on, and we won 1-0 thanks to Daniel Powell's first-half strike.

Our good form helped propel us into the play-off spots but, more importantly than that, it validated the work that Karl, John and the coaching staff had been doing.

I was really enjoying my football and felt as fit as I'd ever felt. I still got a buzz every time I put the shirt on and stepped over the white line. I never got bored of the excitement I felt on a matchday. The one thing I didn't enjoy was having the TV cameras around. Karl loved the media attention and part of his remit was to increase the profile of the club. I had a little sulk one day when Sky Sports were allowed into the dressing room before a match. I was moaning, telling everyone that it wasn't the right way to prepare for a game. Another time, the *Soccer AM* cameras turned up at the training ground to film us doing the crossbar challenge, a popular segment of their show. I refused to take part because of the Soccerette incident the year before.

Towards the end of the season, I was dislocating my shoulder on a weekly basis again. I was a little concerned because I'd had surgery a couple of years earlier that was supposed to fix it, but it wasn't a massive problem because I knew how to manage it. In the lead-up to our last home game of the season, we trained inside, and my shoulder came out of its socket. I managed to pop it back in and wanted to carry on playing. Karl told me to go back to the changing room and rest and we had a bit of an argument. Even at that stage of my career, I still loved playing football. He ended up winning the argument.

We finished the season in fifth place and faced Peterborough in the play-off semi-final. Both league games had been close – we lost 2-1 at London Road and won 1-0 at Stadium MK – but we were confident that we had enough to beat them.

In the first leg, at Stadium MK, we came from behind to lead 3-1. With ten minutes to go, Stephen Gleeson conceded a penalty that should never have been given. To make it worse, the referee also sent him off. They scored from the spot, and we had to settle for a 3-2 win. We'd battered them in the second half and had so many chances to put the tie to bed, so there was a feeling of disappointment. In the last couple of minutes of the game, I blocked a free kick and walked down the tunnel with my shoulder hanging off its joint!

We were confident going into the second leg, but I'm sure Peterborough also felt they had a chance as there was only one goal in it. Unfortunately, they were the better team on the night and beat us 2-0 to secure their place in the final. The mood in the dressing room afterwards was like a funeral parlour. To lose in a semi-final is devastating. At least in a final you have additional revenue, and the fans have a day out. There were a fair few guys in our side who'd lost to Scunthorpe at the same stage two years earlier, and the feeling was the same.

On a personal note, I'd played 52 games in all competitions and also won the player-of-the-year award for the second year running. I may not have played the full 90 minutes in every match, but I was as fit as I'd ever been. The No.10 role, or a free role in the wide positions, was perfect for me at that stage of my career. My understanding of the game allowed me to get into good positions. The majority of our opponents lined up in a 4-4-2 formation and they often found it difficult to pick me up playing through the lines. I also played on the on the right or left as a wide man. Not in a traditional winger's role, though. Karl gave me the freedom to roam on my side of the pitch. I came inside quite often, which caused problems for the opponents as the full-back was forced to follow me inside or they had to use a deep-lying midfielder.

For the first time in my career, I'd found the elusive blend of fitness *and* form. I just hoped it would continue.

Chapter 25

Heartbreak Again

WE RETURNED to Ireland in July 2011 for our pre-season training camp, where Damo once again put us through our paces. It was intense, but we knew what to expect this time. I loved it. I was the fittest player in the squad, even though I'd entered my 30s. It gave me a real buzz to see my name at the top of the fitness stats.

It was a fairly quiet summer on the transfer front, with just a handful of major signings, as Karl was keen to keep the momentum that we'd built up the previous season. Dean Bowditch was the first arrival. Dean had been a striker at his previous clubs, but he played in a wider role for us and excelled in his new position.

The fans took to him from day one and he weighed in with more than his fair share of goals. Darren Potter came in from Sheffield Wednesday. It was obvious from his first training session that Potts was a really good player. He held the middle of the pitch and was able to make passes from seemingly impossible angles. Potter and Gleeson were the two holding midfielders and they combined well with me in the No.10 role. Angelo Balanta rejoined us on loan from QPR. Angelo was a gifted boy who played on the left. A free spirit in many ways and someone John Gorman knew very well.

With the disappointment of the previous season still in our minds, it was important to get off to a good start. And we did just that, winning five of our first six league games. We also beat Norwich City 4-0 at Carrow Road in the League Cup. Norwich were a Premier League side, so that was an excellent result. They lined up with one or two fringe players and played a diamond in the middle of the pitch. We took it apart, found loads of space and could have scored even more.

That was one of my best performances in an MK Dons shirt and I managed to score a brace against my old club. Hayley and Louis were in the away end, and it was nice to run over and celebrate my goals with them. I know that players don't celebrate goals against their former clubs these days, but I wasn't being disrespectful. I wasn't shushing the fans, nothing like that. I was sharing the moment with my family. I was somewhat of a footnote in Norwich's history and most of their fans probably didn't even know who I was anyway.

It was quite a big story for a League One club to beat a Premier League side by such a large margin. After the game, Karl told me that the Anglia news team wanted to come to my house to do an interview about me scoring against my former team. I politely declined as it wasn't something I was comfortable with. I never really liked the attention off the pitch.

We were brimming with confidence, but suffered a huge blow when we lost Sam Baldock. Sam had been our top scorer the previous season, which had led to some of the bigger clubs sniffing around. He'd been linked with various clubs over the summer and there was a reluctant acceptance that he'd be going.

Sam got a great move to West Ham United and helped them win promotion back to the Premier League in his first season.

Karl had already planned for life without Sam and had a ready-made replacement lined up – Charlie MacDonald. The former Brentford striker was small in stature, but very strong. He typified the style that Karl wanted to play, passing the ball into the box, rather than going direct. Charlie's debut came against Stevenage on 27 August 2011. We rode our luck a bit – I even cleared two off the line – before finally finding the breakthrough early in the second half. Steven Gleeson played a nice chippy pass over the top of the defence. I got on the end of it and ran towards the goalkeeper. I saw Charlie out of the corner of my eye and squared it to him to tap into the empty net for his debut goal. We won 1-0. That's one of my favourite assists because I couldn't have made it any easier for him.

Three days later, we played Brentford in the Football League Trophy. I scored my fifth goal of the season in a 3-3 draw, although we went out of the competition on penalties. Up until then my best-ever return had been six in a season, and I'd now scored five before the end of August. Surely I was going to smash that record? No. I didn't score again that season! When I look back on my career, I noticed that my goals all came in clusters, usually at the start of the season. I can't explain why.

September began with a 3-1 win away at Carlisle. It was such a long coach journey, but one of the lads noticed that we could get home a couple of hours earlier if we took the train back instead of the team bus. So, as soon as we got changed, a few of us ran to the train station and travelled by rail. I doubt Karl would have allowed us to have done that had we lost, so it's a good job we won.

Travelling is a big part of life as a professional footballer. We spend a lot of time on the road, and it can get a bit dull and monotonous. For the games against the Lancashire clubs, we'd travel up on the train and stay overnight at the Malmaison Hotel, near Piccadilly station. I always quite enjoyed that and looked forward to the games against teams like Bury, Rochdale and Oldham. We'd travel back by coach, which was fine for a Saturday afternoon kick-off, but not great when we played in the evening.

On Monday, 10 October 2011, we played Oldham live on Sky. We had a couple of injuries, so I lined up at right-back for the first time in my career. We lost 2-1 and Karl wasn't happy. He told us to report for training the next morning. We arrived back at Stadium MK around 2am and then I had to drive home. I was fuming as I drove along the A428 because I knew I'd be doing the reverse journey a few hours later. Every single traffic light was red, which did nothing to improve my mood.

When I was only 20 minutes away from home, my car began to shake and then the engine conked out. I phoned the RAC and stood waiting in the cold by the side of the road for what felt like hours. Eventually, a bright orange van pulled up behind my car and the mechanic opened the bonnet to identify the problem. It turned out to be something quite simple – I'd run out of petrol! I hadn't noticed the light on the dashboard because I was so tired. I managed about an hour's sleep before my alarm woke me up, telling me that it was time to drive back to Milton Keynes. I arrived late and incurred a fine, so I was a massive grump for the next few days.

Injuries had mounted and we were going through a bad patch that saw us drop out of the automatic promotion places. When we travelled to Bramall Lane to take on promotion favourites Sheffield United at the end of October we were struggling. That was another night match and during the warm-up the floodlights went out and we trained in the dark. When I was a kid, even though I absolutely loved playing football, I always got a buzz when a game was called off. I have no idea why, but when the lights went out that night, I felt a little bit of excitement that we wouldn't be able to play.

The lights were fixed, and the game took place, although maybe it would have been best if it had been postponed because we lost 2-1 and slipped further down the table. To be fair, the Blades were a very good side with Matt Phillips up front and Harry Maguire in defence. Harry was a huge presence at the back. He was calm and carried an air of authority that's rare for such a young defender. Fast-forward a few years and he was the captain of Manchester United and a mainstay of the England squad. After the Sheffield United defeat, we only lost one of our next ten games, and promotion was once again in our grasp.

In January 2012, Alan Smith joined us on loan from Newcastle. Alan was a good player, with a high profile, and his experience proved invaluable for the younger players. I'd played with Alan for the England Under-18s and 21s, and we were also together briefly at Manchester United. He became a big part of the squad, even though he didn't start every game. Alan was quiet, but a leader, and he got on well with everyone. He was a positive role model; he trained properly and was 100 per cent committed. He was quite happy to ruffle a few feathers on the pitch with his all-action displays.

Despite Alan's arrival, we suffered another little blip in January and February that meant that the automatic promotion spots were out of our reach. But we still had the play-offs to aim for.

In March, I felt some pain in my knee during the warm-up ahead of a game against Hartlepool. I managed to play most of the game, but it was agonising, and I knew something wasn't right. I went for a scan and discovered that I'd torn my meniscus, a knee ligament. The surgeon's advice was for me to have an operation, but that would rule me out for four to six weeks and then I'd have to rehab. We were approaching a crucial part of the season – hopefully the play-offs – so the idea was to manage it and then have the surgery in the summer.

From then on, my season was stop–start. With the toe injury I'd suffered in my first season with the Dons, I'd been able to take an injection to numb the pain, but it wasn't advisable to inject my knee. I couldn't train at all. Instead, I spent my days in the treatment room with an ice pack on my knee. I could play, but it was painful and took a long time to recover. It was a case of picking and choosing which games I could play, and that was frustrating.

We secured a play-off position with a few games to spare. On the last game of the season, at home to Walsall, I came on for the final 25 minutes. Unfortunately, my knee gave way and, with hindsight, I probably should have had the operation.

Straight after the game, we had a team night out at Sopwell House, St Albans. I was absolutely scrambling. I was struggling to walk up and down the stairs and I was worried that I wouldn't have any chance of playing in the play-offs. I met with Karl and the coaching staff, and the plan was for me to rest completely and hopefully be back in time for the final, assuming we could beat Huddersfield in the semi-final. That would be no mean feat as Huddersfield were the favourites. They'd recruited really well and, in Jordan Rhodes, had one of the most prolific strikers in the country. He scored 40 goals in all competitions that season, which is incredible.

I found it difficult not being involved in the first leg at Stadium MK. I was in the dressing room giving the lads some encouragement before the match, but as they stepped onto the pitch, I took my seat in the stand, feeling totally powerless as Rhodes and Jack Hunt helped Huddersfield to a 2-0 victory.

The defeat meant that the plan for me to rest went out the window. I hadn't trained at all since injuring my knee, but I took part in the session the day before the second leg. I did really well, and John Gorman told me that Karl was considering starting me. In the end I was named on the bench and came on for the last 20 minutes with the score level at 1-1. We needed another two goals to take the game to extra time.

Alan Smith put us 2-1 up on the night in injury time but, despite our best efforts, we couldn't add another. As the clock ticked down, I could see the Huddersfield fans gathering at the side of the pitch, ready to run on at full time. I edged myself towards the tunnel so I could make a sharp exit. When the ref blew the final whistle, I was first down the tunnel and went straight into the dressing room. Alan Smith got into a bit of a kerfuffle with some of the home fans, which was disappointing. I have no problem with supporters celebrating with their players, but it becomes a problem when they target the opposition. We'd just lost in the semi-final for the third time in four years and the last thing we wanted was for the home fans to be in our faces, rubbing it in.

There was a sombre mood on the coach ride back from Huddersfield and the lads got pretty well oiled. We were all devastated. I travelled to London the following morning – with a huge hangover – to have the operation on my knee. Everything went well and I spent the summer resting and recuperating, ready to go again.

Chapter 26

End of an Era

WE ONCE again returned to Ireland for our pre-season training camp ahead of the 2012/13 season. I spent the first few days with the physios as I was still recuperating, and they worked me incredibly hard. Damo displayed the GPS stats each morning and I was covering more ground than the lads who were doing the full training! I was trying to prove a point to the gaffer. *I'm ready to return to full training.*

There were some new faces on the trip. My old team-mate from Norwich Jon Otsemobor, a right-back, was one. He had incredible pace and power and I enjoyed linking up with him when I played on the right-hand side. Jon began his career at Liverpool and had worked with Karl before, as had Ryan Lowe, who joined us from Sheffield Wednesday. Defender Antony Kay was recruited from Huddersfield. Antony was a solid centre-back who went on to make over 100 appearances for the Dons.

Karl's final summer signing was midfielder Jimmy Bullard. Unfortunately, Jimmy was struggling with his knees, and he only played three times for us before being forced to retire. But he more than made up for that with the impact he had off the pitch. Jimmy was hilarious with his banter, and I saw him destroy lads on a regular basis. One evening we went out to a darts evening at Stadium MK. Most of the lads went along and it was a good night. Gary MacKenzie, a big, strong, Scottish centre-half, an absolute tank of a man, made the mistake of wearing a dodgy jumper. Jimmy started getting into him about it. He was absolutely rinsing him, it was relentless. Gary eventually caught a taxi home so he could change his top!

We were probably suffering with a play-off hangover as we had a mixed start to the season and struggled to get any kind of run going. One highlight was beating Blackburn Rovers in the League Cup. I scored both goals in a 2-1 win over the Championship club. I always seemed to do well when we played teams in the higher divisions. It wasn't about me raising my game, I always gave 100 per cent. I think the main reason was that I was closely marked by League One opponents, whereas the bigger teams ignored me and focused on playing their own game. That opened up more space and allowed me to have more of an impact on the game.

I got on the scoresheet again against Carlisle a few days later, helping us to a 2-1 win. After a win, a draw and a loss, we smashed Bury 4-1 at Gigg Lane. The brilliant Dean Bowditch helped himself to a hat-trick and I got the fourth. I always enjoyed playing against Bury. I'd played a lot of games for Manchester United's reserves at Gigg Lane, and the memories came flooding back every time I returned. David Healy had played alongside me in most of those reserve games, and he lined up for Bury against me that day. We reminisced after the game, which was nice.

The Bury goal took my tally for the season to four, and a month later I added two more, although it should really have been three. Despite my goalscoring prowess as a kid, I never scored a hat-trick in English football (I'd scored a hat-trick in my first season at Antwerp). I scored two on numerous occasions, but that third goal always seemed to elude me. The best chance I ever had was against Scunthorpe on 27 October 2012.

Going into the match, we'd been on a six-match winless run. We were desperate for a win. With 17 minutes on the clock, I tapped home from close range after their keeper made a mistake. By the half-hour mark I'd doubled our lead with a nice strike into the top corner. Alan Smith made it three in the second half and then Angelo Balanta was tripped in the box. The referee awarded a penalty. With three points already in the bag, Karl shouted over, telling me to take it. I collected the ball, placed it on the spot and ... I took a terrible penalty that their keeper saved quite comfortably. I think Karl regretted his decision afterwards! In my career I took two penalties and scored zero.

Towards the end of the game, I was substituted and, as I walked off the pitch, I received a rousing round of applause from both sets of supporters. It was a lovely gesture and something that sticks in my mind today.

After my disastrous spot kick, I was as surprised as anyone when Karl gave me additional responsibility for our next match – the captain's armband. Dean Lewington was our usual skipper, but we'd been drawn against Cambridge City in the FA Cup and the manager thought it would be a nice gesture for me to lead the team out when we went to my home city.

The tie was played at Milton Road, Cambridge, a pitch that held fond memories for me. I'd been spotted by Manchester United scouts when I played there for Cambridge Schools. I knew quite a few of City's players too, as I lived in the area. It would have been nice to have played against Cambridge United at the Abbey Stadium, but there's a little rivalry between United and MK Dons and I'm not sure how I'd have felt if I'd been booed by the Cambridge fans!

Despite dominating possession and hitting the woodwork, we were unable to find the breakthrough and Cambridge City held us to a 0-0 draw. The one highlight was that a 16-year-old by the name of Dele Alli made his debut as a second-half substitute. So, my claim to fame is that I was Dele's captain when he began his career!

Dele had trained with the first team when he was still a schoolboy and we all instantly recognised the immense talent that he possessed. We had several talented boys at that time, including Brendan Galloway and George Williams, but Dele was the pick of the bunch. He was fearless in the way that he trained and played. He was a free spirit who enjoyed playing football. He was so confident and thought nothing of knocking the ball through the legs of the senior players. In return, he'd get smashed. Every time he got clattered, he'd get straight back up – no moaning or crying – and try to do it again.

Dele's attitude was great. I was shocked when I watched the Spurs documentary on Amazon and I saw Jose Mourinho questioning his work ethic. I'd only ever known him to be hard-working and dedicated.

Five days after the draw with Cambridge, Ryan Lowe scored the only goal of the game against Leyton Orient. Our next match was against Sheffield United, who were top of the league. As part of our preparation for the big game, the club had arranged for us to spend some time at the luxurious health spa

Champneys in Tring. Unfortunately, relaxation wasn't on the agenda when we arrived at Champneys. As we walked to the cryochamber, I cast an envious glance towards the hydropool, steam rising from the inviting water.

Cryotherapy is supposed to be good for reducing inflammation and for muscle recovery. It's also bloody cold! Spending three minutes in temperatures of -150°C is not much fun! After a minute or so, my feet started to hurt. I looked down and noticed that the other lads were wearing Crocs or flip-flops, whereas I was barefoot. When I left the chamber, the member of staff looking after us looked at my bare feet and stared at me in disbelief. 'You need to have something on your feet inside the chamber or they'll burn,' she said. *You could have told me before*, I thought.

By the time I got home, I was in absolute agony. I couldn't put any weight on my feet because they'd been burnt to a crisp. I missed training for three days and the only way I could play against the Blades was by wearing boots that had been specially insulated with foam. It was the most bizarre injury I've ever had. We beat the league leaders 1-0, so it was all worth it.

A fortnight later, I scored two goals in a 5-1 win over Colchester. That took my tally up to eight goals for the season, which was my record haul as a pro. Making his debut for us that day was 19-year-old Patrick Bamford, who'd joined on loan from Chelsea. Bamford was different to the typical footballer; he was a very well-spoken, polite guy. He was also a very gifted player, physically strong, mature beyond his years and a great finisher. Patrick stayed with us until the end of the season and then returned the following year on another loan. He made a big impact during his time at MK Dons.

In the FA Cup we beat Cambridge City 6-1 in the replay (I missed the game through suspension), and our reward was a home tie against AFC Wimbledon. The media made a big deal out of it because it was the first time the clubs had ever met. There was quite a lot of animosity towards us from the Wimbledon fans, and the police were expecting some trouble. We had our pre-match meal in a hotel in the town centre, before being given a police escort to the stadium.

We were poor on the day. Steve Gleeson gave us the lead with a wonder goal on the stroke of half-time, but the visitors equalised midway through the second half. The game looked to be heading to a replay when Jon Otsemobor scored a crazy backheeled goal in the last minute that sparked wild scenes. Jon became a cult hero, and fans still refer to his goal as 'The Heel of God'.

Two weeks later, in December 2012, I injured my knee in training following a challenge with Daniel Powell, my roommate. The pain was so intense that I needed gas and air. I was convinced that I'd done my cruciate, which would have meant almost a year out, but fortunately a scan showed it was just a torn ligament that didn't require surgery. I was out for six weeks. My absence coincided with a dreadful run where we couldn't buy a win, and I was rushed back to the side a little earlier than planned. I only lasted a few games before I tore a hip muscle and was in and out of the team for the remainder of the season.

We'd spent most of the campaign skirting in and around the play-offs, but that poor run of form between December and March cost us and we finished in eighth position, four points behind the play-off places. It was a disappointing season.

Over the summer, I suffered with a couple of illnesses and didn't have the best pre-season. For the first time in my MK Dons career, I wasn't number one in the fitness stats. That crown now belonged to Deli Alli.

Karl brought in Ben Reeves on a free transfer from Southampton. Ben was a good player, who also played in the No.10 role. He was told that he'd be playing when I was out, but he came in and did really well.

After a poor pre-season, I had a bad game in the 2013/14 opener away at Shrewsbury. After the match I was called into Karl's office and told that I wasn't going to be starting the next couple of games. I was almost 33 and for the first time it dawned on me that maybe I was coming to the end of my playing career.

After a run of games where the best I could hope for was a cameo appearance, I found myself back in the starting line-up at the beginning of September 2013. I scored my first goal of the season against a Notts County side featuring a young Jack Grealish, and I remained a regular until November, when I picked up another injury that kept me out of action for ten weeks.

While watching the lads from the stands, I pondered my future. I loved MK Dons. I loved the people, the fans, the club, and I'm sure they'd have offered me a coaching role when I eventually hung up my boots. I wasn't ready for that, though. I was proud of what I'd achieved in my career, but there was one dream I was yet to fulfil – playing for my beloved Cambridge United. I'd wanted to join them when I was a kid but didn't get in following the farcical trial. The next time I seriously considered joining Cambridge was during my early days at United when I felt homesick. I thought about it again when I realised that my time at Old Trafford was coming to an end.

Towards the end of my season at West Ham United, when I was struggling for form, I pulled on my Cambridge shirt (Hayley got me the latest shirt every year for Christmas) and went into the back garden for a kickabout, trying to recapture the joy I'd experienced as a youngster.

And when I left Stoke and Norwich, I'd suggested Cambridge as a potential new club to my agent. Sadly, Cambridge had tumbled down the leagues after those glory days under John Beck, and it didn't make sense from a career or financial sense for me to drop down to the National League when I was considered a good Championship player.

But now, things were different. With Ben Reeves and Deli Alli seamlessly slotting into the MK Dons first team, I wasn't as important to the side as I had been previously. I was still an effective player, though, and I knew that if I was going to achieve my childhood goal, now was the time to do it.

On 14 January 2014, I returned to action against Wigan in the FA Cup. The Latics had shocked everyone when they won the famous trophy six months earlier. I opened the scoring with what turned out to be my final goal in an MK Dons shirt. It would have been brilliant to have scored the winning goal against the cup holders, but they outclassed us and came back to win 3-1.

Shortly after the Wigan game, I had a really open and honest conversation with Karl. I told him that I'd always dreamed of playing for Cambridge and I knew that my career was coming to an end, so now was the time. I wanted to go there while I could still have a positive impact and I wanted to help the club return to the Football League. Karl was quite taken aback but he respected what I said. He told me that he appreciated everything that I'd done for him and told me he'd do what he could to make my dream a reality. The only problem with my plan was that Cambridge hadn't actually expressed a desire to sign me, so I had to engineer the move.

A family friend named Jimmy Carter was an agent and he put me in touch with Jez George, Cambridge United's chief executive. Cambridge could only afford to pay £700 of my £3,300-a-week wages, but MK Dons agreed to pay the rest. I have a huge debt of gratitude to Karl and our chairman, Pete Winkelman, for helping me to achieve a lifelong ambition.

On 15 March 2014, I came on for the last half an hour of a 2-0 defeat to Peterborough. I didn't know it at the time, but that was the final time I'd play for MK Dons. I'm gutted that I signed off my Dons career with a loss against one of our biggest rivals. Everything was kept very quiet, and no one knew that I was leaving. My big regret is that I wasn't able to say a proper goodbye to the fans.

A few days later, Karl pulled me aside after training and said, 'The deal is done.' And that was it. I was going home.

Chapter 27

Coming Home

JUST AFTER my first meeting with Jez George where I floated the idea of joining my boyhood club, I travelled to Cambridge's training ground to meet with their manager, Richard Money. I arrived after training had finished, when the lads had gone home, so that no one would see me.

Jez wasn't at the training ground, so I went straight to Richard's office to introduce myself. He was in a meeting with the groundsman, Robbie Nightingale, who, coincidently, I'd played alongside for Cambridge Schools. Richard asked me where Jez was. When I replied that I didn't know, he asked me to wait outside. He didn't seem that excited at the prospect of signing me.

When Jez finally arrived, we went in to see the manager. Richard achieved great things at Cambridge, but he wasn't the most personable of characters and the conversation didn't flow smoothly. It was such a strange situation and I wonder whether Richard was questioning my motives. I had no intention of ever becoming a manager, but maybe he thought I had one eye on his job.

The frosty reception was not at all what I expected. I was a good League One player with Premier League and Champions

League experience, and I was offering myself to a National League club. I was expecting the red-carpet treatment. I couldn't have been further from the truth.

I'd thought about this moment so many times over the years, but it had always played out differently. I honestly thought that they'd be buzzing that someone who'd played at a higher level was coming in, but it wasn't like that at all. In my prima donna mind, I thought my arrival would have been like the king of Cambridge returning home after battle.

The National League is a very tough division to get out of. There are some fantastic clubs in the league and, with only one automatic promotion spot up for grabs, teams can get stuck there for years. Cambridge had fallen at the play-off stage twice during their nine-year exile from the Football League, and with Luton Town the runaway leaders, it looked like Cambridge would be in the play-offs again by the end of the 2014/15 season.

I was still a huge supporter of the club, and my motivation was to help the team to finally get over the line. I didn't have any illusions that it was going to be easy. I certainly didn't expect to be the best player in every game, but I knew that I was capable of making a difference in that division.

After my discussions with Jez and Richard, I returned to MK Dons while the two clubs sorted out the terms of my loan spell. On Tuesday, 18 March 2014, I'd just finished a double training session with MK Dons when Karl told me that the deal was done. I signed the papers at Stadium MK and then drove over to the Abbey Stadium to meet Richard. My new manager told me that I'd be making my debut against Welling United that evening!

I was kept out of the dressing room until the entire team had arrived and then I was introduced to the lads. It was so surreal. Obviously, I knew who they all were because I'd followed the club all my life. They were shocked – in a good way – that I'd signed.

My excitement was building with each passing second. It reached a crescendo when I saw the gold shirt with my name on the back hanging on a peg. During the latter part of my career, I liked playing in a tight-fitting shirt, but no such luck at Cambridge.

The deal had gone through so quickly that the kit man had to grab a shirt from the club shop and have them print my name and number on the back. It was extra large and I looked like a small child wearing his dad's shirt! Regardless of the size, when I pulled that jersey on the reality hit me – I was finally was going to play for Cambridge United.

I received a fantastic reception from the fans during the warm-up, which made the occasion feel even more special. Hayley and the boys were sitting in the stands, and that meant a lot. The memories came flooding back as I looked around the stadium: the Newmarket Road End where I'd cheered on my heroes, the touchline where I'd been the ball boy. I'm grateful for the career that I had, playing for some huge clubs in big games, but making my debut for Cambridge is one of the proudest moments of my career.

I was shattered after the first 20 minutes following the morning's double training session, but I played the entire 90 in a scrappy game that we won 2-1. I applauded the fans as I left the pitch, and they responded by singing my name. That was a real hairs-on-the-back-of-your-neck moment.

I immediately felt at home in the dressing room. They were a special group of people. Tight-knit, with everyone pulling in the same direction. There was a lot of quality within the squad too, and when you have that combination you can achieve anything. Luke Berry, another local lad, had progressed from the youth ranks to the first team and eventually made it to the Premier League with Luton Town. Luke was a brave, talented player. I'd watched Josh Coulson when I was at Norwich, and he was breaking into the Cambridge City development squad. He moved across to United and spent over a decade at the club. Josh was a brilliant person to have around. Midfielder Tom Champion brought the dressing room together.

The city was buzzing in the days following my debut, although it was nothing to do with my arrival. Cambridge had reached the final of the FA Trophy, which meant a trip to Wembley. I wasn't registered for the competition, but I'd bought tickets before I signed, so I was planning to cheer the lads on from the stands. However, during training the day before the final, I was struggling with my hips. We were playing Salisbury City a few days after the final and I wanted to be fit for that. I was shitting myself because I'd made this big song and dance about going to Cambridge, played one game and then got injured. I felt really low and decided to stay at home and rest.

So, Hayley and the boys travelled down to Wembley and watched my new team-mates claim a stunning 4-0 victory over Gosport Borough. I listened to the game on Radio Cambridge, while icing, stretching and doing everything I could to get fit.

Unfortunately, I didn't recover in time for the Salisbury game – which we won 3-0 – but I returned to action for our next game, a 1-1 draw at home to Barnet. My hips felt better, and I went on to enjoy a solid run of games.

Playing in either a wide position coming inside, or in a central midfield role, I excelled in the National League and often found that I was the standout player in training and matches. On 1 April 2014, I played really well in the first half of our game against Macclesfield. At half-time, Richard's team talk consisted of him telling everyone to give me the ball. It was a huge compliment, but I didn't know whether it was a good idea because my legs weren't what they once were and I wasn't sure that I could keep running with the ball, playing one-twos and making things happen. We won 1-0 thanks to Luke Berry's late penalty.

Four days later I scored my first goal for Cambridge United in a 3-1 win over Southport. It was a scrappy goal, but to me it felt like the best goal I ever scored. It was the most incredible feeling in the world. When the ball hit the back of the net, I ran to the fans in the Newmarket Road End, just like my heroes had done before me. An immense feeling of pride and joy washed over me as I stood, arms aloft, taking in the acclaim of the supporters. That goal alone vindicated my decision to join Cambridge.

I scored again in our next match against Woking. A 3-0 victory was enough to secure a play-off place and the manager decided to make five or six changes for our next game, which was against struggling Hyde. The lads who played did amazingly well, smashing Hyde 7-2, but the changes took away some of the flow and momentum that we'd built. It disrupted our rhythm, and we lost the last four league games without scoring a single goal. The wheels were coming off. In training we'd work on shape and the team would change on an almost daily basis. The manager was just searching for a way of getting a result. We'd accumulated enough points to ensure a second-place finish, but we wanted to enter the play-offs with a bit of form.

Halifax, who'd finished in fifth place, were our opponents for the two-legged semi-final. The pressure in the build-up to those games was more intense than I'd ever known it. Richard was quite regimented and if things weren't right, he'd tell everyone in no uncertain terms. We were walking on eggshells each morning, wondering what mood the manager would be in when he arrived. Things probably needed to ease up a bit.

Will Norris, our goalkeeper, got injured during the end-of-season run-in so we signed Adam Smith, a young keeper, on loan from Leicester City. Adam went straight into the team. Another Smith who probably hadn't expected to be involved in the play-offs was Sam, a striker who'd spent the season on loan at Hereford until they were expelled from the National League for failing to pay creditors. Sam was a surprise inclusion in our starting line-up for the first leg at Halifax.

Despite our best efforts, we lost 1-0.

If the build-up to the first leg was intense, the second leg was off the charts. On the day of the match, I found out that I'd been dropped to the bench, which was incredibly disappointing. I was praying that we could sneak through, and we did thanks to an unlikely hero – Delano Sam-Yorke. Delano had spent the bulk of the season on loan at Lincoln City and had only been recalled by Cambridge a few months earlier. His two first-half goals were enough to give us a 2-1 aggregate victory.

The mood in the dressing room afterwards was sheer relief. No joy. We still had one game to go. One game to achieve what we'd set out to.

Wembley was the venue for Cambridge's biggest game in a decade. Gateshead, who'd finished third, were all that stood between us and a return to the Football League. I'm sure this is the only time this has happened in National League history, but the managers of the two finalists had both won the European Cup during their playing careers. Richard with Liverpool in 1981 and Gary Mills with Nottingham Forest in 1980.

This was my first visit to Wembley as a player and it meant more that I was going there with Cambridge. I was gutted to be named on the bench again as I honestly felt that I could help make a difference. But I had to put my disappointment aside and cheer on the lads. If I'd started, I'd have approached the game the same way as I did any other. But it was hard to separate being a fan and a player when you're watching the game from a plastic seat at the side of the pitch. I was experiencing so many emotions that I felt like a hormonal teenager!

At that point, I wasn't enjoying my spell at Cambridge as much as I thought I would have. It was so different to what I was used to. I'd worked with Karl Robinson for many years and had been put on a sort of pedestal at MK Dons, and it was hard to drop down to non-league and not be a first-team regular. I'd done really well in my first few games for Cambridge and then found myself sitting on the bench. I questioned myself, wondering that if we lost the final, would it have been worth it?

The first half was tense, and although Gateshead had the bulk of the possession, they were unable to transform it into a goal. At half-time the score remained 0-0. We opened the scoring shortly after the break when Liam Hughes headed home Ryan Donaldson's cross. Just after the hour mark, the manager turned to me and said, 'Get ready.' I didn't need to get ready.

I'd been ready for this moment my whole life. I can't explain the feeling as I stood on the side on the touchline, wearing the Cambridge badge on my chest, waiting to step onto the hallowed Wembley turf.

I was playing right midfield, which was the other side of the pitch to the dugouts. As I ran across to get into position, I realised just how big the Wembley pitch is. It seemed to be so much bigger than normal pitches. Although it felt like a dream come true when I stepped onto the pitch, I'd been in football for long enough to know that a dream can very quickly turn into a nightmare.

With 71 minutes on the clock, Donaldson scored a stunning free kick to double our lead. We should have been home and dry, but with ten minutes to play Jack Lester pulled one back for Gateshead to set up a very nervy finish. We were hanging on for dear life. Gateshead were on top, pressing for an equaliser. It got worse when our captain, Ian Miller, snapped his Achilles, which resulted in seven minutes of stoppage time. It was the longest seven minutes of my life.

When the referee did finally blow the full-time whistle, I had the ball in the corner near the Cambridge fans and the noise they made was deafening. I felt so relieved that we'd done it. We may not have done it in the prettiest of ways, but that didn't matter. We'd won promotion. For me, despite the fact I wasn't enjoying it as much as I'd hoped, the result justified my decision to join the club I loved.

There were reporters milling about on the pitch and I did an interview for Radio Cambridge. I couldn't stop crying. I've never felt that emotional on a pitch before. Then we went up to receive our medals and lift the trophy. The awkwardness I always felt while celebrating team achievements returned as we posed for the photos and went round the pitch, sharing the moment with our supporters.

I saw my family in the stands and lifted the boys over the advertising hoardings so they could join in the celebrations on the pitch. Liam was crying his eyes out and that set me off again! It was the first time I'd ever cried in front of my children. The emotions were crazy. A steward told me that the kids weren't allowed on the pitch, so I helped them to return to their seats.

I guess some people may have expected me to hang up my boots after that game. Finish on a high and ride off into the sunset. But I didn't for one moment consider retiring. I naively thought that I'd keep going on forever.

I had an incredible affinity with the Cambridge fans because I was one of them. I had a brilliant relationship with the players, and we'd grown close. I didn't have a huge relationship with the manager or chief executive, but I assumed that I'd sign permanently and stay at the club as long as I could.

Soon after the play-off final, we had a party at the Abbey Stadium and, at the end of the evening, I met Jez George to discuss my future. I was still under contract at MK Dons, but they'd agreed that I could leave on a free transfer to help me make my move permanent.

'Luke, we'd like you to stay for another year, and we can offer you £800 a week,' Jez said, opening the negotiation.

They'd paid £700 towards my wages during my loan spell, so I said, 'It's alright, £700 is fine.'

'No, please let me give you £800,' Jez replied. So, I signed a one-year contract on £800 a week. MK Dons gave me a little bit of money too because they were getting me off their wage bill.

There was a big turnover of players as we prepared for our return to the Football League. Players that the club didn't think could make it in League Two moved on to pastures new and in came lads who had experience of league football.

We played a pre-season friendly against MK Dons as part of my move between the clubs. It was great to see the manager and the lads again, but I didn't really appreciate the enormity of the game at the time, the fact that it was being done for me. I only played the first half of the game, which was a sign of things to come.

I was in really good shape and was the fittest player in the squad during the pre-season running drills. My ability was still there too, but I started just one of our opening six league games. Maybe I was trying too hard because I was desperate to do well, and I perhaps should have been more relaxed, but I wasn't given a huge amount of game time to impress the manager and secure a place in the team.

The one highlight during the early part of the season was scoring against Newport County in September 2014. I reckon I'm the only footballer in history to have scored in the top five English divisions, the FA Cup, League Cup, EFL Cup, and the Belgian First and Second Divisions. I don't think anyone has ever done that and probably never will again. That's another claim to fame!

The final goal of my career came in December 2014 in an FA Cup second-round tie against Mansfield. Tom Champion played a lovely through ball behind the defence. I'd made an inside run from the right wing and finished with my left foot. It was a move that we'd worked on in training and it was nice to pull it off in a game. It was an important goal as it helped us to a 2-2 draw. We saw off the Stags 1-0 in the replay and then defeated Luton in the third round.

We were hoping to draw one of the big boys in the next round. A home tie would be perfect. I was glued to the TV when the draw was made. The big clubs had their numbers displayed on the side of the screen and I'd memorised our number. When Cambridge came out of the hat first, I was buzzing. I held my breath in anticipation.

'Cambridge United will play,' said the presenter, 'number four. Manchester United.' It was unbelievable. I'd never played against United before.

The following day I was inundated with media requests as I became the poster boy for the game. The story became about me, which I wasn't very comfortable with because I didn't want to take the spotlight away from the lads.

I've never seen the Abbey Stadium rocking like it was on 23 January 2015 when United came to town. I wasn't massively shocked to be named as a substitute because I was in and out of the side by then, but I managed to come on for the last 15 minutes and experience that amazing atmosphere. United weren't at full strength, but there was still a wealth of talent within their side, including David de Gea, Michael Carrick, Ángel Di María, Robin van Persie and Luke Shaw.

We fought to a deserved 0-0 draw, which was a fantastic result. Chris Dunn, our keeper, was in inspired form, making a host of saves to keep the Red Devils at bay. Josh Coulson had a great chance to win it for us but he claims he missed it on purpose so we could have a replay at Old Trafford!

A few days later we travelled to Manchester for the replay. In the hotel before the game, the manager took me and Robbie

Simpson to one side. It was a strange conversation. He told us that he didn't really want to play us, but he was going to because of our experience.

We all dreamed of a providing a shock, but we were under no illusions that it was going to be tough. On the bus to Old Trafford, I was hoping that it was written in the stars that I was going to have a worldy and help inspire one of the biggest cup upsets of all time. But the reality was that I was run ragged by Paddy McNair, who was playing right-back. He was supposed to be marking me, but he kept running forward causing me to track back. I was subbed after 50 minutes and, to my utter surprise, I received a standing ovation from the whole stadium. I didn't even think the Manchester United fans would remember who I was. It was a really special moment. United, with Juan Mata and Wayne Rooney in their starting line-up, beat us 3-0 to end our hopes of an upset.

When I walked into the dressing room after the game, I suddenly felt very low. I can't put my finger on why, but I just felt a wave of sadness wash over me. I later bumped into Dave Bushell, the man who'd done so much for me when I'd joined Manchester United, and he asked how I was. 'I don't know what to do, Dave,' I replied. 'I think I'm finished.'

The coach took us from Old Trafford back to our hotel where we were staying overnight. I was rooming with Robbie, and he said he was going to the lobby to knock about with the lads. I didn't want to go, so I stayed in my room feeling subdued. I don't know whether it was the emotion of returning to Old Trafford, or what, but I felt very uneasy. I phoned Hayley and told her that I didn't know what was wrong with me. I still can't explain it.

A week later I came on as a sub in a 2-2 draw away at Exeter. And that was the last game I played as a professional.

I'd been having some problems with my hip again, and the pain had spread to my groin and back. It didn't really help that I was still training at 100 per cent. I went for a scan after the Exeter game and that's when I discovered that there was a tear in my hip that required surgery. It wasn't anything major, but my season was over, nonetheless, and the low feeling returned. I wouldn't call it depression; it was just a realisation that I wasn't going to be able to play football forever.

My contract was up at the end of the season, but I fully expected to be fit for the start of the new campaign. When I signed for Cambridge, the idea that had been spoken about, but never put in writing, was that I'd stay at the club in some capacity when I did eventually hang up my boots. But after my operation, it all went quiet.

I was on a coaching course at St George's Park in April 2014 when Richard phoned me. We had a one-minute conversation where he told me that my contract wouldn't be renewed. My football career was over.

On paper, it looks like I had the fairy-tale ending, finishing my career with my hometown club, but it wasn't like that in reality.

I felt that the wind had been knocked out of my sail. For the first time in my professional career, I'd been rejected. I wasn't wanted. And to make it worse, the rejection came from the club that I'd supported all my life. It was one of the toughest moments of my career.

I briefly considered joining another League Two club, but I felt so let down that I decided I just didn't want to do it anymore. I didn't want to up sticks and play for another club miles away from home.

So, that was it. I was no longer a professional footballer. And then it hit me: *If I wasn't a footballer anymore, what was I? Who was I?*

Chapter 28

What Next?

THERE WERE no 'breaking news' banners on Sky Sports News when I retired. That's because I didn't officially announce my retirement from the game. Deep down I knew that I'd never play professional football again, but I never said it aloud. I didn't want to admit that my career had come to an end. As a result, I didn't have the closure I perhaps needed at the time.

Retiring from being a professional footballer is strange. I spent my whole life striving to become a pro and, when I made it, I thought I could go on forever. I was so absorbed in my career that I didn't ever really consider a life after football. My focus was always on the next game, the next season. And then one day it was all over. It happened overnight. That's the industry and I was quickly forgotten. The game moves on and I realised that I wasn't as important as I thought I was. Hundreds of players retire each season, and I became just another ex-footballer. Someone who used to kick a ball around.

For the first time since I'd been with Hayley, we had a two-week family holiday, in July 2015. It felt strange being on holiday when I'd usually be in a pre-season camp, preparing for the season ahead. I felt numb and spent a bit of time in a daze.

During my final season at Cambridge, I'd finished my level two coaching qualification, and when I found out that my contract wasn't going to be renewed, I signed up for some more courses. The Professional Footballers' Association helped me to get on the UEFA B course and I'm grateful to them for that. I didn't have a particular passion for coaching, it was more that I felt I should do it. I was only 34, and I needed to do something to fill my days. Football was all I knew so I decided to focus on becoming a coach.

When I returned from my holiday, I signed up to every course going, and I read every coaching manual I could get my hands on. Anything to distract myself from the fact that I wasn't playing or training each day. I was trying to avoid the negative thoughts that invaded my mind when I didn't have anything to do.

I went from feeling to numb to feeling bitter and anger that I hadn't been offered another contract at Cambridge after what I'd given up for them. I'd always assumed they'd look after me when my playing days were over. I felt so much animosity towards the club because of the way I'd been cast aside. I felt guilty because if I'd remained at MK Dons, I'm sure they'd have found a role for me. I'd be working. Money had never mattered to me during my career, but I knew that if I'd stayed at MK Dons, I'd be earning money to support my family. Instead, I was unemployed and had given up tens of thousands of pounds for my selfish crusade to play for Cambridge. No one had twisted my arm. I'd done this myself, but I needed someone to blame.

I felt lonely and isolated. I hadn't kept in touch with my former team-mates, so I didn't have that network of people who were going through the same thing. I always found it hard to admit that I was struggling. Never wanting to show any kind of vulnerability. I just put on a brave face and tried to get on with it. I could have gone back to Cambridge or MK Dons to train and be around the lads, but it didn't feel right because I wasn't a footballer anymore.

I lost my identity at this stage. If I wasn't a footballer, what was I? A lot of my team-mates played golf, were into the horses or were involved with businesses. I didn't have that. My life had revolved around family and football. That was it. Without any focus or targets, without anything to work towards, I lost motivation. My confidence was at rock bottom, and I lacked the belief that I could do anything else.

The biggest loss was not playing football. I was used to getting up, going to work and coming home absolutely shattered. Going off to sit in a classroom all day and taking a coaching course didn't give me that sense of satisfaction. I still associate hard work with that feeling of exhaustion that follows.

I started to do some voluntary coaching with the Cambridge University football team, which was a really good experience. At the same time, I started playing futsal. That was quite an experience, playing a slightly different game to what I was used to.

Then, in November 2015, my old mate Robbie Nightingale phoned and asked me to meet him in a coffee shop for a chat. Robbie was the manager of non-league Soham Rangers, and over a coffee he asked if I'd play for them and have some fun. Robbie's assistant was Dave Theobold, a friend of my brother. My legs felt good, so I signed the forms and made my debut a few days later against Witham Town.

Soham played in the seventh tier of English football and, although it was obviously very different to what I was used to, I really enjoyed it. My team-mates were a great bunch of lads. I didn't train, I just turned up on the Saturday and played. After my first game, Robbie handed me an envelope containing £250. I hadn't signed a contract and wasn't expecting anything, but I gratefully accepted it. I received an envelope after every game. I didn't tell Hayley about it, so I had a bit of cash to spend as I wished. One time, Hayley was in the clubhouse having a drink with me when Robbie threw the envelope down on the table. With speed no one had seen since my Manchester United days, I scooped it up and put the cash in my jacket pocket before anyone could see it.

I used to get kicked about a bit. It was obviously quite nice for the opposing players to have the opportunity to put a former United player on his arse. It was all light-hearted, though, and I certainly gave as good as I got.

Away games were an experience. We didn't travel as a group by coach; instead we'd make our own way to the ground. I often travelled with Robbie and Dave. There was one match when we were playing a team based in London. Dave was driving and the traffic was horrendous. He started to lose his head as we were running late. We finally arrived at the ground and walked into the dressing room. We didn't recognise anyone so assumed they must have been the home team. We went into the other dressing room but didn't recognise anyone in there either. It turned out that we'd gone to the wrong place! We eventually managed to find the right ground with less than five minutes until kick-off.

Another time, we were playing an away game – I can't remember who the opponents were – and the place was as rough as you like. I went over to take a corner and there was a little lad watching the game next to his dad. As I put the ball down near the corner flag, the boy shouted, 'Chadwick. You're a wanker.'

I looked at him and reckon he was no older than ten. I turned to his dad and said, 'Are you going to let him speak to me like that?'

The dad put his arm around his son's shoulders and replied, 'Yes, I am.'

Another time, I got caught with an elbow that split my eye open. We didn't have a physio, so Dave ran onto the pitch and smeared Vaseline over my eye to stem the bleeding so I could continue. It was great fun.

Later that season, I got my first paid coaching job working part-time in the Cambridge United Development Centres in Royston. I got that job through a guy called Jonny Martin. Another friend, James Cutting, brought me in to help him with the sessions that he delivered with Cambridge. I needed a certain number of hours in order to get my coaching qualifications.

While I was doing my UEFA A licence, I went away for a residential. There are usually quite a lot of ex-pros on these courses and this one was no different. I checked into the hotel and took the lift up to my room. When I opened the door, there was someone lying on the bed, which was strange. It was the former Everton footballer Nick Chadwick! The receptionist hadn't realised there were two Chadwicks on the course.

A year or so later, in 2016, I saw a job advertised within the Cambridge United academy. I had the relevant coaching badges, so I submitted my CV. Jez George invited me in for a chat. It was the first time we'd spoken for over a year. I explained why

I wanted the job and what I thought I could bring to the role. Jez said it seemed like a good idea.

That meeting led to an interview with the academy manager, and he offered me a job as the foundation phase lead coach. I'd be in charge of the eight to 12-year-olds. I was delighted and proud, although I had no experience and felt completely out of my depth. On the pitch I was fine, of course, but in the office doing the admin I was so out of my comfort zone. I found it incredibly difficult to begin with but that feeling of pride helped me get through it.

One of the big advantages of the role was that I got to spend time with Louis and Liam. Louis was already in the academy when I joined, and Liam came in while I was there. I know first-hand what pro football is like and I think it was quite nice for them to have someone who loved them more than anyone else in the world that was in a position of authority within the club.

Louis had started playing football when he was six and I got roped in to help with the coaching at his grassroots club. I was playing for MK Dons at the time, and I became a terrible football parent. I was constantly on his back, having a go at him for not working hard enough. I thought that he should be the best player on the pitch because I was a pro. After five weeks I realised that he didn't want me going to his games anymore, and that was heartbreaking. I quickly changed how I acted towards him and his brother, and football became more about just having fun and enjoying it.

Watching them play football, particularly when they were little, was something I really enjoyed. Now that they are older, I don't enjoy the experience of watching them play as much. I probably feel a little bit of the pressure that they feel on the pitch. I think the world has changed now, so TV shows wouldn't be able to do to others what they did to me, but social media seems to be the place where footballers are abused these days. Fortunately, the boys haven't inherited my looks, so they won't receive the same abuse I received!

They both absolutely love football and are still involved in the game. But I do worry whether they're doing the right thing. Don't get me wrong, there are some huge benefits to being a footballer, but there are also the big highs and lowest of lows that you have to deal with. If I was given a choice, I'd rather they went down different career paths. Professional footballers enjoy some wonderful experiences, but it's a ruthless industry, particularly for young players, and your career can come grinding to a halt because of the decision of just one person. I try to manage their expectations because all I want is for them to be happy.

I'm not one of those parents who think their kids are going to be England internationals and become world-class superstars. Of course, it would be fantastic for them if they did, but whatever they do and whatever they achieve on a football pitch makes no difference to how I feel about them. I'm proud as punch of both of them because of who they are as young men.

I spent three and a half years at Cambridge as a coach within the academy. I started with the little ones, then moved up to 12 to 16-year-olds and then the under-18s. I was offered the role of youth-team manager, but I turned it down. By then I'd accepted that I wasn't a footballer anymore and decided that I no longer wanted to be involved in the professional game. Maybe I needed the coaching role to close that chapter of my life.

Academy football is a very demanding job with long hours – I found myself out of the house six days a week. I loved engaging with the young people I was working with, but I didn't like the job. I didn't like who I became on the side of the football pitch. I'm generally a nice guy, but I became quite arrogant as a coach, thinking that my background meant my teams should win. I started to hate the sound of my own voice, moaning at the kids and the ref. That wasn't the real me. The challenge was that I thought the team's performance was a reflection on me personally, but I didn't have any control of the game once the boys had taken to the pitch. As a player, I could control my own performance, but as a coach, I was powerless.

Everything just seemed so serious for the young kids. They'd train three times a week and play a game at the weekend. The focus was on the destination of becoming a pro footballer, whereas the reality is that it will only happen to a very small percentage. The journey was being ignored. There are so many fantastic opportunities within that environment; you build relationships, you can learn life skills to take to a career outside football. But they weren't being learned because it was all about being retained at the end of the season and taking another rung on the ladder to becoming a footballer.

Too many parents and children go into that system believing they'll make it. The messaging needs to change. They need to realise that they'll have a fantastic experience, playing with and against some talented kids, but they're still children. Yes, they might be wearing the badge of a professional club on their shirt, but they're not playing for that club. It's just a badge. They're so far away from ever making it that the focus should be on developing skills and enjoying the experience. The kids need to start the journey with the full understanding that it might last a year, maybe two, possibly five. But there's a 99.9 per cent chance that it won't end in a glittering career. Of course, that's going to happen to a few, and that's brilliant. But for everyone else, the journey will end in disappointment. That's why it's so important that every child has a positive experience.

I became disillusioned and walked away from professional football. Stepping out of that intense environment was like a breath of fresh air. My time spent coaching had rebuilt my confidence and I was ready to start the next adventure.

Chapter 29

Putting the Fun Back into Football

I HAD no idea what I was going to do when I decided to leave Cambridge. I was close friends with another guy who worked in the academy called Jonny Martin. When I told Jonny that I was leaving he said he was going too. Jonny explained that he was going to work with James Cutting, another former colleague, on something called the Football Fun Factory. He thought it would be good for us all to have a chat.

James had worked on the commercial side at Cambridge United. He was highly thought of and had earned the club a lot of money through the various initiatives he'd developed. In 2017, James created the Football Fun Factory, a children's coaching organisation where the focus is on fun. He was running it as a one-man band until 2019 when Jonny joined him.

I was intrigued and met the pair for a chat. They were so passionate about their plans for the future, and it really captured my imagination. It was all about engaging children in a pressure-free, fun environment. It reminded me so much of my early experiences at Melbourn Tigers when I loved running around chasing a ball about with my friends. There was no technical or tactical coaching. To have a chance to be a part of that but on a mass scale excited me. James's and Jonny's energy and enthusiasm wore off on me. I'm now the company's third director.

We've achieved great success so far and I'm highly motivated to move forward and continue to grow the company. We've got huge ambitions to become the world's leading children's football coaching organisation and the thought of that really excites me. We're building a hugely successful business, but it's all about the why that sits behind it. That why is to give the kids a positive first footballing experience in an inclusive environment, and to help them to fall in love with the beautiful game. Just as I had.

The Football Fun Factory has filled that football-shaped hole in my life. I don't miss the game now that I've finally come to terms with the end of my pro career. Mind you, I still enjoy lacing up my boots and playing for Manchester United's legends. I always feel like an imposter playing for the legends as I only played 39 times for the club, but I still get a buzz every time I pull on a shirt with the United badge. The team is a real mixed bag consisting of players from different eras. Russell Beardsmore, Lee Martin, David May, Wes Brown, Danny Webber, Chris Eagles and Danny Simpson are usually involved. Sammy McIlroy played a few games for us while in his 60s, and he's still fit as a fiddle.

I don't get invited to the matches against Liverpool at Old Trafford; they bring the big guns out for those games, but I've been on several fantastic trips. I played a match out in Dubai with Dwight Yorke, Mikael Silvestre and Raimond van der Gouw, and another in Finland where I was managed by the legendary Bryan Robson. Even though I'm a middle-aged man now, I still felt under pressure to give everything I had to impress him.

I'm constantly trying to get myself fit again, but always seem to fail miserably. As soon as I've got my kit on, I feel like a 21-year-old again. When the game kicks off, I fly around trying to get the ball, and that's what kills me. Within 20 minutes I realise that my legs aren't what they once were. I need to remind myself that it's a sprint not a marathon. There's always a good amount of banter and it's nice to catch up with other players who have played for the club.

I also have the opportunity to reconnect with former team-mates in my role with MUTV. I never saw myself becoming a pundit nor did I have any aspirations to do so. But one day I received an email out of the blue from MUTV asking if I'd like to do some studio work. I wasn't sure but I went up to Manchester to meet them and I've been doing it for a while now. I wouldn't say I'm brilliant and I'm not sure how many people actually listen to my insights, but it's good fun. I never say anything too outspoken, and I don't criticise players because I know how hard it is for them out on the pitch. It's interesting work and I have to watch the games with a greater attention span than I would at home so that I have something to say.

I was nervous to begin with, but the MUTV guys are a great bunch, and everyone is so relaxed. There are two former players on each show, so there's always support. Some I'm meeting for the first time, others I haven't seen for 20 years. Ben Thornley, a member of the famous Class of '92, does the commentary for most of the games. I bumped into him before one of my early appearances and he said, 'You're here as the talent.' I thought he was taking the piss, but that's what the pundits are called: the talent.

I went to the London Stadium in 2023 to cover the West Ham United vs Manchester United game for MUTV. That was my first visit to West Ham's new ground, and I saw quite a few people who were at the club when I was there, which was nice. The game was being broadcast by Sky and I always feel awkward when I bump into the top, top pundits, such as Gary Neville, Rio Ferdinand and Peter Crouch. I get a bit of imposter syndrome when I'm trying to do my thing next to these highly skilled people.

I can't see myself ever doing any work for Sky or the BBC. I'm not sure they'd be interested in taking me, to be honest. The only time I've ever tried to draw the circles on the screen with one of those gizmos, I had an absolute nightmare. And I can't imagine BT would invite me back after my one and only appearance. When Cambridge United played Dover Athletic in 2016, I was asked to be a pundit. I was really nervous and wore my best suit. There wasn't a TV studio at the ground, so we were set up at a table in the supporters' lounge. Before the game, I sat there while a lady applied make-up, surrounded by Dover fans enjoying their pre-match pint! I was heavily biased towards Cambridge in my analysis – I was a fan, a former player and coach, of course I was going to be on their side – and they never invited me back! At least with MUTV, I can be as positive about United as I want to be.

In 2020, I received a message from a sports agency asking whether I'd be interested in mentoring their clients. I've spent a long time in the professional game and it's great to have the opportunity to share my experience to help others. The game has given me so much and I enjoy giving back. It's all for the players' benefit and we talk about what they want to discuss.

Sometimes it's about tactics or technical elements within their game, other times it's about some challenges that they may be facing in their personal life. I'm there to listen and offer support and guidance. Even if the players only get a tiny benefit from our sessions, it makes it worthwhile.

My clients and our conversations are completely confidential, but one of my mentees who has spoken publicly about our work together is England women's player Georgia Stanway. Georgia is a brilliant person who I've really enjoyed working with. She's achieved so much: winning the Euros, playing in a World Cup Final, and has multiple domestic winners' medals. I'm truly humbled by her kind words towards me as a mentor.

Writing this book has allowed me to look back and reflect on my career and life. When I think back to that young boy who dreamed of becoming a professional footballer, I think he'd be proud of the career that I've had. I haven't got a trophy cabinet full of medals, but I've achieved more than I ever could have wished for.

All these years later, I'm still in love with the game of football. My first love.

Acknowledgements

TAKING THIS trip down memory lane has reminded me of the many wonderful people I've encountered on my journey. There are far too many to mention, but I'd like to say a special thank you to the following people:

My wife, Hayley, who has been by my side from the very beginning. Together, we've experienced the highs and the lows, and I wouldn't have been able to achieve what I did without her. To my children, Louis and Liam. I'm so proud of the men they've become.

To my mum and dad for all their support and for encouraging me to follow my dreams. To my brother, Carl and best friends, Barnes and Lurch. To all my friends and family. Too many people to mention, but you know who you are.

To Dion Dublin for providing the foreword to this book. Dion was my first hero, an absolute legend, and I'm proud to call him a friend.

To Mathew Mann for listening to my stories and turning them into this book. To Jane Camillin, and the team at Pitch Publishing.

To all my former team-mates, managers, coaches and the officials at all the clubs I had the privilege of representing (I'd need another book to list everyone, as I played for so many teams!). And, most importantly, to the fans of all the clubs I played for. I always gave 100 per cent and I hope I gave you all some treasured memories.

Luke Chadwick has collaborated with Mathew Mann to write his autobiography. Mathew would like to thank:

Luke for taking me into his confidence and giving me the opportunity to help tell his story. Paul and Jane at Pitch Publishing. My nanna Reneé for giving me my love of reading. My wife Holly for her continued support and encouragement. My children, Dylan and Eve, who are my inspiration.

Career Stats

Club	Years	Games	Goals
Manchester United	1999–2004	39	2
Royal Antwerp (Loan)	2000–2001	27	7
Reading (Loan)	2002–2003	17	1
Burnley (Loan)	2003–2004	40	6
West Ham United	2004–2005	36	1
Stoke City	2005–2006	55	6
Norwich City	2006–2008	18	2
MK Dons	2008–2014	246	24
Cambridge United	2014–2015	40	4
England Under-18s	1998–1999	5	1
England Under-21s	1999–2001	13	0
Total		536	54

Honours

Club	Honour	
Royal Antwerp	Belgian Second Division Champions	2000
Manchester United	Premier League Champions	2001
	Community Shield Runners-Up	2001
West Ham United	Play-Off Winners	2005
MK Dons	Player of the Year	2010 & 2011
Cambridge United	Play-Off Winners	2014